LUCIAN
SATIRICAL SKETCHES

LUCIAN

SATIRICAL SKETCHES

TRANSLATED
WITH AN INTRODUCTION BY

PAUL TURNER

INDIANA UNIVERSITY PRESS
Bloomington and Indianapolis

First Midland Book edition 1990

The paper used in this publication meets the minimum requirements
of American National Standard for Information Sciences—Permanence of
Paper for Printed Library Materials, ANSI Z39.48-1984.
∞ ™

Manufactured in the United States of America

Library of Congress Cataloging-in-Publication Data

Lucian, of Samosata.
[Selections. English. 1990]
Satirical sketches / Lucian ; translated with an introduction by
Paul Turner.—1st Midland book ed.
p.   cm.
Reprint. Originally published: Harmondsworth, Middlesex, England :
Penguin Books, 1961.
ISBN 0-253-36097-8 (hard).—ISBN 0-253-20581-6 (pbk.)
1. Lucian, of Samosata—Translations, English. 2. Satire. Greek—
Translations into English. 3. Satire, English—Translations from
Greek.   I. Turner, Paul. II. Title
PA4231.A58   1990
867'.01—dc20
89-26834
CIP

CONTENTS

CONTENTS

STORIES

INTRODUCTION

I

THE earliest surviving biography of Lucian appears in a tenth-century encyclopedia, and reads as follows:

> Lucian of Samosata, otherwise known as Lucian the Blasphemer, or the Slanderer, or, more accurately, the Atheist, because in his dialogues he even makes fun of religion. He was born somewhere about the time of Trajan. He practised for a while as a barrister at Antioch in Syria, but did so badly at it that he turned over to literature, and wrote no end of stuff. He is said to have been torn to pieces by mad dogs, because he had been so rabid against the truth – for in his *Death of Peregrinus* the filthy brute attacks Christianity and blasphemes Christ Himself. So he was adequately punished in this world, and in the next he will inherit eternal fire with Satan.

If we try to disentangle probable facts from pious hopes, we may infer from this that Lucian was born at Samosata, now the village of Samsat in Turkey, shortly before A.D. 117; that he was once a barrister at Antioch; and that he eventually died. His literary output was certainly immense: about eighty of his works survive. His attitude to religion was always satirical, though his references to Christianity are not particularly abusive. He may have been a failure at the bar, but he himself gives other reasons (p. 181) for his change of profession.

Any further information about his life must be extracted from his works, and this is rather a risky process. In *The Dream* we are told that he was fond of making wax models as a child; but this charming biographical detail turns out to be a reminiscence of a passage in Aristophanes. He says in the *Nigrinus* that he went to Rome to consult an oculist; but he so often plays upon the metaphorical meaning of bad eyesight that his visit to an oculist may be merely a literary device to prepare for the later statement that Nigrinus opened his eyes to the truth. In the *Alexander* he says that the Prophet tried to murder him; but such accusations were almost a convention in polemical writing, and we need not take this one much more seriously than Alexander's counter-accusation that Lucian was only interested in 'Beds of lust and midnight orgies'. Admittedly, it is stated in *The Double Charge* that Lucian married a rich woman, who then sued him for desertion, and accused him of irregular relations with an older man; and both of these crimes have been taken literally by simple-minded biographers. But the woman in the case was called Rhetoric, and the man's name was Dialogue. On a more sophisticated level, it is equally rash to deduce from the *Nigrinus*, as some scholars have done, that at the age of twenty-five Lucian was 'converted' to Platonism, and like Peter Bell,

> Forsook his crimes, renounced his folly,
> And after ten months' melancholy,
> Became a good and honest man.

However, from a cautious use of internal evidence, we can reconstruct the main outlines of Lucian's career. He went to a primary school at Samosata, until he was about fourteen. He then left home, and took a course in rhetoric, either at Tarsus, the nearest educational centre, or in some other town of Asia Minor, or by attaching himself to some itinerant teacher. This course involved the study of Greek literature, and the composition and delivery of recitations on a variety of set themes.

Once fully trained, he began to earn his living partly as a barrister, and partly as a travelling lecturer. In this capacity he toured Greece and Italy, and finally landed a well-paid Professorship of Literature somewhere in France. By this time he was famous throughout the Roman Empire, though not perhaps quite as famous as he liked to think.

On a visit to Rome, he met and was greatly impressed by a philosopher whom he calls Nigrinus, but who is probably a Platonist known from other sources as Albinus (Mr Black for Mr White). When he was about forty, he settled at Athens. There he came into contact with an eclectic philosopher called Demonax, who further stimulated his interest in philosophy. Soon afterwards he invented his own particular brand of Dialogue, and gave a very successful series of public readings.

In his old age he accepted a post on the staff of the Governor of Egypt. It was an important job with a high salary, and he even had hopes of becoming Governor himself. But he still felt rather uneasy about joining the Establishment, after a lifetime of opposition. In the *Alexander* he speaks of 'his late majesty Marcus Aurelius', so his own death must have occurred after A.D. 180. That is all we know about it: Dryden's suggestion that he died of gout has rather less authority than the mad-dog theory.

2

Lucian spends so much of his time making fun of philosophy and religion, that one wonders what precisely he was up against. Was it merely a personal obsession, or did philosophy and religion really play so large a part in the second-century climate of opinion? In this respect at least, Lucian was quite objective.

The importance of philosophy during this period was both symbolized and enhanced by the Stoic Emperor, Marcus Aurelius. At last Plato's prescription for an ideal government had been dispensed, and a philosopher was king. He established Chairs of Philosophy throughout the Empire for the four chief schools, the Stoics, the Epicureans, the Academics, and the Peripatetics; and three others, the Pythagoreans, the Sceptics, and the Cynics, were immensely active, even without state patronage. I have no space here to describe their various doctrines adequately, and can only refer inquiring readers to some such book as A. H. Armstrong's *Introduction to Ancient Philosophy*; but I have summarized in the Glossary all the information that one needs to understand Lucian's philosophical jokes.

All this philosophy might be expected to militate against religion, but it had the opposite effect, for the teachings of the Stoics, the Academics, the Peripatetics, and the Pythagoreans included a strong religious element. All four schools agreed upon the existence of a divine Providence, which controlled human affairs through the agency of *daemons* or spirits. Apuleius, the author of *The Golden Ass*, was typical of his period in being a priest of Isis as well as a Platonist, and combining the study of philosophy with the study of magic. In *Marius the Epicurean*, a novel which accurately conveys the intellectual atmosphere of Lucian's day, Walter Pater makes Apuleius expound Plato in the language of a mystic:

There are certain divine powers of a middle nature, through whom our aspirations are conveyed to the gods, and theirs to us. Passing between the inhabitants of earth and heaven, they carry from one to the other prayers and bounties, supplication and assistance, being a kind of interpreters. This interval of the air is full of them! Through them, all revelations, miracles, magic processes are effected.

Such philosophies prepared the ground for an unprecedented crop of new religions. In addition to the rapid growth of Christianity, foreign cults like those of Attis, Bendis, and Mithras became extremely popular, and even the worship of an old Greek god like Aesculapius acquired a new flavour of fanaticism. Apuleius was a priest of Aesculapius, and the Glycon-cult satirized in the *Alexander* was an offshoot of the same religion. All these sects, except Christianity, accepted oracles, prophetic dreams, and magic as normal facts of life, nor was such belief in the supernatural confined to the uneducated: even doctors like Galen used patients' dreams as evidence for diagnosis, and prescribed forms of treatment that were dream-inspired.

Of course there was some opposition to this general tendency. The Epicureans, in particular, campaigned against all forms of religion and supernaturalism. One of them, called Celsus, wrote an attack on Christianity, which provoked a famous reply from Origen, and another Celsus, also an Epicurean, appears from the *Alexander* to have written a book exposing the pretensions of magicians. But such materialists were a deeply unpopular minority, and the spirit of the age could be summed up in Tertullian's phrase: *Credo quia impossibile*, 'I believe it because it is impossible.'

3

Lucian was clearly unsympathetic towards the majority view, but it is not so clear what precisely this implies about his character. To Early and not so Early Christians, his character seemed only too obvious: he was virtually Antichrist. This judgement was based on rather inadequate grounds, for his explicit references to Christianity are confined to two works, the *Alexander* and the *Peregrinus*. In the former he couples Christians with Epicureans as the chief opponents of the fraudulent Prophet, thus paying Christianity a doubtless unintentional compliment. In the latter he mentions Christians as the innocent victims of the unscrupulous Peregrinus, and summarizes their beliefs merely to explain why they let themselves be victimized:

They still worship that great man, the fellow who was crucified in Palestine, for bringing this new cult into the world. . . . When Peregrinus was put in prison, the Christians thought it a terrible disaster, and did everything they could to try and get him out. When this proved impossible, they helped him in every other way they could think of. First thing every morning, you would see a crowd of old women, widows, and orphans waiting outside the prison, and the leaders of the sect used to bribe the warders to let them spend the night with him in his cell. They brought him in all sorts of food, talked to him about their religion, and called 'that good man Peregrinus' (for that was how they spoke of him) a second Socrates. Delegates even arrived from other Christian communities in Asia Minor, to help him by petitioning for his release and trying to comfort him.

They are always incredibly quick off the mark, when one of them gets into trouble like this – in fact they ignore their own interests completely. Why, they actually sent him large sums of money by way of compensation for his imprisonment, so that he made a considerable profit out of them! For the poor souls have persuaded themselves that they are immortal and will live for ever. As a result, they think nothing of death, and most of them are perfectly willing to sacrifice themselves. Besides, their first law-giver has convinced them that once they stop believing in Greek gods, and start worshipping that crucified sage of theirs, and living according to his laws, they are all each other's brothers and sisters. So, taking this information on trust, without any guarantee of its truth, they think nothing else matters, and believe in common ownership – which means that any unscrupulous adventurer who comes along can soon make a fortune out of them, for the silly creatures are very easily taken in.

There is nothing really offensive here, except the patronizing tone: the actual statements made constitute another back-handed tribute to Christianity, for Lucian faithfully records the admirable features of Christian behaviour, although he does not admire them himself. Yet as late as the thirteenth century this passage was enough to send a commentator into fits of indignation, and provoke the marginal note: 'You filthy scoundrel, that's a lie!' He then reels off a string of arguments for the doctrine of universal brotherhood, and concludes with the not very brotherly remark: 'You can't find anything to say against that, even if you try until you burst!'

Once Lucian was seen as a virulent enemy of Christianity, almost anything could be interpreted as a veiled attack on the Faith. The whale-passage in the *True History* became a malicious parody of the Jonah-story; the Island of the Blest became a caricature of the New Jerusalem; and the anonymous Syrian who casts out devils in *The Pathological Liar* touched off another explosion of wrath in the margin:

> Woe to thee, Lucian! Atheist! My Lord and God was a quack, and took money for healing the sick! When you talked such nonsense, why did not the earth split open and swallow you up? Presumably because it found you too disgusting!

A more recent reaction has been to envisage Lucian as a fearless crusader against superstition, an apostle of common sense, a martyr for rationalism: a solitary figure struggling desperately to hold aloft the Torch of Truth, with the Dark Ages inexorably closing in around him. It is a wonderfully romantic picture; but before we can decide whether it is a better likeness of Lucian than the one that highlights his cloven hoof, we must investigate his literary technique.

4

Twentieth-century criticism has increased our understanding of Lucian in three ways: by discovering what literary education was like in Lucian's day, by tracing in detail his debt to previous writers, and by comparing the view of the world expressed in his works with what is known from other sources of the actual world he lived in.

He was educated under a system standardized by a literary movement called the Second Sophistic. For our purposes, the main features of this movement were its doctrine of Imitation, and its use of rhetorical exercises. 'Imitation' was the natural result of a critical theory which stressed, like T. S. Eliot's, the importance of a continuous literary tradition; it meant modelling one's style and content on those of the best Greek authors. The most obvious sign of this practice was a habit of quotation and allusion, but it went much deeper than that, and altered the whole approach of writers to their work. Their aim was no longer to express contemporary experience, but to create literature that was a worthy continuation of previous literature.

Of the many standard exercises used in this training, it will be enough to mention two, which might otherwise be mistaken for original forms invented by Lucian. They are the *dikanikos logos*, which was to dramatize an argument in a law-court scene (as in *Fishing for Phonies*), and the *ekphrasis*, which was to describe a visual object (like the statues in *The Pathological Liar*) as vividly as possible. The other point to register is that though these exercises were usually of a controversial nature, the subject of the controversy was often quite absurd: it did not matter what you were saying, so long as you said it convincingly.

Detailed investigation of Lucian's sources has shown that he deliberately tried to include the maximum amount of literary material in his works. One scholar has compiled a list of Lucian's quotations, allusions, and reminiscences, which covers fifty-five closely printed pages. But apart from such specific references to earlier literature, most of his themes, arguments, illustrations, and plots are also second-hand. The dramatic opening scene of *Fishing for Phonies* was modelled on an episode in a play by Aristophanes; every story in *The Pathological Liar* except that of the sorcerer's apprentice had been used before; and even the comparison of a town to an ant-hill in the *Icaromenippus* was drawn from a common pool of literary images.

How little Lucian thought of originality can be seen from the *Zeuxis*, but nowadays it requires a considerable mental effort to conceive of a great writer who is not original. Shakespeare, we know, seldom invented his own plots, but his case is hardly analogous to Lucian's, for he did not intend his audience to recognize his borrowings. Milton is a rather better parallel, for he, like Lucian, meant his readers to notice and admire his rehandling of traditional material. But perhaps the best analogy is Homer, whose language, as well as his plots, is now generally agreed to have been largely ready-made; that is, he composed, not with words like a modern poet, but with versified verbal formulas, ranging in length from two words to several lines, which had been built up by generations of oral poets to simplify the process of improvisation. Homer's greatness consists in his individual treatment of this prefabricated poetic material, and on a somewhat lower level Lucian can claim a similar form of greatness.

This special attitude to literature affected his attitude to contemporary life. Historical research has proved that he does not give at all an adequate picture of the second-century world. Nor is it merely a matter of personal prejudice, as it doubtless is in his portrait of *Alexander*, who appears from other evidence to have been a sincere if theatrically-minded mystic. It is rather that his references to the actual world around him are extremely rare and, when they do occur, tend to be expressed in literary terms and adapted to pre-existing patterns. For instance, he describes his contemporary Rutilianus in words borrowed from Theophrastus's *Character of the Superstitious Man*, written five hundred years before. He never seems to throw in a detail drawn from his own observation of life – not because he lacked observation, but because his critical taste instinctively rejected material for which there was no literary precedent.

For the same reason, his criticisms of philosophical and religious sects seldom have any topical significance: they are mostly traditional criticisms dating back to the age of Pericles. His delightful mockery of the myths about the Olympian gods served no serious purpose in his time, for such stories had long ceased to be taken literally by any religious believers. Historically, the growth of Christianity was the most noticeable phenomenon of the age, but he mentions it in only two works – doubtless because there were no models in classical literature for treating that particular subject.

He was, in fact, neither Antichrist nor an Apostle of Free Thought, for propaganda was not his main objective. His primary concern was the world of literature: the world he lived in was chiefly interesting as a chaos of raw material from which to select elements that could be fitted into the pattern of existing Hellenic culture. The controversial tone of his writings was a sign, not of emotional involvement, but of a rhetorical training.

We must not, however, go too far in this direction, and picture Lucian as a man with no opinions of his own, no interest in the problems of real life. In that case, how could we explain the remarkable consistency of his viewpoint? Though trained 'to make the worse appear the better cause', why does he always come out so strongly on the same side of the argument? The truth of the matter seems to be briefly this: though he was not a passionate agitator for or against any belief, he had a strong distaste for all forms of obscurantism, and never lost a chance of putting across what he regarded as a realistic view of human life. Personally, though I find some of his judgements rather narrow, and one or two of his jokes a trifle inhuman, I consider his general attitude both sane and valuable, especially when modified by a hint of self-criticism, as on page 177. In his constant variations on the theme of death he is not, I think, merely exploiting a rich source of comedy, but dramatizing the important truth expressed in E. M. Forster's epigram: 'Death destroys a man: the idea of Death saves him.'

5

Besides suggesting subjects for pictures by Botticelli, Dürer, and Degas, inspiring the music of *L'Apprenti Sorcier* by Dukas, and influencing such European authors as Boiardo, Ariosto, Erasmus, Rabelais, Cervantes, Voltaire, and Goethe, Lucian has also played a part in the creation of English literature.

Sir Thomas More, who translated several of his works into Latin, echoes the *True History* in the general form, the fantastic humour, and the quasi-realistic details of his *Utopia*. In the sixteenth century Lucian was on the normal grammar-school syllabus, and several Elizabethan dramatists show how he stuck in their minds. Marlowe's famous line,

> Was this the face that launched a thousand ships?

is practically a straight versification of a remark by Menippus in *Conversations in the Underworld*. Ben Jonson based a scene of his *Poetaster* on Lucian's *Lexiphanes*, and his best play, *Volpone*, derives its plot from the brief dialogue on pages 75–7. It has been plausibly argued that Lucian is one of the sources of the Grave-scene in *Hamlet*, and Shakespeare's *Timon of Athens* is undoubtedly based in part on Lucian's *Timon*.

Some of his works had already been translated into English by John Rastell, the brother-in-law of Sir Thomas More, but the first well-known translation was that of Francis Hickes in 1634. From then on, translations and adaptations followed thick and fast, 'Lucian' became a favourite pseudonym for satirists, and *Dialogues of the Dead, Ancient and Modern: Dedicated to Lucian in Elysium* was the sort of title that constantly appeared in bookseller's lists. *The Works of Lucian, Translated from the Greek by Several Eminent Hands* came out in 1711. The blurb stated that 'Lucian has been the Darling Pleasure of Men of

Sense in every Nation', and his popularity was confirmed by the number of Eminent Hands who had been working on him – twenty-five. Dryden had written a *Life of Lucian* by way of introduction, in which he admitted that Lucian has 'left so little of his own Affairs on Record, that there is scarce sufficient to fill a Page from his Birth to his Death.' So he resourcefully filled up one and a half pages with information about four quite different Lucians, and when he finally ran out of biographical material, padded with scornful allusions to a previous French translator, whom he called a 'Frog-land Wit'.

Gulliver's Travels is an example of the genre initiated by the *True History*, and the scene on the Island of Glubbdubdribb, in which Gulliver interviews Homer, is transparently borrowed from Lucian. Fielding owned nine complete sets of Lucian's works, and planned to translate them; but he did something better, which was to write a Lucianic story of his own, *A Journey from this World to the Next*. In *The Marvellous Travels of Baron Münchhausen* (1785) whole episodes from the *True History* are incorporated almost word for word.

Lucian's common sense was hardly calculated to appeal to a romantic like Shelley; but Lucian the Blasphemer could not be overlooked by a man who once described himself in a hotel register as an atheist, and Charon's 'Homeric' simile (p. 92) duly appears in *Hellas*:

> Worlds on worlds are rolling ever
> From creation to decay,
> Like the bubbles on a river,
> Sparkling, bursting, borne away.

The hint for Shelley's satire on George IV, *Oedipus Tyrannus* or *Swellfoot the Tyrant*, also seems to have come from Lucian's mock-tragedy, *Ocypus*, which describes an attack of gout in Sophoclean verse, with a Prologue spoken by Gout herself.

Shelley's friend, Peacock, found in Lucian a kindred spirit, and his amusing short novels are basically Lucianic dialogues inflated with a few puffs of romantic fiction. Landor's *Imaginary Conversations* clearly stem from the same source, and Lucian's Menippus makes a surprise entrance into Browning's *Pippa Passes*, thinly disguised as an English vagabond called Bluphocks, who says:

Talk to me of the religion of a bishop! I have renounced all bishops save Bishop Beveridge – mean to live so – and die – *As some Greek dog-sage, dead and merry, Hellward bound in Charon's wherry, With food for both worlds, under and upper, Lupine-seed and Hecate's supper, And never an obolus* ... (Though thanks to you, or this Intendant through you, or this Bishop through his Intendant – I possess a burning pocketful of *zwanzigers*) ... *To pay the Stygian Ferry*!

Disraeli wrote two Lucianic skits, *Ixion in Heaven* and *The Infernal Marriage*, and Pater embodied part of Lucian's *Hermotimus* in *Marius the Epicurean*.

The First Men in the Moon, by H. G. Wells, is a remote descendant of the *True History*, and Lucian may thus be held responsible for modern science fiction. He has even found his way on to the screen, in Walt Disney's *Fantasia*, which includes the episode of the sorcerer's apprentice. From now on, however, his influence is likely to be more and more indirect, and reveal itself only in a special blend of fantasy and satire, an oddly farcical approach to grim themes, which has become a naturalized element in English literature. In this sense the most Lucianic work of this century is probably Evelyn Waugh's *The Loved One*.

6

In spite of his popularity in the past, today Lucian is surprisingly little known. To most people his name suggests a vague mental image, which can equally well be activated by the word Lucan, and the operation of separating these ancient Siamese twins seems hardly worth attempting. But Lucian's potential appeal has increased rather than diminished with time. Philosophers and mystics will still think him obtuse, superficial, and frivolous. Scientists and psychologists who have learned to regard Extra-sensory Perception as a reasonable field for research will think his *a priori* rejection of all inexplicable phenomena essentially unscientific. But ordinary people should find his ideas highly relevant to present conditions.

Common sense has always had to fight for survival against unrealistic elements in ourselves, 'the tyrants Hope and Fear', as Lucian calls them; but it has never had to contend with so much external pressure as it has today. Newspapers, posters, films, and television constantly urge us to buy what we do not want; loudspeaker-vans blare into our consciousness conclusive arguments for supporting campaigns of which we do not approve; even the oldest Christian church advertises in the daily press. Under the sheltering wing of big business, miracles and prophecies are having a new lease of life. While medical science denies that baldness can be cured, clinics charge fantastic sums for treatments strongly reminiscent of Alexander's prescription:

> Rub on Cytmis, I command you,
> Sprinkled with the dew of horses.

And even a newspaper which claims to cater for educated readers includes a daily column on what the stars foretell. In such a world Lucian's sardonic realism is a valuable prophylactic.

However, his main appeal must be as a writer, not a thinker; and here we are better qualified to enjoy him than our ancestors ever were. Our great qualification is our increasing ignorance of classical literature. When we first read that Chaucer got up early one morning, for the express purpose of kneeling down on the grass and 'greeting' a newly-opened daisy, we think it charmingly original of him. And when the scholars tell us that the whole thing is merely a literary convention, it is fortunately too late to spoil our enjoyment. So it is with Lucian. To us he gives the impression of being immensely original, and no amount of references to parallel passages in other authors can wholly destroy the illusion. There used to be a catchword: 'It is impossible not to be thrilled by Edgar Wallace'. I think it is still extremely difficult not to be entertained by Lucian.

7

In deciding what to include in this selection, I first short-listed Lucian's most famous works, and then chose from the list the ones that I liked best. The subjectivity of the second criterion may have produced a distorted picture of Lucian; for instance it has meant leaving out the wholly solemn *Nigrinus*. But one cannot do justice in translation to a piece that one finds rather dull in the original, and I can cite a fourth-century authority for presenting Lucian as primarily a humorous writer. 'He was a man', said Eunapius, 'who made very serious efforts to be funny.'

The Lucianic Dialogue is a combination of the philosphical dialogue used by Plato with the fantastic, farcical, and satirical comedy of Aristophanes, and the more realistic comedy of Menander. Like all Lucian's work, it was meant for public reading, not for stage-production. There are no stage-directions, and all the action is ingeniously suggested in the dialogue itself. To be effective in English as it stands, it would have to be read aloud by someone with the histrionic gifts of Dickens, Ruth Draper, or Emlyn Williams, and sold on long-playing records. Rather than propose such a break with the traditions of Penguin Classics, I thought it best to insert full stage-directions, wherever implied by the text, and thus convert the form into something more like a play. In fact these Sketches, as I have called them, vary in character from one-act one-set plays (e.g. *Conversations in Low Society*) to film-scripts involving talk during cross-country flight (e.g. *A Beauty Competition*) and fantasies which only a cartoon film could present in visual terms (e.g. *Charon Sees Life*). I have also supplied titles where Lucian has failed to do so, and expanded his when they seemed unduly elliptical.

Lucian prided himself on the correctness of his Greek, and a ninth-century bishop says of his style: 'It is so harmonious that when read aloud it does not sound like words, but like indefinable music that trickles into the listener's ears.' This quality of his writing I have not attempted to reproduce, since nowadays 'musical' prose seems incompatible with the brisk conversational tone that is even more typical of Lucian. Nor have I allowed a sense of his 'correctness' to rule out modern colloquialisms when they appeared appropriate. Thus I have tried to convey the spirit and over-all effect of his style, while consciously sacrificing some of its literary character.

Much of Lucian's incidental humour takes the form of verbal acrobatics which cannot always be rendered literally into English. In such cases I have given the nearest equivalent that struck me as potentially amusing, and ruthlessly taken advantage of any modern connotations that might have become attached to Lucian's words. Joyce's *Ulysses* and Empson's *Seven Types of Ambiguity* have taught us that *pun* is not necessarily a dirty word, and I felt it essential to retain the habit of centrifugal allusiveness which gives a certain body to Lucian's style, even when his thought seems rather tenuous. As for my occasional sins of anachronism, I doubt if they would worry Lucian, for anachronism is an important part of his own comic technique; and if I come across him in the Underworld, I shall not, on this account, be afraid to meet his eye.

★

Lucian generally explains himself; but he sometimes alludes to myths, historical facts, philosophical theories, and bits of biographical gossip, with which the reader may not be familiar. He will find such allusions explained in the Glossary, under the proper names mentioned in the text. The main function of the Notes is merely to give references for quotations, etc., though a few of them are also explanatory.

P. D. L. T.

TALKS

THE DREAM

OR

A CHAPTER OF MY LIFE

(A talk given by Lucian on revisiting his home-town)

WHEN I was a teenager and had just left school, my father started consulting his friends about my further education. Most of them thought that an academic training took too much time and effort, besides being expensive and requiring considerable capital – whereas we had very little, and needed a quick return for our money. But if I was taught some ordinary trade, I could earn my keep right away, as a boy of my age ought to do, instead of living on my family. And before very long my father would have the benefit of my wages.

So the next question was, which trade was it to be? It had to be something respectable and easy to learn, that didn't require too much equipment and would bring in an adequate income. Various suggestions were made, prompted by personal taste or experience, but as my uncle was there – my maternal uncle, that is, who was supposed to be an excellent sculptor – my father turned to him and said:

'With your example before us, there's no doubt what we must choose. Do take this young man' (indicating me) 'as your apprentice, and turn him into an expert stonemason and sculptor. I'm sure he's capable of it, for as you know, he has quite a gift for that sort of thing.'

He was thinking of how I'd played with wax when I was a child. The moment I was let out of school, I used to scrape all the wax off my writing-tablet, and model it into the shape of a cow or a horse or even a human being – and according to my father the results were quite lifelike. I was always getting into trouble with the teachers about it, but now it was taken as a sign of natural genius, and these early experiments of mine in the plastic arts encouraged everyone to believe that I'd soon learn the technique of sculpture.

It seemed as good a day as any for starting my apprenticeship, so I was handed over to my uncle right away. I had no particular objection to the arrangement. On the contrary, I thought I'd have great fun showing off to my friends, when I was able to carve gods and manufacture statuettes for myself, and for anyone else I cared to give them to.

Well, the first thing that happened was what you might expect. My uncle handed me a chisel and hammer, and told me to start chipping gently away at a small slab of marble that was lying on the floor of his workshop.

'Well begun, you know, is half done,' he assured me.

Through lack of experience I brought the hammer down a bit too hard, and split the slab in two. My uncle flew into a rage, reached for a stick, and went to work on me in no very kindly or encouraging manner, so that the first product of my apprenticeship was a flood of tears. I ran off home still sobbing and crying my eyes out, reported the incident of the stick, and displayed my bruises. I accused my uncle of every sort of cruelty, adding that he'd done it out of jealousy, for fear I turned out a better sculptor than he was. My mother was very cross, and said a lot of rude things about her brother – and eventually I cried myself to sleep.

So far, ladies and gentlemen, my story has been quite childish and absurd. But what I'm going to tell you now is a serious matter, and you must listen very carefully. For, as Homer says,[1]

> Athwart the ambrosial darkness of the night
> Appeared a dream divine,

a dream so vivid that it seemed to be absolutely real. After all these years I can still see it in my mind's eye, and the words I heard that night still ring in my ears. The whole thing was so intensely lifelike.

Two women had got hold of my arms, and were pulling me violently in opposite directions. In fact competition was so keen that they very nearly tore me in two. First one of them would seem to be winning, and about to establish a monopoly – and then the other would grab me back again.

'He's mine!' one of them kept shouting. 'And I mean to keep him!'

'Let go!' shouted the other. 'You've got no right to other people's property!'

One was a rather masculine-looking working-class woman, with her hair in a filthy mess, callouses all over her hands, sleeves rolled up, and clothes covered with dust – in fact just like my uncle, when he was busy polishing stone. The other had a beautiful face, a lovely figure, and most attractive clothes.

Eventually they referred the dispute to me for arbitration – which of them did I want to go and live with? The tough masculine-looking one led off as follows:

'I'm Sculpture, deary, you was introduced to me yesterday, and I'm already one of the family, for your grandad' (here she mentioned the name of my mother's father) 'was a stone-mason, and so are both your uncles, and very well thought of they are too, thanks to me, and if you'll only stop listening to *her* silly nonsense' (pointing at the other woman) 'and come and live with me, first of all I'll make a man of you and give you good strong arms, and secondly you won't get yourself disliked, or ever leave your home and family and go off to foreign parts, and people will respect you for what you can do, not just for what you can say, and don't turn up your nose at me because I'm a bit common to look at and my clothes aren't too clean, because that's how Phidias looked when he was working on his Zeus, and so did Polyclitus when he was doing his Hera, and look at Myron and Praxiteles, how every-one admires them, you'd think they were gods themselves the way people talk, and if you become one of them, what's to stop you being famous all over the world, and making people think your father a lucky man, and being a credit to your country?'

She said a lot more to the same effect, constantly stumbling over her words, using all sorts of bad grammar, and just stringing her remarks hurriedly together in her anxiety to convince me. But I can't tell you exactly what she said, for most of it has slipped my memory.

When she'd finished, the other woman said something like this:

'I, my child, am Culture. You've already made my acquaintance, although you've not had time to get to know me properly. This lady has explained the great benefits that you will derive from being a stonemason. They may be summarized as follows. You'll be an ordinary workman, entirely dependent for your livelihood on manual labour. You'll be quite unknown, and have a wretchedly inadequate income. You'll always be a low-brow, and remain intellectually undeveloped. You'll never be valued by your friends, feared by your enemies, or envied by your fellow-countrymen. You'll just be a working man, a member of the proletariat, always having to kow-tow to the upper classes and lick the boots of educated people – in fact you'll have an absolute dog's life, for you'll be completely at the mercy of your superiors. And even if you do become a Phidias or a Polyclitus, and produce wonderful works of art, your technique may be very much admired, but no one in his senses will want to change places with you. For however successful you are, you'll always be regarded as a common labourer, a mere manual worker who lives by the sweat of his brow.

'But if you'll listen to me, I'll tell you all the wonderful things that men have said and done in the past, and make you practically omniscient. As for the most important part of you, your soul, I'll give it a really effective beauty treatment, using only the very purest spiritual cosmetics, such as wisdom, justice, piety, kindness, virtue, understanding, patience, the love of goodness, and the impulse towards perfection. Past events and present duties will be equally clear to you, and with my help you'll even be able to predict the future. In short, I'll soon make you familiar with every sphere of knowledge, both human and divine.

'At the moment you're poor, the son of a nobody, and you've even thought of practising a wretched trade like this. But before long you'll be a general object of admiration and envy, praised and respected by the aristocracy, and looked up to by your social and financial superiors. You'll be able to dress as well as I do' (pointing to her own clothes, which were certainly very fine) 'and you'll be asked to join the government, and given front seats at everything. Even if you go abroad, you'll still have plenty of publicity, for I'll make you such an unmistakable figure that everyone who sees you will nudge his neighbour, and point at you, and say: "Look! There's Lucian!"'

'At any serious crisis affecting your friends or the whole community, everyone will turn to you. Whenever you make a speech, the whole audience will listen open-mouthed, astonished at your eloquence, and think what a lucky man your father is. And you know those stories about human beings who become immortal? Well, I can arrange that for you too. Even after your death you'll still move in intellectual circles, and associate with all the best people.

'Think how great I made Demosthenes, in spite of his humble origin. Think of Aeschines, whose mother's only accomplishment was playing the drum – and yet I made Philip of Macedon go down on his knees to him. Why, even Socrates was once under the influence of this lady's sculpturesque charms, but as soon as he learned to discriminate, he deserted her for me – and you know how everyone sings his praises now.

'Are you going to ignore the example of great men like

these, and renounce the hope of splendid achievements, noble speeches, gorgeous clothes, praise, honour, and glory, power, position, and privilege, literary fame, and intellectual triumph? Are you going to put on a dirty overal, and work like a slave with hammers and chisels and crowbars, always bent down over your work, earth-bound, earth-orientated, and low in every sense of the word, and never raising your eyes or your thoughts to anything worthy of a free man's contemplation? Are you going to concentrate exclusively on making your statues graceful and well-proportioned, and never think of doing the same for yourself? Are you really less important than a block of stone?'

Before she had finished speaking, I rose and gave my verdict. Turning my back on that common, ugly woman, I flung myself gladly into the arms of Culture – all the more gladly when I remembered the episode of the stick, and thought how Sculpture had treated me the day before. In her rage at being deserted, she shook her fist at me and ground her teeth – but eventually she followed Niobe's example, and turned into stone. It may sound rather improbable, but you must take my word for it, for strange things happen in dreams.

'And now,' Culture told me, 'I'm going to reward you for making such a wise decision. Come over here and get into my chariot.' She pointed to the vehicle in question, which was drawn by winged horses of the Pegasus variety. 'I want to show you what you'd have missed by not coming to me.'

I climbed in, and she picked up the reins and drove off. I found myself lifted up to a great height, from which I surveyed all the towns and countries of the world from East to West, and like Triptolemus scattered seed over the earth. What sort of seed it was, I don't remember. All I know is that wherever I went, people gazed up at me admiringly, and gave me an enthusiastic send-off when I left.

Having shown me all this, and shown me off to my public, she brought me home again. I was now dressed like a very important person, though I'd been wearing quite ordinary clothes when I started off. My father was standing waiting for me, so she showed him how I was dressed, and how famous I'd become, and reminded him what a disastrous choice of career he'd nearly made for me.

Well, that was my dream. I suppose it was the result of emotional disturbance caused by the shock of the beating – for I was still almost a child.

While I was telling you all this, I heard one of you say:

'Good Lord, what a very long and boring dream!'

Then someone else chipped in:

'A Midwinter Night's Dream, presumably! He must have had it on the longest night in the year. Or perhaps, like Hercules, it took three whole nights to conceive! But what on earth possessed him to go maundering on so long about this childish dream of his? He must be getting senile – it's all so stale and uninteresting. Who does he think we are? Dream-analysts or what?'

No, sir, let me explain. Do you remember that passage[2] where Xenophon records a dream about his father's house being on fire, and so on? Of course you do. Well, that wasn't just a bit of play-acting, or just an excuse to talk nonsense. Obviously not, considering the context – a desperate situation in wartime, with the Greeks totally surrounded by the enemy. No, the dream was told for a purpose, and so was the dream that I've been telling you. That purpose was to encourage young men to make the right choice and go all out for culture, especially those who may be inclined through poverty to take the course of least resistance, and waste their natural gifts by choosing an inferior way of life. Any such person will, I'm sure, be fired by my example and think it worth following, when he considers how, undeterred by poverty, I pinned my faith on culture and set off in pursuit of perfection – when he considers what I was then, and what you see me today – as famous, at least, as any sculptor I know of!

ZEUXIS

OR

CENTAURS AND ELEPHANTS

(*One of a series of talks*)

I WAS just going home after giving my last talk, when several members of the audience came up to me – I'm sure there's no harm in saying this sort of thing among friends, as you all are by now – well, as I say, they came up to me, shook me warmly by the hand, and seemed much impressed by my performance. They followed me down the road, calling out all kinds of complimentary remarks, until I began to feel quite embarrassed, realizing how little I'd done to deserve it. But the chief point they made, the one feature they all picked out for special praise, was the paradoxical nature of my ideas. Perhaps I'd better quote their actual words:

'Such originality!' they exclaimed. 'So wonderfully unusual! The man's a genius! How on earth does he think of such things?'

They made several other such comments, which evidently expressed their genuine reactions to my talk – for what reason had they to lie? Why should they wish to flatter a perfect stranger, who wasn't worth bothering about from any other point of view? However, I must admit that I found this praise of theirs extremely annoying, and when they finally went off and left me to myself, I started thinking:

'So the one and only charm of my productions is that they're off the beaten track! As for any beauty of phrasing, conceived on classical lines, any acuteness, or profundity, or Attic grace, or polished style, or architectonic skill, apparently there's nothing of that sort in my work whatever! If there were, they wouldn't ignore it, and only praise the novelty of my material.'

Of course, I always realized, when people jumped up and clapped me, that this aspect of my work had probably something to do with it, for Homer was quite right when he said[1] that novelty always goes down well with an audience. But I was foolish enough to imagine that this was not the chief or the whole secret of my success, but merely an extra attraction which contributed towards it – and that what they were really applauding were the qualities I've mentioned. The result was that I became quite conceited, and almost believed them when they told me that I was the greatest man in Greece, and things like that. But now it's all turned to dust and ashes, for I realize that I'm merely regarded as a sort of conjurer.

I'd like to tell you a story about Zeuxis. This great artist was seldom, if ever, content to paint ordinary, everyday things like heroes, or gods, or wars, but was always trying to do something different. His method was to think of some really outlandish subject, and then use it as a means of displaying his virtuosity. One of his many such daring experiments was a picture of a female Centaur – and what's more she was depicted in the act of suckling two Centaur-babies. An extremely accurate copy of it is still to be seen at Athens. The original is said to have been packed off to Italy by the Roman general, Sulla, along with several other art treasures, but the ship went down, somewhere off Cape Malea I think, and the whole cargo was lost, including this work. However, I've at least seen a picture of the picture in question, and I'll do my best to describe it to you – not that I know anything about art, goodness knows! But I remember this particular painting very well, for I saw it quite recently at the house of an artist-friend of mine at Athens, and it made such an impression on me at the time that I may be able to give you a fairly clear idea of it.

The mother Centaur was shown with her horse-part lying on some soft grass, and her hind legs stretched out backwards. The woman-part was slightly raised from the ground and propped on its elbow. The front legs weren't stretched out as

they would have been if she'd been lying on her side, but one
of them was folded under her with the hoof tucked away out
of sight, and the other was raised in the act of pawing the
ground, as horses do when they're trying to get up. She was
holding one of the new-born babies in her arms, and breast-
feeding it in the normal human manner, but the other was
sucking away at the horse-part like an ordinary foal. In the
upper half of the picture, on a bit of rising ground, appeared
a male Centaur, presumably the husband of the lady who was
suckling a baby at each end of her anatomy. The hind quarters
of his horse-body were out of the picture, but the rest of it
was visible, and he himself could be seen bending down with
a smile on his face. In his right hand was a lion cub, which he
was waving about over his head, as if in a playful attempt to
scare the babies.

Not being an art critic, I'm in no position to judge the
technical merits of the picture, though it's doubtless dependent
on them for its total effect. I mean things like accurate
draughtsmanship, appropriate choice of colours, efficient
brushwork, proper use of light and shade, correct proportions,
satisfactory relation of the parts to the whole, and harmonious
composition. All that I must leave to the experts, whose
business it is to understand such things. But what impressed
me was this: in his treatment of a single theme he'd given so
many subtle indications of his extraordinary talent. For
instance, he'd made the male a wild and terrifying figure, with
a magnificent great mane, and its body all covered with hair,
not only the horse-part but the human part as well. And there
was something about the shoulders, and about the facial
expression, in spite of the smile, that made it look completely
animal, like some savage creature of the mountains.

The female was quite different. Her horse-component was
extremely handsome, like the horses that you see in Thessaly,
which have never to this day been broken in or ridden, and
her upper half was that of a beautiful woman, except that the

ears were pointed like a satyr's. As for the fusion of the two
types of body, the human and the equine, the transition from
one to the other was contrived by such minute gradations as
to be almost imperceptible.

I was also much impressed by the treatment of the Centaur's
young. They were simultaneously babyish and savage, tender
and yet already formidable. And there was something exquis-
itely childlike about the way they were looking up at the
lion cub, while still nestling close against their mother, and
never letting go of the teat.

When this picture was first exhibited, Zeuxis hoped that it
would make a big sensation. And sure enough, as soon as
people saw it, they started uttering cries of astonishment.
What else could they do, when confronted by such a master-
piece? But like my own admirers the other day, what they all
selected for special praise was the strangeness, the novelty of
the conception, the fact that such a thing had never been done
before. Realizing that the unusual subject was distracting
attention from the technique and making people overlook
the accomplishment of the execution, he turned to one of his
students and said:

'All right, Miccio, you can wrap it up now and take it home.
These people only admire the raw material of our art. What
we're trying to do with it, and how far we succeed, are
questions that they never bother to ask. A sensational theme
means far more to them than genuine artistry.'

Well, that was how Zeuxis saw it – though perhaps you
think he shouldn't have lost his temper. A rather similar thing
is said to have happened to Antiochus Soter, in his battle
against the Galatians. I'll tell you that story too, if you like.
Antiochus knew that his opponents were very good fighters,
and could see that they were there in great strength. They
were drawn up in a solid mass, with twenty-four ranks of
heavy-armed infantry in front, twenty thousand cavalry on
each wing, and in the centre, all set to come racing out at him,

eight four-horse chariots fitted with scythes on their wheels.

When he saw all this, his heart sank and he thought he'd
never be able to face them, for his own troops had been
mobilized at very short notice, and he'd arrived on the battlefield with quite inadequate forces, mostly light-armed infantry – and more than half of them had no proper equipment.
So he thought he'd have to come to terms, and find some
excuse to end the war without losing too much face.

However, he had a Rhodian on his staff called Theodotas,
a brave man and a great tactical expert, who wouldn't hear
of such a defeatist policy. Now Antiochus had sixteen elephants. Theodotas gave orders for these to be temporarily
concealed, so that they wouldn't be seen towering above the rest
of the army. But when the trumpet sounded the signal to en-
gage, when the Galatian cavalry began to charge and their front
line opened to let out the chariots – at that moment four elephants on each wing were to be driven against the enemy cavalry,
and the remaining eight were to counter-attack the chariots.

'If we do that,' said Theodotas, 'their horses will take fright
and bolt back among their own infantry.'

And that is precisely what happened. The unexpected sight
of the elephants, even at long range, completely unnerved the
Galatians and their horses. The moment they heard them
trumpeting, and saw their great tusks gleaming white against
the blackness of their bodies, and saw their trunks waving
about in the air, as if in search of prey – without even waiting
for them to come within bowshot, they turned and retreated
in disorder. The infantry were impaled on one another's
spears and trampled underfoot by the cavalry, who fell back
on them in blind panic. And the chariots wheeled round too,
and went charging about among their own troops, adding
considerably to the bloodshed. Then, as Homer says,[2]

Many a car of war was overthrown.

The horses were quite unable to face the elephants, and once out of control, they soon got rid of their drivers and galloped off

With empty chariots rattling behind them,[3]

slashing and dismembering with their scythes anyone who got in their way – and in the general confusion only too many *did* get in their way. The elephants lumbered after them, trampling men underfoot, or seizing them with their trunks and hurling them into the air, or goring them with their tusks. Finally, by sheer brute force, the elephants gave Antiochus the victory.

By this time, most of the Galatians had been killed and the rest had been taken prisoner, except for a very few who managed to escape into the mountains. So the Macedonians raised a song of triumph, and started crowding round Antiochus, presenting him with wreaths of victory and calling him a mighty conqueror. But Antiochus, we're told, burst into tears.

'Men,' he said, 'we should all be ashamed of ourselves. We owe our lives entirely to these sixteen animals. If their strange appearance hadn't sent the enemy into a panic, what on earth could we have done?'

And all he let them engrave on the trophy was a picture of an elephant.

So I must make sure I don't find myself in the same position as Antiochus, inadequately equipped in every respect, except that I've got a few elephants, a few outlandish oddities, a few conjuring tricks to surprise my audience with – for that's all they ever praise me for. They pay no attention whatever to the virtues I've always relied on. All that interests them is that I've painted a female Centaur. That seems to them very strange and wonderful, and so indeed it is – but apparently everything else this poor Zeuxis has tried to do has been a waste of time. Not entirely a waste, though, for some of you, I know, examine every detail of my work with the eye of a connoisseur. I only hope I can show you something worthy of your scrutiny.

SKETCHES

Conversations in Low Society

MOTHER KNOWS BEST

OR

A YOUNG GIRL'S GUIDE TO SUCCESS

Scene: A shabby living-room in Athens. Crobyle, a middle-aged woman, is talking to her teenage daughter, Corinna.

CROBYLE: There now, Corinna, that wasn't as bad as you thought, was it – going to bed with a nice young man and earning your first mina? And I'm going to spend some of it right away to buy you a new necklace.

CORINNA: Oh, thanks, Mum. Can I have one like Lycaenis's, with lots of jewels in it?

CROBYLE: That's just the kind it will be. But first I want to give you a bit more advice on how to behave with men. You see, dear, it's our only source of income. You know what a struggle we've had to make ends meet these last two years, since your poor father died. So long as he was alive, we never went short of anything, for he'd made quite a name for himself in the Piraeus – in fact everyone swears there'll never be a blacksmith to touch him. When he died, I sold his hammer and tongs and anvil for two minas, and that kept us going for a while. Then I did various odd jobs like dressmaking and spinning and weaving, to scrape together enough for us to live on. But all the time I was struggling to bring you up, this was what I was hoping for.

CORINNA: This mina, do you mean?

CROBYLE: No, not just that. I reckoned that once you were grown up, as you are now, you'd soon be able to support me, and buy your own jewellery, and have lots of money and servants and gorgeous clothes.

CORINNA: Why, however did you expect me to do that, Mum? I don't understand.

CROBYLE: Simply by going about with young men, and having drinks with them, and getting paid to sleep with them.

CORINNA: What, like that girl Lyra!

CROBYLE: Yes.

CORINNA [*bursting into tears*]: But she's a prostitute!

CROBYLE: Well, what's so dreadful about that? It means that you'll be rich like her, and always have plenty of boy-friends. Oh, what on earth are you crying for, Corinna? Don't you realize what important people prostitutes are these days? Don't you know what a great demand there is for them, and how much money they make? Why, goodness me, I remember how shabby Lyra's mother Daphnis used to be before Lyra grew up, and now look at her – masses of jewellery, wonderful clothes, and four servants to wait on her!

CORINNA: But how did Lyra manage to earn all that?

CROBYLE: Well, first of all by dressing nicely, and being polite and charming to everyone – not going off into hoots of laughter at the slightest pretext, as you tend to do, but just smiling in a pleasant, attractive sort of way. And then, by knowing how to behave – giving every client his money's worth, but never throwing herself at a man's head. If a client takes her to a dinner-party, she doesn't get drunk – for that makes a girl look ridiculous, and men hate her for it – and she doesn't forget her manners and stuff herself with food. She picks up each morsel delicately with the tips of her fingers, instead of cramming the whole lot in until both cheeks are bulging. And she takes her wine in tiny sips, instead of just opening her mouth and pouring the stuff down.

CORINNA: But what if she's thirsty, Mother?

CROBYLE: She's all the more careful how she drinks, Corinna. And she never talks too much, or makes fun of the other

guests, and she always keeps her eye on the man she's with.
That's what they like about her. And when she's sleeping
with anyone, she's careful not to seem either too interested
or not interested enough, and concentrates on leading the
man on and encouraging him to make love to her. That's
another thing about her that they all appreciate. If you can
only learn to behave like her, you'll make both our fortunes,
for in other respects she's not a patch – but touch wood,
I'll say no more. All we want is enough to live on.

CORINNA: I say, Mother, will all my clients be as nice as
Eucritus, the boy I slept with last night?

CROBYLE: Not all of them. A few will be even nicer, but
some will be middle-aged, and mayn't be particularly good-
looking.

CORINNA: Shall I have to sleep with the ugly ones too?

CROBYLE: Of course you will, dear. They usually pay much
better. The handsome ones seem to think it's enough to pay
in kind. But you must always stick out for as much money
as possible, if you want to have all the other girls pointing
at you before long and saying: 'Oh look, there's Corinna,
the one that's got all that money! What a blessing she's
been to her mother!' Well, what do you say? Will you do
it? I know you will, and you'll do it far better than any of
the others. So now off you go and have a bath, in case
young Eucritus pays you another visit tonight. He said he
would.

THE LANGUAGE OF TRUE LOVE

*Scene: A street in Athens. Ampelis, a prostitute in her late thirties,
is talking to a younger one, Chrysis.*

AMPELIS: But look here, Chrysis. Suppose he never got jealous
or lost his temper – suppose he never knocked you about,

or cut off your hair, or tore your clothes, would you really call that being in love with you?

CHRYSIS: Why, is that the only way you can tell?

AMPELIS: Of course it is. That shows he's really in a state about you. Things like kisses and tears and promises and constant visits are merely the first symptoms. It's only when they start getting jealous that you know they're really in love. So if Gorgias has been knocking you about as much as you say, it's a very good sign. Let's hope he goes on like that.

CHRYSIS: Goes on knocking me about, do you mean?

AMPELIS: Not necessarily, but goes on being upset if you ever look at another man. For if he weren't in love with you, why should he care how many lovers you had?

CHRYSIS: Well, actually, I haven't any. But he's got a silly idea into his head that that rich gentleman's in love with me, just because I happened to mention him the other day.

AMPELIS: Oh, that's splendid, if he thinks someone rich is after you. He'll be all the more upset, and start offering you better terms. He won't want his rival to outbid him.

CHRYSIS: Well, all he's done so far is get cross and knock me about. He hasn't given me a thing.

AMPELIS: He will, don't you worry. They always do if they're jealous – especially if you make them really miserable.

CHRYSIS: Darling, I don't quite see why you're so anxious for me to be knocked about.

AMPELIS: I'm not, but the way I see it is this. If you want him to develop a real passion for you, you must pretend not to care for him. If he thinks he's got a monopoly, he'll very soon lose interest. You can take my word for it – I've had twenty years' experience in the trade, and you can't be more than eighteen, if that.

Shall I tell you what happened to me a few years ago? I was having an affair with Demophantus – you know, that money-lender who lives at the back of the Town Hall. He never gave me more than five drachmas a time, and for that he seemed to regard me as his personal property. But his feelings for me never went at all deep. There was never any question of sighing or weeping or turning up on my doorstep in the middle of the night. He merely slept with me from time to time – and at pretty long intervals too.

Then one night I refused to let him in – I'd got an artist called Callides with me, and he'd given me ten drachmas. Well, all he did at the time was go off shouting abuse, but when several days went by without his hearing from me, Demophantus began to get rather hot under the collar. When he reached boiling-point, he suddenly burst into the house one day – he'd been watching for the door to open – and started crying, and hitting me, and threatening to murder me, and tearing my clothes, and goodness knows what else. Finally he gave me a whole talent, on the strength of which I lived for eight months exclusively with him. His wife told everyone I'd given him an aphrodisiac and sent him crazy with it. But all I'd actually given him was a dose of jealousy. So I suggest you use the same prescription on Gorgias. He'll be quite a rich young man when his father dies.

THE RESULTS OF SHOOTING A LINE

Scene: A public house in Athens. Two soldiers on leave, Leontichus and Chenidas, are sitting having drinks with two girls that they have picked up, Hymnis and Grammis.

LEONTICHUS: Tell her about that battle with the Galatians, Chenidas. Tell her how I led a cavalry-charge on that white horse of mine. They were no cowards, those Galatians, but they all turned tail at the sight of me. There wasn't a single man that stood his ground. So then I let fly with my javelin at their commander-in-chief – it went straight through his body and through his horse as well. After that I drew my sword and made a furious charge at what was left of them – for though they'd all broken ranks, a few of them were trying to reform in a hollow square. With the sheer momentum of my horse I knocked down seven or eight of their best men, and then I came slashing down with my sword and neatly bisected the head of a cavalry-lieutenant, helmet and all. By the time you turned up, Chenidas, their whole army was on the run.

CHENIDAS: What about that duel you had with the Persian Governor, Leontichus, somewhere in Paphlagonia? You put up a pretty good show on that occasion too.

LEONTICHUS: Oh, thanks for reminding me. No, that wasn't a bad bit of work either. You see, this Persian Governor was a huge great fellow who was generally thought to be the best fighter they had. So thinking nothing of us Greeks, he came swaggering out into no-man's-land and offered to fight a duel with anyone who felt equal to it. All our company commanders and platoon commanders were absolutely terrified, and so was the general himself, although he wasn't at all a bad type. He was an Aetolian called Aristaechmus, an expert javelin-thrower, and our commander-in-chief, for at that time I was only a colonel. But I accepted the challenge, and shaking off the friends who were trying to hold me back – for they felt rather anxious about me, when they saw that huge savage in his glittering gold-plated armour, with a fearful great crest on top of his helmet, brandishing his spear at me –

CHENIDAS: Yes, I felt pretty anxious myself, Leontichus. Do you remember how I clung to you, and begged you not to take such a risk? If you're killed, I said, life won't be worth living any more.

LEONTICHUS: Even so, I accepted the challenge. Out I went to meet him, and in fact my armour was every bit as good as his, for it was made of solid gold. Immediately a great shout went up from both armies, for the Paphlagonians recognized me the moment they saw me, by my shield and helmet and crest. I forget who they all said I looked like at that moment – do you happen to remember, Chenidas?

CHENIDAS: Why, Achilles, of course! Who else? Your helmet seemed to blaze out just like his,[1] and then there was that gorgeous red cloak round your shoulders, and that flashing shield on your arm!

LEONTICHUS: When we started fighting, the Persian drew first blood with his spear – but it was merely a scratch, just above the knee. I replied by driving my pike straight through his shield and into his chest. Then I leapt on him, and without the slightest trouble sliced off his head with my sword. The next moment I was on my way back, carrying his armour in one hand, and with the other waving his head about on the top of my pike – and giving myself a shower-bath of blood in the process!

HYMNIS [*jumping up*]: Ugh! Get away from me, Leontichus! What a horrible disgusting story! If you enjoy killing people as much as that, I never want to see you again, let alone have drinks with you, or go to bed with you! I won't stay here a moment longer!

LEONTICHUS: I'll give you double the usual rate.

HYMNIS: No, I couldn't bear to sleep with a murderer.

LEONTICHUS: There's no need to be frightened, Hymnis darling. All that was in Paphlagonia. And it's peacetime now.

HYMNIS [*going towards the door*]: I don't care. There's something nasty about you. You were all splashed with blood from that Persian's head, when you waved it about on your pike! Do you expect me to put my arms round you after that? Do you expect me to kiss you? Good gracious, I might as well kiss the public hangman!

LEONTICHUS: If you'd only seen me in that golden armour, I'm sure you'd have fallen in love with me.

HYMNIS [*at the door*]: It makes me feel quite sick even to hear about it, Leontichus. It's horrible – I can almost see the ghosts of your victims, especially that poor cavalry lieutenant with his head chopped in two! How do you suppose I'd have felt if I'd actually been there – if I'd actually seen the blood, and all those corpses lying on the ground? I think I'd have died – why, I've never even seen a chicken being killed!

LEONTICHUS: Are you really such a little coward, Hymnis? I thought the story would amuse you.

HYMNIS: I dare say it would, if I were a murderess. Go and see if you can find one. Personally I'm going home to Mother, this moment, before it gets dark. And you'd better come with me, Grammis. As for you, my brave Colonel, good-bye – you wholesale murderer!

LEONTICHUS: Wait a minute, Hymnis. Do wait –

[*Exit Hymnis, with Grammis in tow.*]

She's gone.

CHENIDAS: Well, what did you expect, Leontichus – frightening the poor child stiff with your waving plumes and incredible feats of prowess? The moment you started that bit about the cavalry lieutenant, I saw her turn pale, and the mere mention of chopping his head in two made her screw up her face and shudder.

LEONTICHUS: I thought it would add to my charm. Anyway, it was partly your fault, Chenidas, for suggesting that duel.

CHENIDAS: Well, I had to back you up, didn't I? I could see what you were driving at. But you made it far too gruesome. It was all very well cutting off that wretched Paphlagonian's head, but why did you have to stick it on the end of your pike, with the blood pouring down all over you?

LEONTICHUS: Yes, that bit really *was* rather disgusting, Chenidas, but you must admit the rest made a jolly good story. Well, see if you can persuade her to come back and sleep with me?

CHENIDAS: Shall I tell her you invented the whole thing, because you wanted her to think you a hero?

LEONTICHUS: Wouldn't that be rather a come-down, Chenidas?

CHENIDAS: Maybe, but it's the only way to get her back. So take your choice. Do you want to be a hero that she hates, or a liar that she's willing to sleep with?

LEONTICHUS: I'm not too keen on either alternative. But on the whole I'd rather have Hymnis. So off you go, Chenidas, and tell her that I just made it up – but not quite all of it.

Conversations in High Society

THE NEW SLEEPING PARTNER

Scene: The grounds of the royal palace in heaven. Ganymede, a good-looking boy scantily dressed in a sheep-skin, stands registering bewilderment. Behind him, with his hands on the boy's shoulders, is a tall bearded man, Zeus. Hermes, a handsome youth with wings on his sandals and hat, is waiting in the background.

ZEUS: All right, Ganymede, now that I've got you here, you can give me a kiss – just to make sure that the hooked beak and sharp claws and wings have really gone.

GANYMEDE [*turning round and staring*]: Why, you're a human being! But weren't you an eagle a moment ago? Didn't you come swooping down and whisk me away from my sheep? Then what's happened to all your feathers? Are you moulting, or what? You look completely different all of a sudden.

ZEUS: No, my boy, I'm not really an eagle. Nor am I a human being. [*Grandly.*] You see before you the king of all the gods. [*Reverting to an ordinary tone.*] That eagle business was just a temporary disguise.

GANYMEDE: Do you mean to say you're the great god Pan? Then why haven't you got a Pan-pipe and horns? And why aren't your legs more hairy?

ZEUS [*contemptuously*]: Is that fellow really your idea of a god?

GANYMEDE: Of course he is – or we shouldn't sacrifice a perfectly good billy-goat to him, in that cave where his image is. But I know what you are – you're a kidnapper!

ZEUS: Come now, haven't you ever heard of Zeus? Haven't you ever seen his altar on Mount Gargarus? The god that sends the rain, and the thunder, and the lightning?

GANYMEDE: Oh, so you're the kind gentleman that's been sending us all the hail lately? The one that lives in the sky and kicks up such a racket? The one that my father sacrificed a ram to the other day? Well, what have I done now, Your Majesty? What have I been summoned up here for? The wolves will be tearing my sheep to pieces if I don't get back pretty soon.

ZEUS: Are you still worrying about your sheep? Don't you realize that from now on you'll be an immortal, and live up here with us?

GANYMEDE: Why, won't you be taking me back to Ida at all today?

ZEUS: Certainly not. A god like me doesn't turn himself into an eagle for nothing.

GANYMEDE: But my father will be wondering where I am, and he'll be awfully cross if I don't turn up, and I'll only get a beating afterwards for leaving the sheep on their own.

ZEUS: Ah, but how's he going to find you?

GANYMEDE: No, really, I must get back. I couldn't bear never to see him again. If you'll only take me back, I promise he'll give you another ram in exchange. You can have the big three-year-old that leads the flock to pasture.

ZEUS [*over his shoulder to Hermes*]: How delightfully innocent he is! In that respect he's still quite undeveloped. [*To Ganymede.*] No, Ganymede, you must say good-bye to all that, and forget about your sheep on Mount Ida. Now that you're one of us, you'll be in a position to do your father and your country a lot of good. Instead of eating cheese and drinking milk, you'll live on a diet of ambrosia and nectar – in fact you can be responsible for the nectar supply yourself, and pour out for the rest of us. Best of all, you'll be immortal, and I'll make your star the most beautiful one in the sky – and altogether you'll have a wonderful time.

GANYMEDE: But will there be anyone to play with, if I feel like it? There were lots of boys on Mount Ida.

ZEUS: Of course. You can play with Cupid. And you can have as many toys as you want. Only do try to look a bit more cheerful, and stop wishing you were back down there.

GANYMEDE: But what possible use shall I be to you? Have you got any sheep for me to look after, or what?

ZEUS: No, but you can pour out our drinks, and take charge of the cellar, and help generally at parties.

GANYMEDE: That doesn't sound very difficult. I'm quite good at pouring milk into a jug and handing it round.

ZEUS: There he goes again! Always talking about milk and imagining he's going to wait on human beings! This is heaven, I tell you, and what we drink here, as I said before, is nectar.

GANYMEDE: Is nectar nicer than milk, then?

ZEUS: You'll soon see. Once you've tasted it, you'll never want to drink milk again.

GANYMEDE: And where shall I sleep at night? With that boy Cupid?

ZEUS: No, the whole point of bringing you up here was for you to sleep with me.

GANYMEDE: Why, can't you get to sleep by yourself? Or do you find it nicer to sleep with someone else?

ZEUS: I certainly find it nicer to sleep with a beautiful boy like you, Ganymede.

GANYMEDE: What on earth has beauty got to do with it? Does it help you to sleep?

ZEUS: Yes, it acts like a charm, and makes me sleep far more soundly.

GANYMEDE: That's funny, because my father always hated sharing a bed with me. He used to complain every morning that I'd kept him awake all night by tossing about and kicking him and talking in my sleep. So he usually made me sleep with my mother. If that's what you've brought me up for, you'd better send me back quick, or you'll never get a wink of sleep. I'll drive you mad with my constant twisting and turning.

ZEUS: There's nothing I'd like better than to stay awake all night, kissing you and holding you in my arms.

GANYMEDE: Well, you should know. But I'll probably go to sleep while you're doing it.

ZEUS: I'll know what to do about that. In the meantime, Hermes, just take him along and give him a dose of immortality, will you? And then bring him back to pour out drinks for us. But first of all, do show him the proper way to handle a wine-glass.

ZEUS IS INDISPOSED

Scene: A corridor in the palace. Enter Hermes from the royal bed-chamber, shutting the door behind him. A bearded gentleman, rather wet and carrying a trident, comes hurrying along the corridor. It is Poseidon.

POSEIDON: Oh, Hermes, could I have a word with Zeus, do you think?

HERMES: Out of the question, I'm afraid, Poseidon.

POSEIDON: All the same, just let him know I'm here.

HERMES: He mustn't be disturbed, I tell you. You've chosen a very awkward moment – you simply can't see him just now.

POSEIDON: Why, is he in bed with Hera?

HERMES: No, it's something quite different.

POSEIDON: Oh, I see what you mean. He's got Ganymede in there.

HERMES: No, it's not that either. The fact is, he's feeling rather unwell.

POSEIDON: Why, Hermes, what a terrible thing! What's the matter with him?

HERMES: Well, I hardly like to tell you.

POSEIDON: Oh, come on, I'm your uncle – you can tell *me*.

HERMES: All right, then – he's just had a baby.

POSEIDON [*roaring with laughter*]: Had a baby? Him? Who-ever by? Do you mean to say he's been a hermaphrodite all these years without our realizing? But there wasn't any sign of pregnancy – his stomach looked perfectly normal.

HERMES: You're quite right. That wasn't where he had it.

POSEIDON: Oh, I see. He produced it like Athena, out of his head. It's a very prolific organ.

HERMES: No, he's been carrying this child of Semele's in his thigh.

POSEIDON: What a splendid chap he is! He can produce babies from every part of his anatomy! But who, exactly, is Semele?

HERMES: A girl from Thebes, one of Cadmus's daughters. Zeus had an affair with her, and got her in the family way.

POSEIDON: What? And then had the baby instead of her?

HERMES: Strange as it may sound, yes. You see, Hera – you know how jealous she is – went and talked Semele into asking Zeus to bring his thunder and lightning with him next time he came to call. Zeus did as he was asked, and arrived complete with thunderbolt. The house went up in flames, and Semele was burnt to death. Zeus told me to cut her open and fetch him the embryo – it was only seven months old and pretty undeveloped. So I did that, and he slit open his thigh and popped the little thing inside to mature. Now, two months later, he's given birth, and is feeling rather poorly as a result.

POSEIDON: And where's the baby now?

HERMES: Oh, I've taken it off to Nysa, and put it out to nurse with some Nymphs. It's called Dionysus.

POSEIDON: Then, strictly speaking, my brother is not only Dionysus's father, but his mother as well?

HERMES: It looks like it. Well, I must go and get some water to clean him up, and see to all the other little things that need doing on these occasions.

THE RELUCTANT PARENT

Scene: A street in heaven. Hermes is strolling along, looking very elegant, when he is stopped by a stranger whose appearance is positively sub-human.

STRANGER: Morning, Dad.

HERMES [*coldly*]: Good morning to you, sir. But why did you call me that?

STRANGER: Well, you're Hermes of Cyllene, aren't you?

HERMES: Of course I am, but how does that make me your father?

STRANGER [*chuckling*]: I'm a little love-child, specially designed for you!

HERMES: Specially designed for a couple of goats, I should think! You can hardly be anything to do with me, with those horns on your head – and a nose that shape – and a great shaggy beard – and cloven hooves – and a tail dangling over your backside!

STRANGER: You can jeer at me as much as you like, Dad, but you're only fouling your own nest. It's not my fault that I'm like this – if it's anyone's fault, it's yours.

HERMES: Then who was your mother, may I ask? Have I inadvertently had an affair with a she-goat?

STRANGER: No, not exactly – but have you forgotten that young lady you raped in Arcadia? Oh, do stop biting your nails and pretending not to remember! You know perfectly well whom I mean – Penelope, the daughter of Icarius.

HERMES: In that case, why do you look like a goat? Why don't you take after me?

STRANGER: Well, I can only tell you what she told me, when she packed me off to Arcadia. 'My child,' she said, 'it's time you knew who your parents are. My name's Penelope, and I come from Sparta, but your father's a god called Hermes, the son of Zeus and Maia. So even if you have got horns and rather peculiar legs, don't let it worry you. The fact is, your father disguised himself as a goat to preserve his incognito, and that's why you've turned out like this.'

HERMES: Good Lord, I seem to remember doing something of the kind. Well, it's a fine situation, I must say. I've always prided myself on my physical charm, and to all appearances I'm still a beardless youth – but as soon as it gets about that I'm your father, everyone will laugh at me for producing such a handsome son!

STRANGER: But really, Dad, I'm nothing to be ashamed of. I've got quite a good ear for music, and I can make a tremendous noise on my shepherd's pipe. Dionysus says he can't get on without me, and has made me one of his Bacchants – in fact I do most of his choreography. And you've no idea what beautiful sheep I've got round Tegea and Parthenius. And I govern the whole of Arcadia. And only the other day I fought with the Athenians at Marathon, and put up such a good show that they voted me a special cave below the Acropolis, in recognition of my services. If you ever go to Athens, you'll find that Pan is a very important person there.

HERMES: But tell me, Pan – for I gather that's your name – are you married yet?

PAN: No fear, Dad! I'm far too highly sexed to be satisfied with just one wife!

HERMES: Then I take it that you confine your attentions to the she-goats?

PAN: There you go again, making fun of me! But I've been to bed with Echo, and Pitys, and every single girl in Dionysus's chorus – and they all think I'm terrific.

HERMES: Well, my boy, do you know the first favour that I want to ask you?

PAN: No, Dad. What is it?

HERMES [*looking round anxiously*]: Let's keep all this to ourselves, shall we? Come and give me a kiss, but – mind you never call me Dad when there's anyone listening!

A BEAUTY COMPETITION

Scene: The royal drawing-room in heaven. Zeus is standing by the fireplace. Seated on golden chairs about the room are his wife, Hera, a dignified, matronly figure with very large eyes and very white arms; his daughter, Athene, a grey-eyed, severe-looking intellectual type, wearing a helmet with a huge feather in it; and his younger daughter, Aphrodite, a seductive blonde, heavily made up, whose contours are emphasized by the girdle round her waist. Enter Hermes.

ZEUS: Oh, Hermes, will you please take this apple to Phrygia and give it to that cowherd-son of Priam's? You'll find him with his cows on Mount Gargarus.

[*Hermes takes the apple.*]

Tell him that in view of his own good looks and sexual experience I want him to judge a beauty competition between these goddesses. The winner gets the apple. You ladies had better go along too, so that he can do the job right away. I won't do it myself, because I'm equally devoted to all of you, and if I had my way, you'd all get first prize. There's also the further point that, whichever I declared the winner, I'd be bound to make myself unpopular with the other two. So it would be quite unsuitable for me to judge between you. But this young Phrygian is a member of a royal family – in fact he's distantly related to our friend Ganymede here. However, having always lived in the mountains, he's quite simple and unspoilt, and well-qualified to decide a question like this.

APHRODITE: As far as I'm concerned, Zeus, I'm perfectly prepared to face the most captious critic in the world – for how could anyone find fault with *me*? But I don't know how the other two feel about this particular young man.

HERA: Personally, Aphrodite, I shouldn't be in the least upset if the matter were referred to your own boy-friend, Ares. And I'm quite willing to accept the verdict of this Paris person, whoever he is.

ZEUS [*to Athene*]: And what about you, my dear? Do you agree? Come now, speak up!

[*Athene turns away, blushing.*]

Oh well, I suppose it's only natural for a virgin goddess to feel shy about these things. But just nod if you agree.

[*Athene nods.*]

That's all right then. Off you go, and mind you don't get cross with the judge if you don't win, and start beating the poor young man up. It just isn't possible for you all to be equally beautiful.

[*The three goddesses get up and follow Hermes out of the palace. Once in the open air, he starts up the wings on his sandals and takes off. The goddesses fly after him.*]

HERMES: Right, full speed ahead for Phrygia! I'll lead the way, and please don't start lagging behind. There's really no need to be nervous. I know Paris quite well – he's a most attractive young man, extremely interested in sex, and an excellent judge of such matters. You can rely on him to make the right decision.

APHRODITE: Good for him – and that's certainly a point in my favour. But tell me [*flying closer to Hermes and whispering in his ear*], is he a bachelor or a married man?

HERMES: Well, I wouldn't exactly call him a bachelor, Aphrodite.

APHRODITE: What do you mean?

HERMES: He's said to be living with a girl from Mount Ida – not bad-looking, but terribly countrified, as you might expect, considering where she comes from. Still, he doesn't seem to take her very seriously. But why do you want to know?

APHRODITE: Oh, I just thought I'd ask.

ATHENE [to Hermes]: Now, my good man, no collusion! No talking to her in private!

HERMES: There's nothing sinister about it, Athene. We weren't saying anything against you. She merely asked if Paris was a bachelor.

ATHENE: What does she want to know that for? What's it got to do with her?

HERMES: I've no idea. She says it just came into her head – there was no special reason.

ATHENE: Well, anyway, *is* he a bachelor?

HERMES: Apparently not.

ATHENE: By the way [flying closer to Hermes and whispering in his ear], has he any military ambitions, do you know, or is he content to be a cowherd all his life?

HERMES: I can't say for certain, but I should imagine that, at his age, he probably has some leanings in that direction, and would like to distinguish himself in action.

APHRODITE [to Hermes]: Please note that I haven't the slightest objection to your talking to that lady in private. Some people are always complaining – but I'm not like that.

HERMES: She merely wanted the same sort of information as you did. So don't be cross and think you've been done down, just because I gave a simple answer to a simple question. But while we've been talking, we've come a long way. The stars are far behind us, and we're almost over Phrygia. I can distinctly see Mount Ida, and the whole of

Mount Gargarus, and there, if I'm not mistaken, is the very man we're looking for.

HERA: Where? I can't see anybody.

HERMES [*pointing*]: Over there, Hera, to the left. On the hill-side, not quite at the top, but where that cave is – where you can see that herd of cows.

HERA: But I *can't* see any cows!

HERMES: Nonsense! Of course you can. Now look exactly where my finger is. Don't you see a lot of little cows coming out among the rocks, and a man running down the hill with a stick in his hand, trying to keep the herd together?

HERA: Oh yes, now I see him – if that's really the person we want.

HERMES: Certainly it is. We're getting quite close now, so don't you think we'd better land and finish our journey on foot? He might be a bit upset, if we suddenly came swooping down on him out of the sky.

HERA: Very true. We'll do as you suggest.

[*They touch down on the summit of Mount Gargarus, and start walking towards their objective.*]

Now that we're here, Aphrodite, perhaps you'd better lead the way. You must know the place quite well, considering how often you came here to see Anchises – or so people say.

APHRODITE: Cracks like that don't worry me very much, you know, Hera.

HERMES: No, I'll lead the way myself. I spent quite a lot of time here, when Zeus fell in love with Ganymede. I was always being sent down to keep an eye on him, and when Zeus finally did his eagle-act, I flew along beside him and helped to take some of the weight. In fact, if I remember rightly, this was the very rock that he whisked him up off. Ganymede was busy playing his shepherd's pipe to the sheep at the time. Zeus came swooping down from behind and flung his arms, or rather his talons round him. But he was very gentle about it, and held Ganymede's hat in his beak, to make sure it didn't fall off. Even so it was rather a shock for the boy, and he must have got quite a crick in the neck turning round to stare at him. I picked up his flute, which he'd dropped in his fright, and – but here's our judge in person. Let's introduce ourselves. Good morning, cowherd!

PARIS: Good morning to you, sir. May I ask who you are? And who have you got with you? One doesn't often see beautiful women like that wandering about the mountains.

HERMES: Ah, but those *aren't* women, Paris! Allow me to present – Hera – Athene – and Aphrodite. And I'm Hermes, with a message for you from Zeus.

[*Paris shows signs of terror.*]

Don't be frightened. There's nothing to worry about. It's just that he wants you to judge a beauty competition between these three goddesses. He says that in view of your own good looks and experience in such matters, he's leaving the decision to you. And the winner – but you can read for yourself what's written on this apple.

[*He hands it over.*]

PARIS [*taking it*]: Let's see what it says. [*Reading.*] 'First Prize for Beauty.' But good Lord, Hermes, I can't possibly do it! I'm only a mortal, and an ordinary country chap at that, and this sort of thing is quite beyond my scope. You don't want a cowherd for a job like this – you want someone smart and fashionable from Town. As far as I'm concerned, I might be able to judge at a cattle-show – I can tell which cow or which goat has the best points – but these goddesses are all so beautiful that I simply can't take my eyes off any one of them. Whatever I start looking at, my eyes seem to get stuck there, and refuse to move on. Or if they do move on, the next thing they see is just as beautiful, and they linger on that until they're drawn away to something else. I feel absolutely overwhelmed by their beauty – utterly absorbed by it! I just wish I had eyes all over my body, like Argus! It seems to me that the only fair decision would be to give the apple to all of them. Besides, there's another problem. One of them is the wife and the sister of Zeus, and the other two are his daughters. Doesn't that rather complicate the issue?

HERMES: Well, I don't know about that. All I know is, when Zeus tells you to do a thing, there's no getting out of it.

PARIS: All right, then, but would you do me just one favour, Hermes? Would you ask them not to get cross with me if they're beaten, but merely to take it that I've got defective eyesight?

HERMES [*after a brief consultation*]: Yes, they agree to regard it in that light. But now you really must get on with it.

PARIS: Well, I'll do my best – I can't do more than that. But first of all there's something I want to know. Will it be enough to look them over as they are, or shall I have to ask them to undress, and carry out a thorough examination?

HERMES: That's up to you. You can arrange matters just as you like.

PARIS: Just as I like? In that case, I'd like to see them naked.

HERMES [*to the goddesses*]: Undress, ladies. [*To Paris.*] Go on, have a good look – though personally I shall keep my eyes averted.

[*He does so.*]

HERA: Quite right, Paris. I'll undress first. You'll find that my famous whiteness is not confined to my arms, and that my eyes are not my only attractive feature. I'm equally beautiful all over.

PARIS: You too, Aphrodite.

ATHENE: Just a moment, Paris. Before she does anything else, make her take off that magic girdle of hers. Otherwise she may use it to cast a spell on you – for she's an absolute witch, you know. Besides, she's got no right to come here all dolled up like that, and with all that make-up on, just like a prostitute. This was supposed to be a display of *natural* beauty!

PARIS [*to Aphrodite*]: She's right about the girdle. Please take it off.

APHRODITE: Why don't you take off your helmet, Athene, and let us see how little hair you've got, instead of trying to intimidate the judge by brandishing that feather at him? Or are you afraid those grey eyes of yours won't look so good if people aren't scared of you?

ATHENE [*removing it*]: All right, there goes my helmet.

APHRODITE [*removing her girdle*]: And there goes my girdle.

HERA [*impatiently*]: Oh, come on, let's get undressed.

[*They do so.*]

PARIS: Zeus almighty, what a sight! What beauty! What a wonderful experience! The virgin goddess! Hera, radiant with majesty, every inch a queen – no wonder Zeus married her! And Aphrodite – how absolutely sweet she looks! And there was something so irresistibly attractive about that smile she just gave me – [*Pulling himself together.*] Well, that's about as much as I can take for the moment, but if you agree, I'd like to examine you separately one by one, for I still haven't made up my mind, and I feel so distracted by all this beauty that I simply can't concentrate.

APHRODITE: What a good idea!

PARIS: All right, you two go away, and you stay behind, Hera.

[*Aphrodite and Athene move away.*]

HERA: Certainly I'll stay – and when you've finished your examination, you'd also better consider what you stand to gain by declaring me the winner. For if you do that, I'll make you the master of all Asia.

PARIS: Sorry, my vote's not for sale. You can go away now. I'll do what I think fit. You next, Athene.

[*Hera goes away and Athene takes her place.*]

ATHENE: Here I am, Paris – and if you decide in my favour, you'll never lose a single battle. I'll make you such a good fighter that you'll always win.

PARIS: That's really not much use to me, Athene. You see, it's peacetime now in Phrygia and Lydia, and so far my father's country has managed to keep out of a war. But don't worry. I shan't necessarily decide against you, even if I've turned down your offer. Well, you can get dressed now, and put on your helmet. I've seen all I need. Now it's Aphrodite's turn.

[*Athene goes away to dress, and Aphrodite comes up very close to Paris.*]

APHRODITE: Here I am, right in front of you, and I want you to take a really good look at me. Don't be satisfied with a cursory glance, but let your eyes linger on every part of my body. And then, my handsome friend, let me give you a word of advice. I've always known what a fine young man you were – in fact I don't know anyone to touch you in the whole of Phrygia – and in that respect you have my congratulations. But I feel you're making a mistake not to say good-bye to all these rocks and crags, and go and live in a town, instead of wasting your sweetness on the desert air like this. For what satisfaction can you get out of a mountain? Or what use is your personal charm to a herd of cows? You ought to be married by now, not to some ordinary local girl – you know what they're like around here – but to some Greek lady from Argos, or Corinth, or maybe Sparta. Helen, for instance. She's young and beautiful – just as beautiful as I am – and what's more, she's extremely susceptible. She'd only have to see you once, and she'd be your slave for life – throw up everything, and go and live with you. But you must have heard a good deal about her already.

PARIS: Not a word, Aphrodite. And I'd very much like to hear it all from you.

APHRODITE: Well, she's the daughter of Leda, that beautiful girl that Zeus turned himself into a swan for.

PARIS: And what's she like to look at?

APHRODITE: Very white skin, doubtless inherited from her swan-father – soft and delicate, as a result of starting life in a shell – spends most of her time wrestling in the nude, and consequently has lots of admirers. In fact there's actually been a war about her. Theseus began it, by kidnapping her before she was even grown up. And the moment she was, all the most distinguished men in Greece wanted to marry her. The successful candidate was Menelaus, a man whose pedigree goes right back to Pelops. But if you like, I'll arrange for you to marry her.

PARIS: What do you mean? How can I marry her, if she's married already?

APHRODITE: How very young and innocent you are! I have my methods of doing these things.

PARIS: What are they? I'd be most interested to know them.

APHRODITE: It's quite simple. You go off to Greece to see the sights. When you get to Sparta, Helen sees *you*, and then it will be my job to make her fall in love and run away with you.

PARIS: But that's the part I find most difficult to believe – that she'd be willing to leave her husband and go sailing off with a complete stranger, who isn't even Greek.

APHRODITE: Don't you worry about that. I've got a fine pair of children, one called Love and the other called Sex-appeal, and I'll send them both along to act as guides Love will worm his way right into her heart, and make her fall for you, while Sex-appeal will envelop this whole body of yours, and make you irresistibly attractive. And I shall be there too, to lend them a hand. I'll also ask the three Graces to join us, so that we can all bring pressure to bear on her.

PARIS: I'm still not quite clear how it's going to work, Aphrodite. But I feel I'm in love with Helen already, and in some strange way I can actually see her in my mind's eye – I can see myself setting sail for Greece, and arriving at Sparta, and coming home with my wife in my arms. Oh dear, I do wish it were really happening at this moment!

APHRODITE: You'd better not fall too much in love with her, Paris, until you've paid me for making the match, by giving me the prize. For it's only reasonable, if I'm to help you win your bride, that I should win something myself. Then we'll be able to celebrate your wedding and my victory simultaneously. So it's up to you to decide whether that apple is too high a price to pay for love, beauty, and marriage.

PARIS: I'm afraid you'll forget all about me, as soon as I've given my verdict.

APHRODITE: Do you want me to take my oath on it?

PARIS: No, of course not, but – would you mind just repeating your promise?

APHRODITE: I promise to make Helen marry you, and go and live with you in Troy. I will give the whole thing my personal attention.

PARIS: And you'll bring Love and Sex-appeal and the three Graces with you?

APHRODITE: I will, don't you worry. What's more, I'll bring Passion and Cohabitation along as well. On those conditions, can I have the apple?

PARIS [*handing it to her*]: On those conditions – here you are.

Conversations in the Underworld

NO BAGGAGE ALLOWANCE

Scene: The river Styx. Charon, a scruffy old man with long white hair and a beard, has just brought a derelict-looking boat in to the shore, where a large number of dead men, under the supervision of Hermes, are queueing up to go on board.

CHARON [*after putting out the gangway*]: Now listen to me. Here's the situation. You can see for yourselves how small my boat is. It's also a bit rotten and tends to leak a good deal. What's more, if it develops the slightest list, it's liable to capsize and go to the bottom. But there you are, all turning up at the same time, with any amount of luggage! Well, if you take all that stuff on board, I'm afraid you're going to wish you hadn't – especially those who can't swim!

HERMES: Then what are we supposed to do, if we want to get across?

CHARON: I'll tell you. You'll have to leave all that junk on the shore, take off everything you've got on, and come aboard like that. I'll only just manage to squeeze you in even then. So will you see to it, Hermes? Don't let anyone on to the boat until he's undressed and, as I say, deposited his luggage. You'd better stand at the foot of the gangway and check them over. Make sure they take off everything before they embark.

HERMES: Very well, that's what I'll do. All right, who's first?

MAN AT THE HEAD OF THE QUEUE: My name's Menippus. Well, there goes my stick – and my knapsack. [*He throws them into the water.*] As for my cloak, I took it off before I came – and how right I was!

HERMES: Good for you, Menippus! On you go. You can

have the best seat, up there beside the rudder. Then you can keep an eye on the rest of the passengers.

[*Menippus goes on board and sits down.*]

And who's this gorgeous creature?

NEXT MAN IN THE QUEUE: I'm Charmoleus, the beauty-king from Megara, the boy with the million-dollar kiss.

HERMES: Off with your beauty then. Off with your lips, kisses, and all. Off with that lovely long hair, and those rosy cheeks – in fact off with your whole body. ... That's right, now you're travelling really light. You can go aboard now.

[*The skeleton of Charmoleus goes on board.*]

[*To the next man in the queue.*] And who may you be, with your crown and purple robes and disagreeable expression?

NEXT MAN: I am Lampichus, King of Gelonia.

HERMES: Well, Lampichus, what do you think you're doing with all that paraphernalia?

LAMPICHUS: You can hardly expect a king to travel in the nude.

HERMES: If he's a dead king – certainly I do. Take it all off.

LAMPICHUS [*removing his jewellery*]: There! I have jettisoned the Crown Jewels.

HERMES: You'd better jettison your conceit as well, Lampichus. A mass of arrogance like that will overload the boat.

LAMPICHUS: Very well, but at least let me keep my crown and my royal robes.

HERMES: Certainly not. They must go too.

LAMPICHUS [*taking them off*]: All right. What else do you want? I've taken off everything, can't you see?

HERMES: Oh no, you haven't. There's still your cruelty, and your stupidity, and your insolence, and your bad temper. Off with them as well.

LAMPICHUS: Here I am, then, stripped absolutely bare.

HERMES: Right. You can go on board now.

[*Lampichus goes on board.*]

And who is this great lump of flesh?

NEXT MAN: I'm Damasias, the famous heavy-weight champion.

HERMES: Yes, I suppose you must be. I know I've often seen you in the ring.

DAMASIAS [*complacently*]: I expect you have, Hermes. Well, let me pass – I've got nothing on.

HERMES: Nothing on, my dear chap, when you're wearing all that flesh? For heaven's sake take it off, or you'll sink the boat the moment you set foot in it. And get rid of all those championships and all that publicity too.

DAMASIAS: Take a look at me now, then. This time I'm really stripped and weigh no more than any of the others.

HERMES: Yes, that's much better. It's always healthy to lose weight. On you go.

[*A powerfully-built skeleton goes on board.*]

Ah, Craton! I'm afraid you'll have to leave that money behind, and your luxury and effeminacy as well. You won't be able to bring that expensive shroud or that distinguished pedigree. You must say good-bye to rank and reputation and titles, and to all those flattering inscriptions on your statues. And you'll have to stop talking about the great tomb that they've built for you. The mere mention of such things would be enough to sink us.

CRATON: It's a horrible wrench but – there they go. What else can one do?

[*He goes on board.*]

HERMES [*to the next man, who is a soldier killed in action*]: Hullo, what's the Army doing here? And what's that medal for?

SOLDIER: It's a decoration that I won for distinguished service in the field.

HERMES: You must throw it away. And you won't be needing any of that equipment either – it's always peacetime down here.

[*The soldier grounds arms, removes his medal and battle-dress, and goes on board.*]

And who is this dignified character with his nose in the air, a furrowed brow, an air of deep meditation, and a long, flowing beard?

MENIPPUS [*from his seat in the boat*]: He's a philosopher, Hermes – or rather, that's what he pretends to be, but actually he's quite bogus. Make him undress too. You'll find some very funny things under his cloak.

HERMES [*to the philosopher*]: Yes, let's have the cloak off first of all, and then everything else.

[*The philosopher removes his cloak.*]

Good God, look at all the imposture he's brought with him! Look at all that ignorance and conceit and quarrelsomeness – all those tricky questions and thorny problems and tortuous arguments – not to mention a fair amount of wasted effort, a good deal of nonsense, and a lot of fuss about nothing! But, my goodness, that's not all! Here's some money-grubbing too, and some sensuality and impudence and bad temper and luxury and debauchery. I can see it all, however much you try to conceal it. And here's some lying, and arrogance, and thinking oneself better than other people – they'll have to go too. Why, there'd hardly be room for all that luggage on an ocean-liner!

PHILOSOPHER: Well, I've done as you told me. It's all gone now.

MENIPPUS: Hadn't he better take off that beard as well, Hermes? Just look how bushy it is. There must be at least five pounds of hair there.

HERMES: Quite right. [*To the philosopher.*] Take your beard off too.

PHILOSOPHER: Who can I get to shave it off for me?

HERMES: Menippus here will do it. He can spread it out on the gangway, and chop it off with an axe from the toolbox.

MENIPPUS [*jumping up and opening the toolbox*]: Oh, couldn't I use a saw instead, Hermes? It would be much more fun.

HERMES: No, an axe will do.

[*Menippus performs the operation.*]

[*To the philosopher.*] Yes, that's much better. Why, you look quite like a human being now, instead of a goat.

MENIPPUS [*still fingering the axe*]: Would you like me to take a little off his eyebrows too?

HERMES: Yes, please. He keeps knitting them and raising them in a most supercilious way – I can't think why.

[*The philosopher starts crying.*]

What's the matter now, you wretched creature? What are you snivelling for? Are you afraid you might get killed? Oh, all right, go on board as you are.

[*Menippus replaces the axe and returns to his seat. The philosopher starts walking up the gangway.*]

MENIPPUS: I say, he's still got something tucked away under his arm, and it's the most depressing thing about him.

HERMES: Oh? And what's that, Menippus?

MENIPPUS: Flattery, Hermes. He's always found it very useful in the past.

PHILOSOPHER [*now safe in the boat*]: Well, what about you, Menippus? Hadn't you better leave your frankness behind, and your equanimity, and your courage, and your sense of humour? For you're the only one of us that ever laughs.

HERMES [*to Menippus*]: Don't you do anything of the kind. You hang on to them – they're all quite buoyant, and will help to keep us afloat. [*To the next man.*] And you, I suppose, are a public speaker? Well, you'll have to drop that great mass of verbiage, all those antitheses and parallelisms and perorations and solecisms – in fact the whole of that ponderous style of yours.

PUBLIC SPEAKER: There they go, then.

[*He goes on board.*]

HERMES [*to Charon*]: All right, skipper, you can cast off now. In with the gangway, up with the anchor, hoist sail, and man the rudder! Off we go, and good luck to us!

[*As the boat begins to move the passengers raise a wail of despair.*]

What's the matter now, you silly creatures? Most of the noise seems to be coming from that philosopher who's just had his beard demolished. [*To the philosopher.*] Well, what's your trouble?

PHILOSOPHER [*sobbing*]: It's just that I always thought the soul was immortal, Hermes.

MENIPPUS [*to Hermes*]: Don't you believe it. If you ask me, he's got something very different on his mind.

HERMES: Oh? What?

MENIPPUS: He can't bear to think of never having another expensive dinner, and then sneaking out late at night with his cloak pulled up over his face and going the round of the brothels – and next morning extracting large sums of money from young men under the false pretence of teaching them wisdom!

PHILOSOPHER: Well, how about you, Menippus? Aren't you at all upset at being dead?

[*A confused uproar is heard in the distance.*]

MENIPPUS: Of course not. Why, I came here of my own accord. I wasn't even invited. But didn't you hear a noise just then, as if people were shouting in the world behind us?

HERMES: Certainly we did, Menippus, and it came from several different places. First of all they've called a public meeting in Gelonia, and everyone's roaring with laughter at the news that King Lampichus is dead. His wife's being lynched by the women, and the children are throwing stones at her new-born babies. Then in Sicyon Diophantus has just got a round of applause for his funeral oration over Craton here.

[*A piercing shriek is heard.*]

And, my goodness, that was Damasias's mother starting off the keening over his body. But nobody's mourning for you, Menippus. You're lying there quite peacefully, all by yourself.

MENIPPUS: Don't you believe it. Any minute now you'll hear the dogs howling over me in the most heart-broken manner, and the crows beating their breasts with their wings, when they all turn up for my funeral.

HERMES: That's the spirit, Menippus. Well, here we are on the other side. Off you all go to the Last Judgement. It's straight along that path there. [*He points into the semi-darkness.*] Meanwhile Charon and I will go back for some more passengers.

MENIPPUS [*getting up and moving towards Charon, who is putting out the gangway*]: Have a good trip then, Hermes. Come along, the rest of you.

[*The passengers remain trembling in their seats.*]

It's no use, we've all got to stand our trial – and I'm told the sentences are pretty stiff and liable to involve such things as wheels, stones, and vultures. And all the secrets of our private lives are going to come out.

MENIPPUS GETS AWAY WITH IT

Scene: Charon's boat a few seconds later. Menippus (who has somehow regained possession of his stick and knapsack) has been stopped at the gangway and asked for his fare. He roars with laughter. Unlike the other passengers, he has not been buried with the necessary copper coin in his mouth.

CHARON [*losing his temper*]: Pay your fare, blast you!

MENIPPUS [*tolerantly*]: Go on, Charon, you can shout as much as you like.

CHARON [*doing so*]: Pay me my money, I say, for ferrying you across!

MENIPPUS: It's no use expecting money from a person who hasn't got any.

CHARON: You can't be as poor as all that. Everyone can afford an obol.

MENIPPUS: Well, I don't know about other people, but I know I can't.

CHARON: You dirty cheat! My God, I'll wring your neck if you don't pay up!

MENIPPUS [*calmly*]: And I'll crack your skull open with this stick.

CHARON: You just try! You'll find you've come all this way for nothing.

MENIPPUS: Why shouldn't Hermes pay for me? After all, he made all the arrangements.

HERMES: Well, I like that! It's a fine look-out if I'm to accept financial responsibility for every man who dies!

CHARON [*blocking the gangway*]: I'm not going to let you go until I get my money.

MENIPPUS: Then you'd better put your boat into dry-dock, for you'll have a long time to wait. How do you expect me to give you what I haven't got?

CHARON: Didn't you know the rule about bringing an obol with you?

MENIPPUS: I knew it all right, but I just didn't have one to bring. What was I supposed to do? Stay alive or what?

CHARON: So you want to boast of being the only man who ever got free transport across the Styx?

MENIPPUS: Oh, I wouldn't call it exactly that, my dear fellow. I did quite a lot of bailing, and took my turn at the oars – and what's more, I was the only passenger who didn't cry.

CHARON: That makes no difference to the fare. You've still got to pay your obol. There's no way out of it.

MENIPPUS: All right, then, take me back to life again.

CHARON: And get into trouble with Aeacus? That's a brilliant suggestion.

MENIPPUS: Then stop fussing.

CHARON [*suspiciously*]: Let's see what you've got in that knapsack.

MENIPPUS [*opening it*]: Some lupine-seeds and some offal. Like some?

CHARON [*giving up in despair*]: Where on earth did you find this shameless character, Hermes? Look at the way he behaved during the voyage – laughing and jeering at the other passengers, and whistling when all the rest were whining!

HERMES: You don't seem to realize who he is, Charon. Menippus is always like that – completely uninhibited, and never takes anything seriously.

CHARON [*reluctantly letting him pass*]: All right, but if I ever catch you again –

MENIPPUS: Don't you worry, my dear chap. You won't catch me coming here twice!

A SLIGHT CHANGE OF SEX

Scene: Somewhere in the underworld. Through the semi-darkness crowds of skeletons can be seen wandering aimlessly about a vast plain covered with small white flowers called asphodels. Menippus, however, is using his time more profitably. He is carrying out a scientific investigation into the factual basis of mythology. Catching sight of Tiresias, he hurries up to him.

MENIPPUS: Ah, Tiresias! First of all let's see if you're really blind or not. [*Examining him closely.*] But of course it's not an easy point to decide, since none of us have got any eyes down here anyway, only empty sockets. So one really can't tell if a man was originally as blind as a bat or as sharp as a lynx. However, I'm sure I've read somewhere that you were a prophet, and the only person in the world who has been both a male and a female. So for heaven's sake do tell me which life you enjoyed most, a man's or a woman's?

TIRESIAS: It was much more fun being a woman, Menippus – one had so much less to do. Besides, women can always boss their husbands around, and never have to fight or do sentry duty in wartime, or attend public meetings, or act as jurymen.

MENIPPUS: But Tiresias, haven't you read that passage in Euripides,[1] where Medea is being very sorry for women, and saying what a wretched time they have, and what unbearable agony they suffer in child-birth? Which reminds me of another thing – when you were a woman, did *you* ever have a baby, or were you sterile and childless throughout that period of your life?

TIRESIAS [*suspiciously*]: Why exactly do you ask, Menippus?

MENIPPUS [*innocently*]: Oh, I don't mean any harm, Tiresias – but do just tell me, if it isn't too much trouble.

TIRESIAS: Well, of course I wasn't sterile – but I didn't ever actually have a baby.

MENIPPUS: That's all I wanted to know. But no doubt you had a uterus and everything?

TIRESIAS: Obviously I did.

MENIPPUS: But in course of time your uterus disappeared, and your vagina closed up, and your breasts got whisked away, and you developed male genitals and grew a beard?

TIRESIAS: I don't quite see the point of that question. You seem doubtful whether it ever happened at all.

MENIPPUS: Oughtn't one to be a little doubtful in such cases, Tiresias? Wouldn't it be rather stupid to take them on trust, without inquiring whether they're actually possible or not?

TIRESIAS: But what about all those cases of women being turned into birds or trees or animals – like Philomela, or Daphne, or Callisto? Don't you believe them either?

MENIPPUS: If I ever come across any of the ladies in question, I shall be interested to hear what they have to say on the subject. Meanwhile, my dear sir, do tell me – did you start practising prophecy when you were a woman, or did you adopt a new sex and a new profession simultaneously?

TIRESIAS: There you are! You evidently don't know the first thing about me, if you've never heard how I settled an argument between the gods, and Hera struck me blind, and Zeus made me a prophet by way of compensation.

MENIPPUS: Oh really, Tiresias, are you still sticking to that old story? But all you so-called soothsayers are the same. You never actually tell us a word of truth.

HOW TO ENJOY LIFE AFTER SEVENTY

Scene: As before. Polystratus, a new arrival, has just run into Simylus, an old friend of his.

SIMYLUS: So you finally got here, Polystratus. Why, you must be practically a hundred!

POLYSTRATUS: Yes, ninety-eight to be exact, Simylus.

SIMYLUS: And how have things been going with you these last thirty years? For I seem to remember you were about seventy when I died.

POLYSTRATUS: Strange as it may sound, I've been having an absolutely wonderful time.

SIMYLUS: Strange is hardly the word for it, if you really managed to enjoy yourself at that age, considering that your health can't have been too good, and you'd got no children to look after you.

POLYSTRATUS: Well, the great thing was, I could do exactly what I liked. Also, I had lots of pretty girls, and boys to wait on me, plenty of scent, an excellent cellar, and I kept the best table in Sicily.

SIMYLUS: That's rather a surprise to me. In my day you were always so economical.

POLYSTRATUS: But my dear fellow, it all came pouring in free, gratis, and for nothing! First thing every morning there'd be a crowd of visitors at my door, bringing me all sorts of splendid presents from all over the world.

SIMYLUS: Why, did you become a dictator or something after my death?

POLYSTRATUS: No, but I had a tremendous number of admirers.

SIMYLUS: Admirers? At your age? With only four teeth in your head? Don't make me laugh!

POLYSTRATUS: It's perfectly true, I assure you, and they were all extremely important people. Old as I was and, as you see, completely bald, with watery eyes and a perpetually running nose, there was nothing they liked better than making love to me – and if I so much as glanced at one of them, he was happy for the day.

SIMYLUS: You don't mean to say you're another Phaon? You didn't ferry Aphrodite across from Chios, and get her to make you young and beautiful again in return?

POLYSTRATUS: No, I looked just the same as I do now – but it didn't make me any less attractive.

SIMYLUS: You're talking in riddles.

POLYSTRATUS: It's really quite simple. People are always falling in love with old men who are rich and childless nowadays.

SIMYLUS: Oh, now I understand the secret of your charm, you old rascal! It was a case of *golden* Aphrodite, was it?

POLYSTRATUS [*chuckling*]: But I had a lot of fun out of those lovers of mine, Simylus. They pretty well worshipped me, you know. Sometimes I used to play the flirt and refuse to see them. But they still went on competing for my favours.

SIMYLUS: And who did you leave your money to in the end?

POLYSTRATUS: I kept telling each of them straight out that I was leaving it all to him. They thought I meant it, and flattered me all the more. But what I actually said in my will was rather different. I just told them all to go to hell.

SIMYLUS: And who finally got it? Some relation or other?

POLYSTRATUS: Certainly not. I left it to a nice-looking Phrygian boy that I'd recently bought.

SIMYLUS: And how old was he, Polystratus?

POLYSTRATUS: Oh, about twenty.

SIMYLUS [*with a leer*]: I can imagine the sort of thing that he'd done to earn it!

POLYSTRATUS: Well, he deserved it far more than they did, even if he was a foreigner and an absolute pest. By this time all those important people will be paying court to *him*! Now that he's my heir, he'll have automatically become a member of the aristocracy – and in spite of the fact that he's only just started to shave, and speaks Greek with a horrible accent, people will soon be talking as if he had a longer pedigree than Codrus, more beauty than Nireus, and greater wisdom than Odysseus!

SIMYLUS: Oh, well, never mind. So long as the others don't get it he can be Governor of Greece for all I care.

CHARON SEES LIFE

Scene: A crowded street somewhere on earth. Enter Hermes, invisible. He is in such a hurry that he almost bumps into another invisible figure, which is standing there, roaring with laughter. It is Charon.

HERMES: Hullo, Charon, what's the joke? And what are you doing in our part of the world, miles away from your boat? You don't usually take much interest in things up here.

CHARON: Oh, I just wanted to see what goes on, Hermes – what people do when they're alive, and what they're so sorry to lose when they come down to us – for I've never had a passenger yet that didn't cry. So I did the same as that young chap from Thessaly,[1] applied to Aeacus for twenty-four hours' shore-leave, and came up into the daylight. But what a bit of luck meeting you! You know all about these things, and I'm sure you won't mind taking me round and showing me the sights.

HERMES: Sorry, skipper, I can't spare the time. I've got orders from up top to transact a little business down here for Zeus, and I'm just off to see about it. If I don't get a move on, he's liable to lose his temper and put me permanently at your disposal by consigning me to nether darkness – or, you know what he did to Hephaestus? Grabbed him by the ankle and just slung him out of the front door of heaven! He's developed such a limp as a result that when he went round filling up our glasses the other day, everyone burst out laughing.[2] Well, that might happen to me too.

CHARON: You surely don't mean to let me go wandering about the earth completely at random? Is that the way to treat an old friend and shipmate who's also a professional colleague? And I do think you might bear in mind that I've never asked you to do any bailing or rowing. You just lie snoring on deck, with those great biceps of yours – unless you can get into conversation with one of the passengers, in which case you do nothing but talk the whole way across, leaving an old man like me to do all the rowing by himself. So for heaven's sake, my dear good fellow, don't let me down now, but take me on a conducted tour of human life, and let me really see something before I go back. For if you leave me, I'll be like a blind man stumbling about in the dark and constantly tripping over things – only with me it's the other way round – it's the dazzling light up here that makes it so impossible to see anything. Please do me this favour, Hermes. I'll never forget it.

HERMES: Well, it's going to get me into a lot of trouble. I can see myself being well paid for my services – with a couple of black eyes. Still, I suppose I'll have to give in. What else can one do, when a friend insists? Well now, skipper, you can't possibly see everything in detail – the job would take several years. Long before we'd finished, I'd have been posted by Zeus as a deserter, you'd have lost your job with Death, and Pluto's whole kingdom would have suffered serious damage from the interruption of underground transport, while his Chancellor of the Exchequer, Aeacus, would be furious at the loss of revenue. So the question is, how to show you the most important things that are going on.

CHARON: That's for you to decide, Hermes. I'm a stranger in these parts myself, and have no idea what things are like up here.

HERMES: Well, the main thing is to find somewhere high up, so that you can have a good view of everything. If only I could take you up to heaven, there wouldn't be any problem – you'd have a splendid view of the whole world from there. But a person who's constantly associating with creatures of the underworld just wouldn't be received at

Zeus's court – so we'll have to look round for some high mountain or other.

CHARON: You know what I usually tell you when we're afloat, Hermes. Every time a squall hits us amidships and the waves start getting high, you ignorant land-lubbers are always advising me to take in sail, or loosen the sheet a bit, or run before the wind, to which my answer is, 'Shut up! I know what I'm doing!' Well, now you're the skipper. You must take the same line, and do exactly as you think fit. I'm only a passenger, so I'll just sit quiet and do whatever you tell me.

HERMES: Quite right. I'm certainly the best person to decide, and I'll soon think of somewhere suitable. Would the Caucasus do, I wonder? Or Parnassus? Or Olympus – that's higher than either of them. And talking of Olympus, I've got an idea – not a bad idea at that. Only you'll have to give me a hand and do your share of the work.

CHARON: Just tell me what to do and I'll do it to the best of my ability.

HERMES: Well, Homer says[3] that a couple of children called Otus and Ephialtes once planned, without any outside assistance, to tear up Ossa by the roots and dump it on Olympus, and then put Pelion on top of that, thus hoping to construct a flight of steps up to the front door of heaven. Of course they were merely juvenile delinquents, and were suitably punished. But nobody could accuse *us* of having any sinister designs against the gods, so why don't we attempt a similar feat of engineering? Why don't we roll a few mountains on top of one another, to provide ourselves with a satisfactory observation-post?

CHARON: Do you really think we'll be able to pick up Pelion or Ossa, Hermes – just the pair of us?

HERMES: Whyever not, Charon? Are you suggesting that we're somehow inferior to those two babes in arms – in spite of the fact that we're gods?

CHARON: No, of course not, but – it still sounds to me rather an incredible feat.

HERMES: That's because you've got no poetry in you, Charon. Why, a genius like Homer can do the whole thing in a couple of lines – moving mountains is mere child's play for him. And I can't think why you should find the idea so fantastic, for you must have heard of Atlas, who holds up the whole sky single-handed, including all us gods. And presumably you've also heard how my brother Hercules once relieved him at his post, and took the weight off his shoulders for a bit?

CHARON: I've heard about it all right, but whether it's true or not I wouldn't know. Perhaps you and the poets can tell me?

HERMES: Of course it's true, Charon. Why on earth should sensible people want to lie about such things? So let's follow the instructions in Homer's handbook, and start by prising up Ossa. Then we can put 'leaf-shaking Pelion'[4] on top of that.

[*They tear Mount Ossa from its foundations and roll it up to the summit of Mount Olympus. They then place Mount Pelion on top of Mount Ossa.*]

[*Rubbing his hands.*] There, look how easy it was – and how poetic! Right, I'll just nip up and see if it's high enough yet, or if we'll have to build an extension.

[*He goes to the top.*]

Oh dear, we're nowhere near the sky yet. [*Peering round.*] To the East I can barely make out Ionia and Lydia – to the West I can't see farther than Italy and Sicily – to the North my view stops well this side of the Ister, and over there [*turning South*] even Crete isn't any too clear. Well, skipper, it looks as if we'll have to slap on Mount Oeta as well, and then add Mount Parnassus by way of a top storey.

CHARON: Right you are. Only mind we don't make the storey too tall. If we pile it on too thick, we're liable to bring the whole thing crashing down on our heads and wish we'd never started dabbling in problems of epic structure.

HERMES: Don't you worry. It'll be as safe as houses. Just pass me up Oeta, will you?

[*Charon does so. Hermes fixes it in position and then returns to ground-level.*]

And now let's roll up Parnassus.

[*They roll up Parnassus.*]

There we are. Now I'm going upstairs again.

[*He goes up to the top and looks round.*]

That's splendid – I can see everything. Now you must come up too.

CHARON [*feeling rather nervous*]: Well, give me a hand, Hermes. It's quite a step up in the world for me, you know.

HERMES: Well, you wanted to see things properly, didn't you? And you can't get a decent view without taking a few risks. [*Coming down again.*] All right, hold on to my hand and mind you don't slip.

[*He helps Charon up to the top.*]

Well done! Now you're up. Luckily, Parnassus has two summits, so there's one for each of us to sit on.

[*They make themselves comfortable.*]

Now have a good look round and see the world.

CHARON [*staring down at it*]: Yes, there it all is – a vast expanse of earth with a great sea flowing round it – mountains, and rivers twice the size of Cocytus or Pyriphlegethon – and millions of tiny people swarming in and out of their holes.

HERMES: Those holes, as you call them, are towns.

CHARON [*with a sigh of exasperation*]: Do you know what, Hermes? It was a complete waste of effort bringing Parnassus up here, complete with Castalian Spring, and Oeta, and all the rest of it.

HERMES: Oh! Why?

CHARON: Because I can't see anything properly from so high up. I didn't just want to see towns and mountains spread out like a map. I wanted to see human beings themselves – the way they behave and the kind of things they say. For instance, when you first saw me, I was roaring with laughter and you asked me what the joke was. Well, I'd just heard something very funny.

HERMES: And what was that?

CHARON: I'd heard a man invited by a friend to a dinner-party tomorrow evening. 'I'll be there,' he replied, and just as he said it, someone knocked a tile off a roof on to his head and killed him. It made me laugh, because I didn't see how he was going to keep his appointment. So I think I'll go down a bit lower. Then I'll be able to see and hear things better.

HERMES: You stay where you are. I'll soon fix that. I know a magic spell out of Homer that will give you perfect eye-sight in two seconds. Only while I'm repeating it, you must forget about being short-sighted and concentrate on seeing everything clearly.

CHARON: Go on, then.

HERMES:

'I have dispelled the mist that sealed thine eyes,

So that thou mayst discern both gods and men.'[5]

Well, how's the visibility now?

CHARON: Extraordinarily good. Compared with me, that man Lynceus was positively blind. So now you must explain who everybody is and answer all my questions. I'll put them in the words of Homer, if you like. That'll show you I'm not so uneducated as you think.

HERMES: How on earth do you know anything about Homer? Why, you're only an ordinary seaman!

CHARON: That's right, sneer at my profession! Well, the fact is, when Homer died and I ferried him across, I heard him reciting a lot of poetry and some of it stuck in my mind – although it was in the middle of a storm. You see, his choice of subject wasn't very tactful in the circumstances. It was all about how Poseidon collected the clouds, and stirred up the ocean, using his trident as a sort of egg-whisk, and roused the whirlwinds and so on.[6] His poetry had such a disturbing effect upon the weather that a hurricane suddenly blew up and nearly capsized the boat. Homer was so sea-sick that he brought up most of the *Iliad* and the *Odyssey*, complete with Scylla and Charybdis and the Cyclops. So naturally, with all that stuff being spouted out, I managed to salvage some of it. For instance [*pointing*],

> 'Who is that mighty hero tall and brave,
> That towers head and shoulders o'er the rest?'[7]

HERMES: That's Milo, the famous athlete from Croton. He's getting a round of applause at the Olympic Games, because he's just picked up a bull and is carrying it right across the stadium.

CHARON: Then why don't they clap *me*, Hermes? They've got far more reason to, considering that I'll soon be picking up Milo himself and dumping him in my boat. For eventually he'll be coming down to me, after losing a fight with that unbeatable world-champion, Death – and he'll never even know what hit him! Then, of course, he'll be very sorry for himself at the thought of all his past successes, and all the applause that he got. But now he's enjoying the sensation that he's made by that bull-carrying act of his. Well, what's your guess? Do you suppose he has any idea that he's going to die one day?

HERMES: Why on earth should he think of death at a time like this, when he's feeling at the top of his form?

CHARON: Well, never mind about him. He'll be giving me a good laugh in the near future, when he turns up on my boat, too weak to pick up a gnat, let alone a bull. But tell me another thing [*pointing*],

'Whose is that other yet more stately form?'[8]

By the look of his clothes, he isn't Greek.

HERMES: That, Charon, is Cyrus, the son of Cambyses, who's just annexed Media and made it part of Persia. The other day he conquered Assyria and occupied Babylon, and now he looks like making a drive on Lydia, with the idea of deposing Croesus and becoming a world-dictator.

CHARON: And where is the said Croesus?

HERMES [*pointing*]: Over there. Do you see that great fortress with the triple wall? Well, that's Sardis, and there on a golden couch is Croesus himself, having a conversation with Solon.[9] Would you like to hear what they're saying?

CHARON: I certainly would.

[*Hermes tunes in and turns up the volume.*]

CROESUS: Well, sir, you've seen how rich I am, how much money and gold bullion I've got in my vaults, and how expensively I can afford to live, so just give me your opinion – who would you say was the luckiest man in the world?

CHARON: I wonder what Solon's going to say to that?

HERMES: Don't worry, Charon. He won't say anything to make you blush.

SOLON: Lucky people, Your Majesty, are extremely rare. But I think the luckiest I've ever heard of were Cleobis and Biton, the sons of the priestess at Argos.

CHARON: He means those two boys who died of heart-failure the other day, after pulling their mother all the way to the temple on a cart.

CROESUS [*rather offended*]: All right, let's say that they get first prize for luck. But who would come second?

SOLON: Tellus the Athenian. He had a good life and died fighting for his country.

CROESUS: And what about me, you wretched fellow? I suppose I don't strike you as being lucky at all?

SOLON: It's too soon to tell, Your Majesty. We must wait until the end of your life. The real test in these matters is the way one dies – whether one's luck stays the course, as it were.

[*Hermes fades them out.*]

CHARON: Congratulations, Solon! You didn't forget me. You realize that such points can only be decided in my boat. [*Peering down again.*] But who are those people that Croesus is sending off, and what have they got on their shoulders?

HERMES: Oh, he's sending some gold ingots to Delphi, in payment for the oracles that are shortly going to cause his downfall. You see, the man's got quite an obsession about oracles.

CHARON: So that's what gold is! It's that shiny, reddish-yellow substance, is it? I'm always hearing about it, but I've never seen it before.

HERMES: Yes, Charon, that's the famous stuff that causes all the trouble.

CHARON: But I don't see what's the good of it. All it seems to do is induce curvature of the spine in the people who have to carry it.

HERMES: It does a lot more than that. You've no idea how many wars it's started, how much slavery it's caused, how many plots and thefts and perjuries and murders and prison sentences and long sea voyages and big business deals it's been responsible for.

CHARON: But why on earth should it, Hermes? It looks hardly any different from copper. Copper, of course, I'm quite familiar with, because I'm always getting obols from my passengers.

HERMES: Ah, but there's any amount of copper, so no one is very keen on it – whereas this stuff is pretty rare, and miners have to go a long way down to get it. Not that it makes any difference – it still comes out of the earth, like lead or any other metal.

CHARON: Human beings must be terribly silly to have developed such a passion for a heavy yellow substance.

HERMES: Well, Solon doesn't seem to be very passionate about it anyway. Look, he's laughing at Croesus for being so conceited, and I think he's going to ask him something. Shall we hear what it is?

[*He tunes in again to Sardis.*]

SOLON: Tell me, Your Majesty, do you think Apollo really wants these gold ingots of yours?

CROESUS: Of course he does. There's never been an offering at Delphi on such a scale before.

SOLON: So you think you're going to make him very happy, by giving him some gold ingots to add to his collection?

CROESUS: How can I fail to?

SOLON: From what you say, Your Majesty, they must be very hard up in heaven – if they have to send away to Lydia every time they want a little gold.

CROESUS: Why, what better source of supply could they have?

SOLON [*letting that one go*]: Tell me, is iron among the natural products of Lydia?

CROESUS: No, it isn't.

SOLON: Then you're short of the most precious metal of all.

CROESUS: Why, how can iron be more precious than gold?

SOLON: If you'll answer my questions without getting cross, I'll try to explain.

CROESUS: Go on, then. What do you want to ask?

SOLON: Which is more valuable, something that protects you, or something that needs protection?

CROESUS: Something that protects you, of course.

SOLON: Well now, suppose Cyrus invades Lydia, as it's rumoured that he will, what kind of swords will you equip your army with – gold ones or iron ones?

CROESUS: Obviously they'll have to be iron.

SOLON: And if you can't get any iron, your gold will be taken prisoner by the Persians.

CROESUS: Well, really, sir! What a thing to suggest!

SOLON: Let's hope it never happens. But you seem to admit that iron is more valuable than gold.

CROESUS: What do you propose I should do, then? Have all the gold brought back again, and send Apollo a lot of iron instead?

SOLON: No, he won't be needing any iron either. And if you offer him copper or gold, it'll be a nice little surprise for the Phocians or the Boeotians or the Delphians, or possibly for some future dictator or burglar – but you can't expect a god to take much interest in the products of your goldsmiths.

CROESUS: [*petulantly*]: Oh, you're always down on me for having so much money. You're jealous – that's all it is.

HERMES [*fading them out*]: You see, Charon, he can't bear to be told the truth about anything. It's a strange experience for him to find a poor man who doesn't grovel, but just says frankly whatever comes into his head. Well, he'll be reminded of Solon's remarks very soon, when Cyrus takes him prisoner and arranges for him to be burnt at the stake. I know all about it, for the other day I heard Clotho reading out extracts from the Book of Fate, in which it was laid down that Croesus would be captured by Cyrus, and Cyrus would be killed by that Massagetan female over there. [*Pointing.*] You can see her, can't you – the savage-looking woman riding a white horse?

CHARON: My goodness, yes!

HERMES: Well, that's Tomyris, and she's going to chop off Cyrus's head and put it in a bag of blood. And you see his young son over there? That's Cambyses. He'll succeed his father on the throne, and after various disasters in Libya and Ethiopia he'll finally die insane, as a punishment for killing Apis.

CHARON: What a joke! But at the moment they've got such a superiority complex that one can hardly bear to look at them. Who'd have thought that in the very near future one of them would be a prisoner of war, and the other would have his head in a bag of blood? But who is the gentleman in the crimson robes with the gold clasps, Hermes? He's wearing a crown, and he's just been handed a ring that his chef apparently found in a fish that he was filleting.

'He seems the monarch of a sea-girt isle.'

HERMES: Oh, well done, Charon! You're getting quite good at quotations, aren't you? The man you're looking at is Polycrates, the dictator of Samos. He thinks he's been very lucky – but standing just beside him is a servant of his called Maeandrius – who's going to betray him to the Persian Governor, Oroetes – who's going to have him crucified. So before you can say knife he'll have been tipped out of paradise into sheer hell. That's another thing that I heard from Clotho.

CHARON: Good old Clotho! That's the way, my dear. Keep right on burning them at the stake, and chopping off their heads and crucifying them. That'll show them that they're only human. Meanwhile, up with their opinion of themselves! The further they have to fall, the more it'll hurt. And then how I shall laugh, when I see them all naked in my boat, minus their crimson robes and crowns and golden thrones!

HERMES: Yes, that's what they've got coming to them. And

Charon, do you see all those people employed in navigation, and warfare, and litigation, and agriculture, and money-lending, and begging?

CHARON: All I can see is a complicated muddle – a world full of utter confusion. Their towns are like beehives, in which every bee has a sting of his own and uses it against his neighbour – and some are like wasps, preying on the weaker members of the community. But what are those dim shapes flying round them?

HERMES: Hopes and fears, Charon – stupidities, pleasures, accumulative instincts, rages, hatreds, and things like that. At ground level you have stupidity, which is a fundamental part of their make-up – in fact it's quite inseparable from human nature, and so are hatred, rage, jealousy, ignorance, bewilderment, and avarice. But hopes and fears tend to fly at a rather higher altitude. Fears dive on to their targets and knock them out, sometimes even causing a permanent stoop, but hopes hover overhead, and just as a person thinks he's going to catch them, they shoot up into the air and leave him with his mouth hanging open. You've probably seen Tantalus having much the same sort of trouble with his water down below. And now, if you strain your eyes a bit, you'll be able to see the Fates up there in the sky, working away at a spindle, from which human beings are suspended by fine threads. Can you see the threads I mean, coming down like strands of cobweb on to each individual?

CHARON [after gazing intently for a moment]: Oh yes, now I can see them – incredibly thin, and mostly tangled up with one another.

HERMES: Oh course they are, skipper, for [pointing to each in turn] this chap here is destined to be killed by that fellow over there, and that fellow by another fellow. And this chap's going to inherit the estate of someone with a shorter thread than his, and another chap's going to inherit it from him. So no wonder the threads are all tangled up. You see, everybody's life is quite literally hanging by a thread. This one's got hitched up and is dangling in mid-air, but after a while the thread will snap under his weight, and down he'll go with a tremendous crash – whereas this one's only just off the ground, so his fall won't be at all a noisy business, and even his next-door neighbours will have to listen very carefully to hear him come down to earth.

CHARON: It's really rather a funny situation, Hermes.

HERMES: You've no idea how funny it is, Charon – especially when they make ambitious plans, only to be snatched away by good old Death before any of their hopes are realized. You see, Death has a large staff of agents and representatives, such as malaria, pneumonia, consumption, swords, poisons, gangsters, judges, and dictators. Nobody takes any notice of them, so long as things are going well, but the moment trouble starts, there's any amount of moaning and groaning and grumbling. If only people could get it into their heads right from the start that they're eventually going to die – that after a brief excursion into life they'll have to be off again, and leave this world behind them like a dream – they'd lead far more sensible lives and make far less fuss about dying. But as it is, they assume that the present state of affairs is going to last for ever, so when Death's agent turns up with a warrant for their arrest, claps on pneumonia or consumption by way of handcuffs, and carts them off, they're taken completely by surprise and are most indignant about it. For instance, do you see that man over there, who's so anxious to get his house built, and keeps telling the workmen to hurry up? What would he do if he realized that the house will get built all right, but the moment they put the roof on he'll have to take himself off, leaving all the benefit of it to his heir? For he, poor chap, will never eat a single meal in the new house. Or what about that man who's giving a party to celebrate the birth of a son, and planning to name the child after his grandfather? Do you think he'd still regard it as such a happy event, if he knew that the boy was going to die at the age of seven? The trouble is, he only notices the good things that happen to people, never the bad ones. He knows all about that man whose son was so successful at the Olympic Games, but he hasn't registered the fact that the man next door is just off to his son's funeral. So he doesn't realize that his own happiness is hanging by a thread. And then look at all those people arguing about property and accumulating capital. Before they have a chance to enjoy it, they'll be called away by those agents and representatives I mentioned.

CHARON: You know, seeing all this makes me wonder what they find so attractive about life anyway. Why on earth are they so sorry to lose it? They talk about being as happy as a king – but when you come to look at a king's life, you find that, quite apart from its insecurity and the so-called fickleness of fortune, it has far more pain than pleasure in it, if only because of the fear, anxiety, hatred, intrigue, resentment, and insincerity that always surround a throne – to say nothing of all the sorrows, accidents, and diseases which kings share with the rest of humanity. And if even royalty has such a wretched time, you can imagine what it must be like for ordinary people.

In fact, I've thought of a simile to describe human life as a whole. I must tell you what it is. You know the bubbles that rise to the surface below a waterfall – those little pockets of air that combine to produce foam? Some of them are quite tiny, and burst and disappear immediately, but others last a bit longer, and by absorbing the bubbles round them swell up to a monstrous size, until eventually they burst too – for it's the inevitable end of the process. Well, that's what human beings are like. They're all more or less inflated pockets of air. Some of them stay blown up for an infinitesimal space of time, while others disintegrate the moment they're produced – but sooner or later they're all bound to go pop.

HERMES: I say, Charon, that's every bit as good as Homer's famous leaf-simile![10]

CHARON: And yet look at the way they go on, Hermes – desperately competing for important jobs and distinctions, and fighting over money which will all have to be left behind when they come down to us, with the solitary exception of an obol! Do you think it would be a good idea, while we're up here, for me to shout out some advice to them, as loud as I possibly can – tell them to stop wasting their energy, and live with the thought of death perpetually in their minds? 'You silly fools!' I might say, 'why do you take these things so seriously? Stop wearing yourselves out. You're not going to live for ever. None of the things that you're making such a fuss about are going to last. You can't take any of them with you when you die. You'll have to go off without them, and your houses, your land, and your money will belong to other people, and go on changing hands indefinitely.' Suppose I shouted out something like that for them to listen to, don't you think they'd have a much better time and be far more sensible?

HERMES: My dear chap, don't you realize how impenetrable they are? Why, you could take a drill to them, but you still wouldn't get through to their consciousness. Ignorance and delusion have given them the treatment that Odysseus gave his crew – bunged up their ears with wax, for fear they should listen to the Sirens.[11] So how could they possibly hear you, even if you shouted yourself hoarse? You see, ignorance performs the same function up here as Lethe does down below – though admittedly there's a small minority who refuse to have their ears waxed, because they prefer to face facts, see things clearly, and know what's what.

CHARON: Then let's try shouting at *them*.

HERMES: What's the point? We'd be telling them what they

know already. That's obvious from the way they dissociate themselves from the majority view and simply laugh at what goes on, never making the slightest attempt to conform but evidently planning to emigrate from life altogether and seek asylum with us – for they tend to be very unpopular, because they're always exposing the stupidity of other people.

CHARON: Well done! Splendid fellows! Only there don't seem to be very many of them, Hermes.

HERMES: There are just enough. But now let's return to ground level.

CHARON: Oh, there's just one more thing I wanted to look at, Hermes, and then you'll have shown me all the sights. Could I see some of those holes in the ground where they store away the corpses?

HERMES: It's more usual to call them graves, Charon – or tombs, or sepulchres. Well, do you see those mounds of earth, and slabs of stone, and pyramids outside the towns? They're all receptacles for dead bodies.

CHARON: Then why are people laying wreaths on the slabs of stone, and sprinkling scent over them? And what on earth [*pointing*] do that lot think they're doing? They've made a bonfire and dug a trench beside one of the mounds, and now they're burning a lot of expensive dinners, and pouring wine and what looks like honey and milk into the trench.

HERMES: Well, skipper, I don't know what good it does to the people in Hades – but the theory is that their ghosts come up and dine as well as they can by fluttering about in the smoke and enjoying the smell of cooking, and then wash it down with some milk and honey out of the trench.

CHARON: Fancy thinking that one can still eat and drink, when there's no meat left on one's skull! But that's a funny thing to say to you, considering that you bring them down yourself, every day. Well, would *you* say they were likely to come back, once they were under the ground? It would be a nice situation for you, Hermes, and mean a lot of extra work, if besides bringing them down you had to bring them up again, every time they wanted a drink! But what fools they must be! What absolute idiots! Can't they really tell the difference between a dead man and a live one? Don't they know what things are like in our part of the world? Don't they know that

'The tombless man and he that hath a tomb
   Are both alike in death. King Agamemnon
   Hath no more honour than the beggar Irus.
   Thersites and the son of fair-haired Thetis
   Are equals now, for all are dead, and all
   Flit bare and dry o'er meads of asphodel.'[12]

HERMES: My goodness, what a lot of Homer you can spout! And now you've reminded me, let me show you the tomb of Achilles. There it is [*pointing*], beside the sea, on Cape Sigeum in the Troad. And Ajax is buried just across the way, at Rhoetium.

CHARON: They're not much to look at, are they, Hermes? But now show me some of the famous towns that I've heard of down below, like Nineveh, where Sardanapalus lived, and Babylon, and Mycenae, and Cleonae, and of course Troy. I remember having a lot of passengers from there – in fact for ten years I never got a chance to beach my boat and let it dry out properly.

HERMES: Well, as for Nineveh, skipper, it was wiped out long ago. There's not a trace of it left, and one can't even guess where it was. Babylon's over there [*pointing it out*], the place with great towers and a huge wall round it – but before long it will be just as hard to find as Nineveh. Mycenae and Cleonae I hardly like to show you, and least of all Troy – you might go down and wring Homer's neck, for making such a fuss about them in his poems. Admittedly they were fairly prosperous in the old days, but now they're completely dead – for towns die as well as people, you know, skipper, and so, oddly enough, do rivers. There's not so much as a ditch left in Argos to show where the Inachus used to be.

CHARON: Well really, Homer! After all the fine things you said about 'Troy divine' and 'the broad streets of Troy' and 'the firmly-stablished city of Cleonae'![13] But while we've been talking, some people over there seem to have started a war. Who are they, and what are they killing each other for?

HERMES: Those are the Argives and the Spartans, Charon. And that dying general who's writing an inscription for a trophy in his own blood is Othryades.

CHARON: But what are they fighting for, Hermes?

HERMES: For the piece of land that they're fighting on.

CHARON: How very stupid of them! Don't they realize that if each of them owned an estate the size of the Peloponnese, they still wouldn't get more than a square foot of land per head in the underworld? As for this particular patch of ground, it will be cultivated by an endless succession of different people, and plough after plough will turn up the fragments of that trophy.

HERMES: Yes, that's how it will be. But now let's go down and put the mountains back where they belong. Then I can get on with my job, and you can rejoin your ship. I'll be seeing you very shortly when I arrive with my next party of dead.

CHARON [standing up]: Well, I'm most grateful to you Hermes. I'll put your name on my honours list for outstanding service to the community. Thanks to you I've really enjoyed my holiday. But what a time those wretched human beings do have! And they never give a thought to old Charon.

[He starts picking his way downhill, shaking his head.]

MENIPPUS GOES TO HELL

Scene: A street in Athens. Enter a man wearing a skull-cap and a lion-skin, and carrying a lyre. He stops in front of a house and strikes an attitude, which makes a passer-by called Philonides turn and stare.

THE MAN [*hamming*]:
   'Hail, hearth and home, and blessed light of day!
   How gladly I behold you once again!'[1]
PHILONIDES [*to himself*]: Why, isn't that Menippus the Cynic? Or am I seeing things? No, it couldn't be anyone else. It's Menippus, large as life! But why that extraordinary costume, I wonder? I must have a word with him. [*Aloud.*] Hullo, Menippus? Where have you been? I haven't seen you in town for ages.
MENIPPUS [*as before*]:
   'In darkness have I been, among the dead,
   Pacing the god-forsaken plains of hell.'[2]
PHILONIDES: Good Lord! Do you mean to say you've gone and died, without letting any of us know? And now you've come back to life?
MENIPPUS: 'I visited the dead, but did not die.'[3]
PHILONIDES: What on earth made you choose such an extraordinary place for a holiday?
MENIPPUS: 'Rash youth inspired the plan, more bold than wise.'[4]
PHILONIDES: Oh, come off it, my dear chap. Do stop talking in blank verse, and tell me plainly why you're dressed like that. And why did you really go down there? It can't have been very pleasant.
MENIPPUS:
   'I travelled thither, dearest friend, to hear
   What said Tiresias, the Theban seer.'[5]

PHILONIDES: I say, have you gone quite mad? It just isn't sense to keep talking poetry to an old friend like me.

MENIPPUS [*reverting to normal tones*]: Don't let it worry you, my dear fellow. The fact is, I've been seeing a lot of Homer and Euripides lately, and I seem to have got so saturated with their style that I find myself speaking in verse quite automatically. But tell me, how are things up here? What's the news in town?

PHILONIDES: Oh, everyone's carrying on much the same as usual – lying, cheating, money-grubbing, and charging exorbitant rates of interest.

MENIPPUS: Poor souls! If only they knew of the recent legislation down there! A law's just been passed against plutocrats, and, by Cerberus, it hasn't left them a single loophole!

PHILONIDES: Do you mean to say they're revising the criminal code down below?

MENIPPUS: They certainly are, in lots of ways. But it's not supposed to be generally known yet, and I'd better not divulge official secrets, or I'll be up before Rhadamanthus on a charge of high treason.

PHILONIDES: Oh, for God's sake, Menippus! You surely won't refuse an old friend? I know how to keep my mouth shut – especially since I became an Initiate.[6]

MENIPPUS: Well, it's not an easy thing you're asking me to do, and not a very safe one either. However, for your sake I'll have to risk it. All right then, it's been decided that millionaires and plutocrats who keep their money where Danae's father kept her – in a safe deposit –

PHILONIDES: Just a moment, old boy. Before you tell me the actual terms of the law, there are various other things I'd like to hear. What was the idea of going down there in the first place? Who showed you the way? And then I want a detailed report of what you saw and heard in the underworld. You're quite a connoisseur in these matters, so I bet you didn't miss anything worth seeing or hearing.

MENIPPUS: All right, I'll try my best to oblige. What else can one do, when a friend insists?

[*They go into the house and sit down.*]

Well, first of all I'll explain why I went. When I was a child and read in Homer and Hesiod about wars and revolutions among the gods – real gods, mind you, not merely demi-gods – when I read of them committing rape, theft, and adultery, taking revenge on one another, kicking their fathers out of doors, and marrying their sisters, I thought it all quite in order – in fact it rather tickled my fancy. But when I began to grow up, I found that the law took exactly the opposite line, and said it was wrong to steal, or commit adultery, or start a revolution. This puzzled me very much, and I couldn't think what to make of it. For presumably the gods wouldn't have behaved like that, if they hadn't regarded it as perfectly proper, nor would our government have issued instructions to the contrary, if they hadn't thought there was something to be gained by it.

The problem was so baffling, that I decided to put myself in the hands of our so-called philosophers and tell them I didn't mind what they did to me, as long as they taught me some simple and reliable rule of conduct. With this object in view I started studying philosophy, only to find that I'd inadvertently jumped out of the frying-pan into the fire – for the more I had to do with philosophers, the more aware I became of their ignorance and helplessness, until finally the ideas of the man in the street began to seem positively brilliant by comparison.

You see, one of them would tell me to go all out for pleasure, and concentrate exclusively on that, because pleasure was the *summum bonum*. Another would tell me to go all out for hard work and suffering, to mortify the flesh by living in filth and squalor, abusing everyone else and making myself generally disagreeable. He was always quoting those hackneyed lines of Hesiod's[7] about virtue, and sweat, and getting to the top of the hill. Another would advise me to despise money and regard personal possessions as 'a matter of indifference', while yet another would prove to me conclusively that wealth was itself a form of Goodness.

As for their physical theories, they're hardly worth considering. I heard them holding forth about Ideas, and Insubstantial Essences, and Atoms, and Voids, until I was absolutely sick of it. Yet strangely enough they could all produce perfectly convincing arguments for the most self-contradictory hypotheses. For instance, I found it quite impossible to refute a theory which described a single object as both hot and cold, though I knew that a thing couldn't possibly be hot and cold at the same time. So I just went on nodding and shaking my head at intervals, like a man who keeps dropping off to sleep and then waking up with a start.

Even more absurd, these philosophers turned out, on closer inspection, to be practising exactly the opposite of what they preached. The ones who told me to despise money were hanging on to it themselves like grim death. They were always arguing about rates of interest, refused to do any teaching without a fee, and were prepared to put up with anything for money. Those who told me that fame was an illusion were obviously motivated in everything they said or did by a wish to become famous. As for pleasure, nearly all of them denounced it in public, but in their private lives it was the one thing they really cared about.

When this hope failed me, I felt even more discouraged. However, I consoled myself a little with the reflection that if I was still going around in a state of ignorance and folly, I was doing it in the company of some very eminent thinkers. Then one night, as I lay awake worrying about it, I decided to go to· Babylon and consult an expert in

Zoroastrian magic. I'd been told that such people had methods of opening the gates of Hades, taking anyone they liked down there, and bringing him back safe and sound. So I thought I'd better get one of them to arrange a trip down for me. Then I'd be able to ask Tiresias the Boiotian what was the most sensible way to live. A famous sage and prophet like him would presumably know the answer.

I jumped out of bed right away, and set off at full speed for Babylon. There I had an interview with a very wise and incredibly learned Chaldean, with white hair and a most impressive beard, whose name was Mithrobarzanes. I told him what I wanted, invited him to state his own fee, and with some difficulty persuaded him to act as my guide.

The first thing he did with me was to give me a course of twenty-nine early-morning baths in the Euphrates, beginning at the new moon. As the sun rose he made a long speech, most of which I didn't quite catch, for he rattled it off very fast, like one of those hopelessly inaudible announcers at the circus. But I gathered that he was invoking spirits of some kind. After that he'd spit three times in my face, and then back we'd go to his house, taking care not to meet the eye of anyone we passed *en route*. We lived on a diet of chestnuts, and drank nothing but milk, honey-and-milk, or water from the river Choaspes, and at night we slept out of doors on the grass.

Having completed this regimen, he took me down at midnight to the Tigris, where he washed me, dried me off, and then with the aid of tapers, squill, and various other things made me thoroughly pure and holy, muttering the same old spell under his breath as he did so. After that he drew a magic circle round me, so that the ghosts couldn't do me any harm, and made me walk backwards all the way to his house, where we spent the rest of the night preparing for the voyage. He himself put on a magic robe of the Persian variety, but he fitted me out like this with a skull-cap, a lyre, and a lion-skin, and advised me, if anyone asked my name, to say not Menippus, but Heracles or Orpheus or Odysseus.

PHILONIDES: What was the idea of that, Menippus? I don't quite see.

MENIPPUS: Oh, it's really quite obvious. There's nothing very esoteric about it. It's just that those three gentlemen were the first people to enter Hades alive, so he reckoned that if he made me look like them, I'd find it easier to slip past the guards posted by Aeacus, and be less likely to get held up. Being dressed like a tragic hero would make me seem more familiar, and act as a sort of passport.

By this time it was beginning to grow light, so we went down to our embarkation point on the river. There we found a boat waiting for us, complete with sheep for sacrifice, honey-and-milk, and various other pieces of magical equipment. When we'd got everything on board, we

'Embarked in sorrow, shedding many a tear.'[8]

After sailing downstream for a while, we entered the marshy lake that swallows up the Euphrates, crossed it, and came to a desolate shore, covered with dense woods that shut out the sun. There we disembarked – Mithrobarzanes went first – and proceeded to dig a hole in the ground, which we then filled with blood by cutting the sheep's throats over it. Meanwhile, with a lighted torch in his hand, the wizard began to pronounce, not under his breath this time but at the top of his voice, a comprehensive invocation to all the powers of darkness, including the Furies,

'Black Hecate, and dread Persephone,'[9]

interspersing his remarks with several long words in a language that I didn't understand.

Immediately the whole place started shaking, the ground

split open, and Cerberus was heard barking in the distance. It was a ghastly experience.

'The king of hell trembled upon his throne,'[10]

and well he might, for most of his kingdom was now exposed to view, infernal lake, river of fire, and all. Still, down we went through the crack and found Rhadamanthus practically dead with fright. Cerberus gave a great snarl and came rushing towards us, but I struck a few chords on my lyre and he soon dropped off to sleep.

When we reached the lake, it looked as if we'd never get across, for the boat was full up – in fact it was absolutely jammed with wailing passengers. Each of them had either a broken leg, or a head-wound, or some other part of his anatomy smashed in, so presumably they'd been in a war. However, that splendid fellow Charon caught sight of my lion-skin, and immediately assumed that I was Heracles. So he obligingly made room for us, ferried us across, and showed us the right path to take on the other side.

It was pretty dark by now, so Mithrobarzanes led the way, and I hung on to him, until we came to a large field overgrown with asphodels, where vast numbers of ghosts were fluttering about, squeaking. Eventually we arrived at the court of Minos, which happened to be in session. Minos himself was seated high up on a throne, and the Avenging Furies were beside him on the bench. Through a door on the other side of the courtroom the prisoners were dragged in on a long chain. Apparently they included adulterers, brothel-keepers, tax collectors, parasites, informers, and a whole lot of other socially undesirable types. Plutocrats and financiers, with pale faces, protruding stomachs, and gout, formed a separate procession. They had wooden collars round their necks, attached to chains that must have weighed about a hundred and sixty pounds each.

We stopped and watched the proceedings, and listened

to the speeches for the defence. As for the prosecution, it was conducted by counsel of a rather unusual kind.

PHILONIDES: Why, who were they? Do hurry up and tell me.

MENIPPUS: Well, you know the shadows that our bodies cast in the sun?

PHILONIDES: Of course.

MENIPPUS: When we die, those shadows act as our accusers. They bring evidence against us of all the crimes we've committed during our lives. And as they follow us everywhere and never leave us for a second, they're regarded as most reliable witnesses.

After careful investigation of each case, Minos sent the prisoners off to join the other Damned and undergo appropriate punishment. He was particularly down on the ones whose wealth or political power had given them such an inflated idea of themselves that they'd practically expected people to worship them. He was evidently quite disgusted by their short-sighted arrogance – their failure to realize that they and their possessions were strictly perishable. There they stood, stripped of their splendour, of wealth, rank, and authority, stark naked, hanging their heads. And all their worldly success must have seemed to them like a dream.

Personally, I was very glad to see it, and when I spotted someone I knew, I went up to him and whispered in his ear. I reminded him what he'd been like when he was alive – how proud he'd felt when crowds of people turned up on his doorstep each morning, only to be pushed away by his servants and have the door shut in their faces. Even so, they'd waited until he eventually got up and showed himself in a heavily-embroidered robe of purple or gold. And then, as a great favour, he'd allowed some of them to speak to him, or even to kiss his chest or his right hand! But he didn't seem to enjoy being reminded of it now.

In one case Minos gave a favourable verdict. Dionysius of Syracuse had been accused by Dion of several monstrous crimes, his shadow had produced corroborating evidence, and he was just being handed over to the Chimaera, when Arisitippus of Cyrene appeared in court. He's much respected down there, you know, and has a great deal of influence. Well, he had the sentence quashed, by pointing out that Dionysius had always been very generous to intellectuals.

Finally we left the court and proceeded to the punishment area. And there, my dear fellow, I heard and saw some very distressing things. The whole place resounded with the cracking of whips and the screams of people being roasted. Racks, wheels, and pillories were everywhere in operation, the Chimaera was tearing its victims limb from limb, and Cerberus was gnawing away at human bones. Every class was equally represented – kings, slaves, paupers, plutocrats, beggars were being punished side by side – and they all appeared to be repenting of their sins. I recognized some of the more recent arrivals, but they either hid their faces and turned away, or if they brought themselves to meet my eye, their expression was very humble and obsequious. And this, mind you, from people who'd been pompous and overbearing all their lives! But poor men had half of their sentences remitted, which meant that they were given a rest from time to time, and then their punishment would begin again. Oh yes, and I saw those fabulous characters, Ixion, Sisyphus, Tantalus, and the giant Tityos – and my goodness, he really was a giant! His body must have covered several acres.

We made our way past these unfortunate people to the Acherusian Plain, where we found the Heroes and Heroines and all the other dead, grouped according to their nationalities. Some of them were extremely old and beginning to moulder away – I suppose that's what Homer means when he calls them 'frail'[11] – but others were still quite fresh and firm, especially the Egyptians, because they'd been mummified.

It wasn't very easy to distinguish between individuals, for being nothing but bare bones, they all look practically alike. However, after prolonged examination we finally managed to tell one from another. They lay huddled on top of one another in vague, shapeless heaps, without any trace of the beauty they possessed up here. In fact, with such a mass of skeletons lying around, all looking much the same, all staring horribly through hollow eye-sockets and displaying lipless teeth, I despaired of ever being able to distinguish between Thersites and Nireus, Irus and Odysseus, Agamemnon and the local butcher. For all differentiating features had disappeared. They were just a collection of bones, obscure and anonymous, no longer capable of identification.

Seeing them like that gave me the idea that human life is a vast sort of pageant organized by Chance, who provides the people taking part in it with various different costumes. She picks out one man at random and dresses him up as a king, puts a crown and diadem on his head, and supplies him with a bodyguard. She dresses another as a slave, makes up another to look beautiful, and another to look ridiculously ugly. The great thing is, I imagine, that the show should have plenty of variety.

Then, instead of letting everyone wear the same costume throughout the performance, she often changes things round half-way through. For instance, she makes Croesus switch from being a king to being a slave and a prisoner, and after letting Maeandrius be a slave for a while, she makes him put on the costume that Polycrates has been wearing, and try being a tyrant for a bit. When the show's over, everyone returns his costume, strips off the body that goes with it, and becomes just like he was before, quite indistinguishable from anyone else. But some people are silly enough to feel angry and aggrieved when Chance comes up to them and asks for her things back, as though they were being robbed of their own property instead of merely repaying a short-term loan.

I expect you've often seen the same thing on the stage, where an actor has to be prepared to play Creon, or Priam, or Agamemnon, according to the needs of the programme, and a man who's just given a most dignified performance as Cecrops or Erechtheus may find himself required by the producer to appear a few minutes later in the role of a slave. But when the play's finished, each actor removes his gold-embroidered robe, his mask and his high boots, and comes down to earth, where he goes about like a perfectly ordinary person who's rather short of cash. He's no longer King Agamemnon, the son of Atreus, or King Creon, the son of Menoecius, but plain Polus from Sunium or Satyrus from Marathon. Well, that's what human life is like, or so it seemed to me when I saw those skeletons.

PHILONIDES: But I say, Menippus, what about the ones who've got large and expensive tombs up here – monuments, statues, epitaphs, and so on? Aren't they treated with any more respect than ordinary people down there?

MENIPPUS: My dear chap, what a silly question! You know Mausolus, the Carian who's buried in the famous Mausoleum? Well, you'd never stop laughing if you could see him now. There he is, stuffed away among the lower orders, and as far as I could see, the only difference that his tomb had made to him was that he'd got squashed flat by the weight of all that masonry. You see, once a man has been given his ration of space – and Aeacus never lets anyone have more than a square foot – he has to be content with it, and huddle himself up until he fits into the area prescribed.

But I fancy you'd be even more amused if you could see how poor the ex-kings and ex-governors are. They're reduced to selling kippers or teaching the alphabet, and people are always being rude to them and knocking them about – in fact they're no better off than slaves. What was almost too much for me was the spectacle of Philip of Macedon sitting in a corner, trying to make some money by mending rotten shoes – though admittedly there were plenty of other people like Xerxes, Darius, and Polycrates to be seen begging on the streets.

PHILONIDES: It sounds almost incredible. But what about philosophers like Socrates and Diogenes? What were they doing?

MENIPPUS: Oh, Socrates is still going round proving that everyone else is wrong. He's usually to be found in the company of talkative characters like Palamedes, Odysseus, and Nestor. But his legs still look rather puffy and swollen from that poison he drank. As for that splendid fellow Diogenes, he lives next door to Sardanapalus, Midas, and various other ex-millionaires. When he hears them moaning about how much money they once had, he roars with laughter and thinks it a wonderful joke. He spends most of his time lying on his back and singing in a harsh and discordant voice, to drown the sound of their grumblings – which makes them so cross that they're seriously considering moving house to get away from him.

PHILONIDES: Well, that's enough about them. Now tell me about the law that you said had been passed against the rich.

MENIPPUS: Oh, thanks for reminding me. I was meaning to tell you about it, but somehow I seem to have drifted off the subject. Anyway, while I was there, the local authority called a public meeting to discuss various matters of policy. When I saw everyone rushing off in the same direction, I naturally went along too and attended the meeting myself. The last item on the agenda was this question of what to do about plutocrats. After several serious offences had been laid to their charge, such as fraud, assault, arrogance, and injustice, a left-wing speaker proposed the following resolution:

> THAT in view of the many illegal acts committed by the rich during their lifetime, including theft, assault, and the display of utter contempt for the poor, their bodies be punished after death in accordance with the existing criminal code, but their souls be sent back to life and introduced into donkeys, there to remain for the next TWO HUNDRED AND FIFTY THOUSAND years, passing from one donkey to another, being employed as beasts of burden and driven to and fro by the poor; AND THAT after the expiry of that period they be allowed to die. Proposed by Councillor Skull, and seconded by Councillors Corps, De'Ath, and Skelton, all of the Mortuary Ward.

The Chairman put the resolution to the vote, and it was carried by a substantial majority. Cerberus barked agreement, Persephone pursed her lips, which is her normal manner of giving the Royal Assent, and the resolution became law. So much for the meeting.

Finally I did what I'd come to do. I went up to Tiresias, and after explaining the whole situation, asked him what he thought was the best way to live. The question made him cackle with laughter – he's a little old man, you know, quite blind, with a white face and a squeaky voice.

'I know what's the matter with you, my boy,' he said. 'It's those wretched philosophers – always contradicting themselves! But I can't tell you the answer. It's strictly against the rules.'

'Oh, don't say that, sir,' I pleaded. 'You surely can't let me go on being even blinder than you!'

So eventually he drew me aside, and then reached up and whispered in my ear:

'The best way to live is to be an ordinary human being. So give up all this metaphysical nonsense. Stop worrying about first principles and final causes, and forget all those clever arguments – they don't mean a thing. Just live in the moment and get along as best you can, trying to see the funny side of things and taking nothing very seriously.'

'Thus spake the seer Tiresias, and back,
Returned across the fields of asphodel.'[12]

It was growing late, so I turned to Mithrobarzanes and said:

'Well, what are we waiting for? Let's get back to life.'

'Don't worry,' he replied, 'I'm going to show you an easy short-cut.'

He led me to a place that was even darker than the rest of the underworld, and pointed to a tiny ray of light in the distance. It looked as if it was coming through a keyhole.

'That's the Cave of Trophonius,' he told me. 'It's the entrance normally used by the Boeotians. Go up that way, and you'll be back in Greece in a few seconds.'

I was very glad to hear it, so I said good-bye to him, and with some difficulty crawled up through the mouth of the cave. And there I was, goodness knows how, at Lebadea.

ICAROMENIPPUS

OR

UP IN THE CLOUDS

Scene: A street in Athens. Menippus is walking slowly along, thinking aloud. A friend of his is following close behind, trying to catch what he is saying.

MENIPPUS: So my first hop, from here to the moon, was about three hundred miles, and from there to the sun would be, say, fifteen hundred. And from the sun to Zeus's headquarters in the sky is a non-stop eagle-flight of approximately twenty-four hours.

FRIEND [*drawing level and falling into step beside him*]: For goodness' sake, Menippus, what *are* these astronomical problems that you're working out under your breath? I've been walking behind you for some time, and you've kept on muttering about the sun and the moon, and using ordinary words like 'hop' and 'mile' in a most extraordinary context.

MENIPPUS: You mustn't be surprised, my dear chap, if I seem rather up in the clouds, for I'm just trying to calculate the total distance that I covered on my recent expedition.

FRIEND: Why, have you been learning to navigate by the stars, old boy, like the Phoenicians?

MENIPPUS: Not by them. Among them. That's where I went on my expedition.

FRIEND: Good Lord, that must have been a pretty long dream! Fancy travelling all that distance in your sleep!

MENIPPUS: So you think I've been dreaming, do you? Well, I'd have you know that I've just this moment arrived from the palace of Zeus.

FRIEND [*treating it as a joke*]: No! You don't mean to say that our old friend Menippus has dropped on us out of the blue? What a god-send!

MENIPPUS: It's perfectly true. I had a personal interview with Zeus today, and I've only just got back, after some most remarkable experiences. And if you don't believe me, I'm delighted to hear it, for it only goes to show how incredibly lucky I've been.

FRIEND: But how could I possibly doubt your word, my dear old Olympian superman? After all I'm only a poor terrestrial creature, and you live up in the clouds – in fact you're what Homer would call a Celestial. But do explain to me how you managed to get up there? Where on earth did you find a long enough ladder? You don't look much like Ganymede, so you can hardly have been snatched up by an eagle, for future employment as a wine-waiter.

MENIPPUS: I quite realize you're making fun of me, and I don't blame you for thinking it rather a tall story. But the fact is, I didn't need a ladder, nor did I find it necessary to have an affair with an eagle. You see, I had wings of my own.

FRIEND: Now you're going one better than Daedalus. So on top of everything else you've been turned into a hawk or a jackdaw, without any of us noticing!

MENIPPUS: Well done, old man! That was a pretty good guess – because it was Daedalus that gave me the idea of making myself some wings.

FRIEND: But you daredevil, weren't you afraid of falling into the sea, like Icarus, and giving the world a Menippean Ocean?

MENIPPUS: Certainly not. His feathers were only stuck on with wax, so as soon as the wax melted in the sun, he naturally moulted and crashed. But my wings were the genuine article – there wasn't any wax about *them*.

FRIEND: What do you mean? I can't think how, but you're gradually inducing me to take you seriously.

MENIPPUS: Well, it was like this. I caught a large eagle, and a very powerful type of vulture. I amputated their wings, *radius*, *ulna*, and all, and – but if you can spare the time, I'd rather start at the beginning and tell you how I got the idea in the first place.

FRIEND: Please do. I'm all ears. I'm listening open-mouthed to hear what happened. For pity's sake don't leave me hanging in mid-air, at this point in the story.

MENIPPUS: All right, I won't. It's certainly not a pretty sight to see a friend hanging in mid-air – especially if, as you say, he's got his mouth open. Well, the moment I started thinking about life, I realized that the things most people care about, wealth, position, and power, were absurdly unimportant and ephemeral. I soon began to regard them as mere obstacles to the pursuit of what really mattered, and tried to look beyond them and contemplate Nature as a whole. But at this point I became desperately puzzled by what scientists call the physical universe. I couldn't make out how it had come into existence, who had created it, when it had started, or when it was going to end. And some individual aspects of it were even more puzzling. For instance, there were the stars, scattered about at random all over the sky. Then there was the sun – I longed to know what it was actually made of. Above all, I was completely baffled by the odd behaviour of the moon – yet there must, I felt, be some obscure reason why it appeared in so many different shapes. And then, of course, there were such things as lightning darting across the sky, thunder bursting overhead, rain, snow, and hail pouring down – they all seemed very baffling and inexplicable too.

In the circumstances I naturally thought I'd better consult the scientists, who were presumably in a position to tell everyone the truth about such things. So I picked out a few scientists who, to judge from the grimness of their expressions, the paleness of their faces, and the luxuriance of their beards were at the very top of their profession – and it was obvious enough from the way they talked that their knowledge of astronomy was quite out of this world. I placed myself in their hands, put down a large deposit, and agreed to pay the balance on completion of my scientific education. I hoped I'd soon be able to talk intelligently about the stars, and understand the organization of the universe.

But far from relieving my ignorance, the scientists merely picked me up and dumped me in a worse state of muddle than ever, by filling me up with all kinds of technical terms like First Principles, Final Causes, Atoms, Voids, Matter, and Ideas. Worst of all, from my point of view, no two scientists ever said the same thing, but all their statements were utterly conflicting and contradictory. Yet they still expected me to believe them, and each worked hard to convince me that his own particular theory was true.

FRIEND: It's certainly a ridiculous situation, when the experts disagree about the facts and hold opposite views about the same objects!

MENIPPUS: Yes, but wait until you hear what absolute frauds they are. That'll really make you laugh. To start with, though these scientists were ordinary people like the rest of us, with no more than average eyesight – in fact some of them were positively myopic, either because of their age, or because they were just too lazy to use their eyes – that didn't stop them from claiming first-hand knowledge of events in outer space, measuring the sun, and tramping about on the other side of the moon. They described the shape and size of the stars in such detail that you could only imagine they'd just dropped down off one, and though they probably couldn't have said for certain how many miles Megara was from Athens, they were perfectly prepared to give you the distance between the sun and the moon, correct to the nearest foot. They measured the height of the atmosphere, the depth of the sea, and the circumference of the earth. Not content with that, by describing circles, constructing triangles on top of quadrilaterals, and inventing a complicated system of spheres, they actually claimed to measure the sky itself.

Another thing about them that was surely rather stupid, if not absolutely crazy, was that in spite of the difficulty of ascertaining the facts, they never put forward a theory as a tentative hypothesis. On the contrary, they struggled desperately to prove that no other theory could possibly be true, and were practically willing to swear that the sun was a lump of red-hot metal, that the moon was inhabited, and that the stars were teetotallers, drinking nothing but water, which the sun hauled up out of the sea, like a bucket out of a well, and distributed to them all in equal rations.

As for the contradictions between them, they're only too obvious. Just see if you can find any way of reconciling theories like these, or if they're totally incompatible. Take first of all their views about the universe. Some of them say it's uncreated and indestructible. Others postulate a creator, and even specify the exact method of creation. They're the ones that astonish me most, for having introduced a divine technician to assemble the universe, they never bother to tell us where he came from, or where he stood while he was doing the job – for before the universe existed, space and time are both inconceivable.

FRIEND: From what you say, Menippus, they certainly sound like a lot of shameless impostors.

MENIPPUS: That's putting it mildly, old man. You should have heard them holding forth about Ideas and Immaterial Essences, or distinguishing between the Finite and the Infinite! Another thing, of course, that they argue hotly about, is whether or not the universe will ever come to an end. There was also a school of thought which posited any number of different universes, and poured scorn on those who used the word in the singular. Then there was another gentleman,[1] presumably not a pacifist, who attributed the existence of the universe to a war between the elements.

I need hardly point out the diversity of their theological doctrines. Some identified God with a certain number,[2] while others swore by dogs, or geese, or plane-trees.[3] Then there was a sect that kicked out all the gods except one, to whom they handed over the control of the universe. It rather upset me, I must admit, to think of gods being in such short supply. However, another sect went off to the opposite extreme, and were positively over-generous in their output of gods, whom they graded according to the degree of divinity displayed. The one who came out top received the title of God, and the rest merely got Second- or Third-Class Honours. Then there were some who thought that the deity was formless and incorporeal, while others regarded it as a physical entity. There wasn't any general agreement that the gods take an interest in human affairs, for some thinkers relieved them of all responsibility, just as we exempt elderly people from civic duties – thus reducing the gods to extras, and giving them only walk-on parts. Others go even further, and refuse to believe there are any gods at all, leaving the universe to function as a fully automatic mechanism.

When I heard a lot of impressively bearded genetlemen thundering out this type of information, I didn't care to disbelieve them. But I couldn't find a single one of their statements that seemed incontrovertible and was not in fact disproved by someone else. The result was a bad attack of Homeric indecision – for every time I started being convinced by one of them,[4]

'Another voice within me held me back.'[4]

The whole thing was so baffling that I finally despaired of ever hearing a word of truth on such matters from any-one on earth, and decided that the only solution was to get

a pair of wings and go straight up to heaven. My hope of
bringing it off was based not merely on wishful thinking,
but also on Aesop's Fables,[5] which made it clear that heaven
was perfectly accessible to creatures like eagles and beetles,
and occasionally even to camels. It was obviously out of the
question to grow wings of my own, but if I borrowed some
from an eagle or a vulture – for no other bird's would be
strong enough to support the weight of a human body –
the experiment might possibly succeed.

So I caught a specimen of each variety, and carefully
amputated the right wing of the eagle and the left wing of
the vulture. These I attached to my arms, fitting them with
handgrips at the outer ends, and securing them with stout
straps at the shoulders. I then gave myself a preliminary
flight-test, by jumping into the air and flapping my arms
up and down, so as to flutter along like a goose, half flying
and half walking on tiptoe. After this successful experiment,
I tried something a little more enterprising. I went up on to
the Acropolis, launched myself over the edge of the rock,
and glided right down into the theatre, where I landed
quite safely. I now developed more lofty ambitions. I
practised taking off from mountains, like Parnes or Hymet-
tus, and flying as far as Geraneia, then up to Acrocorinth,
then over Pholoe and Erymanthus, and finally landing on
the summit of Taygetus. By this time I was most efficient at
it, and now that I was fully fledged I became impatient to
leave the nest. So I climbed up to the top of Mount Olympus, and having supplied myself with food for the journey
in the lightest possible form, I set off at full speed for
heaven.

The height made me rather giddy at first, but I soon got
used to it. When I was well above the clouds and approaching the moon, I began to feel a bit tired, especially in my
left wing, the one I'd got off the vulture. So I landed on the
moon and sat down for a short rest. I felt just like Zeus in

Homer,[6] gazing down at the earth and turning my attention first to

'The savage Thracians, busy with the horse,'

then to the Mysians, and then, if I liked, to Greece, Persia, and India. All of which gave me a great deal of entertainment.

FRIEND: Oh, do tell me about it, Menippus. I'm very anxious to hear the whole story of your travels, including any information that you may have picked up *en route*. I bet you've found out all kinds of interesting things about the shape of the earth and its contents, as seen from above.

MENIPPUS: You're absolutely right, my dear fellow. So try to imagine yourself up there with me in the moon, and let's have a look at the whole state of affairs on earth. First of all, you must picture the earth as something very small indeed, far smaller than the moon, I mean. In fact, the first time I glanced down, it took me several minutes to locate those great mountains over there, and that great expanse of sea. Why, if I hadn't caught sight of the Colossus of Rhodes and the lighthouse at Pharos, I assure you I shouldn't have known it was the earth at all! However, those two landmarks were high enough to stand out fairly clearly, and convince me that it really was the earth I was looking at. Another thing that helped me to identify it was the faint sparkling of the sea in the sunshine. But once I'd got my eyes properly focused on it, the whole of human life came into view, not merely countries and towns, but actual individuals sailing about, or fighting, or working on the land, or taking part in law suits. I could even make out dear little women and wild animals – in short

'All creatures nourished by the fruitful earth.'[7]

FRIEND: But that's quite incredible. You're contradicting yourself. A moment ago you were trying to identify the earth, which had shrunk to a tiny point in the distance. If it hadn't been for the Colossus of Rhodes, you might have been looking at something completely different. But now you've suddenly turned into a lynx, and can see everything there is to be seen on the earth, human beings, animals – you'll be seeing gnats' eggs next!

MENIPPUS: Oh, thanks for reminding me. Somehow or other I seem to have left out the one thing I should have mentioned. It's this. When I found I was looking at the earth, but was too far away to see anything properly, I was terribly upset and didn't know what to do. I felt so depressed that I practically burst into tears – when suddenly the famous scientist, Empedocles, appeared from behind me, coal-black, covered with ash, and obviously done to a turn. I must admit the sight of him gave me rather a shock. I thought he must be some sort of lunar deity.

'It's all right, Menippus,' he said.

'"No god am I: misdeem me not immortal."[8]

I'm Empedocles, the scientist. You see, when I jumped into that volcano, it erupted me in a cloud of smoke and deposited me up here. So now I live on the moon, spending most of my time in space travel, and subsisting on a diet of dew. I've come to help you solve your problem – for you're evidently in agony at not being able to see things clearly on earth.'

'My dear Empedocles,' I replied, 'how extremely kind of you! As soon as I get home, I'll remember to pour a libation to you over a smoky fire. And I'll pray to you regularly once a month, opening and shutting my mouth three times in the direction of the new moon.'

'But, Man-in-the-moon knows,' he said, 'I didn't come here wanting to be paid. It just broke my heart to see you looking so miserable. Anyway, do you know how to give yourself perfect eyesight?'

'I certainly don't,' I answered. 'That is, unless *you* can somehow clear away the mist from my eyes. As it is, I seem to be half blind.'

'You don't need me to do it for you,' he said. 'Good eyesight is already in your possession. You brought it with you from the earth.'

'Where is it then?' I asked. 'I can't see it anywhere.'

'Don't you realize that your right wing belonged to an eagle?'

'Of course I do,' I said. 'But what's the connexion between wings and eyes?'

'Just that the eagle has stronger eyes than any other living creature,' he replied. 'It's the only one that can look straight at the sun. That's why it's the king of birds, and that's how one can tell if any given specimen is a legitimate heir to the throne – by seeing if it can stare at the sun without blinking.'

'Yes, so I've been told. And now you mention it, I'm sorry I didn't take out my own eyes and pop in the eagle's instead, before I started up here. As it is, I'm only half-equipped – I haven't a full set of kingly attributes. So apparently I'm just a poor bastard.'

'Still, you can soon acquire at least one kingly eye,' he told me. 'All you have to do is stand up for a moment, keep the vulture's wing stationary, and flap the other up and down. That'll make your right eye as strong as your right wing – though the left one's bound to give you a rather inferior bird's-eye view.'

'I'll be quite content to be even semi-eagle-eyed,' I assured him. 'It'll do just as well, for I fancy I've often seen carpenters shutting one eye deliberately, when they're trying to get a plank straight.'

While I was saying this, I was already carrying out his instructions, whereupon he began to fade away and finally went up in smoke. However, the moment I started flapping my right wing, everything became brilliantly illuminated, and I found I could see things that I couldn't see before. For instance, when I looked down at the earth, towns, human beings, and human actions were clearly visible to me – not merely what went on out of doors, but what people were doing inside their own houses, where they thought no one could see them. I saw Ptolemy going to bed with his sister, Agathocles planning to murder his father, Antiochus the First making a secret signal to his stepmother, Stratonice, Alexander of Pherae being killed by his wife, Antigonus having an affair with his daughter-in-law, and Attalus being poisoned by his son. Elsewhere I saw Arsaces cutting his pretty little wife's throat, and the eunuch Arbaces drawing a sword to kill Arsaces. Spatinus the Mede was being dragged feet-first out of a dinner-party by his own bodyguard, after having his skull smashed in with a golden cup. The same sort of thing was happening in the palaces of Libya, Scythia, and Thrace, where people were equally busy committing adultery, murder, high treason, theft, and perjury, going in constant fear of their lives, and being informed on by their nearest and dearest.

So, as you may gather, royalty gave me a lot of quiet amusement, but even funnier were the private individuals. For I saw Hermodorus the Epicurean perjuring himself for the sake of a thousand drachmas, Agathocles the Stoic suing one of his students for non-payment of fees, Clinias the Professor of Literature snitching a piece of sacramental plate from the temple of Asclepius, and Herophilus the Cynic spending the night in a brothel. As for the rest – but there's no point in trying to tell you about all the people I saw burgling houses, lending money, going to law, and begging. It's enough to say that it was a spectacle of infinite variety.

FRIEND: It would be nice if you could tell me a bit more about it, Menippus. You seem to have found it extremely entertaining.

MENIPPUS: Well, I couldn't possibly describe it all, my dear fellow. I had my work cut out just to see it. But the main items were much the same as you'll find on the Shield of Achilles, in Homer.[9] At one point there'd be a wedding or a party going on, at another a trial or a public meeting. One man would be at a thanksgiving service, his next-door neighbour at a funeral. Every time I looked at the Getans, they were having a war. Every time I looked at the Scythians, they were trailing about in their covered wagons. Shifting my gaze a few degrees to the South, I could see the Egyptians engaged in agriculture, the Phoenicians in commerce, the Cilicians in piracy, the Spartans in flagellation, and the Athenians in litigation. With all these different things going on simultaneously, you can just imagine what a hotch-potch it seemed. Suppose you collected a large number of singers, or rather of massed choirs, and told each member of them to forget about harmony and concentrate on singing his own tune, what would you expect it to sound like, with every performer trying to execute a solo of his own, and shout down the man next to him?

FRIEND: I should think it would be a pretty nasty noise, Menippus.

MENIPPUS: Well, that's what things are like on earth, old chap. It's not just that people sing out of tune, but that they all sing *different* tunes, each with its own rhythm and its own meaning – until eventually the conductor chases every one of them off the platform, saying he has no further need for their services. Then at last they do achieve some sort of unison, for they all keep equally silent, and instead of the hideous racket that they've been making, there's a long rest.

Needless to say, in this great variety show of human life there are some very funny turns. But what made me laugh most of all was the way people squabbled about land, and were terribly pleased with themselves for having a farm on the Plain of Sicyon, or owning an estate near Oenoe on the Plain of Marathon, or possessing a thousand acres at Acharnae – when the whole of Greece appeared from up there to be about four inches across, of which Attica doubtless represented only a tiny fraction! It made me wonder what grounds for self-satisfaction our rich men had really got, considering that the biggest landowner of them all seemed to be busily engaged in cultivating one of Epicurus's atoms. Then, as I glanced at the Peloponnese, the district of Cynouria caught my eye, and I thought of all the Argives and Spartans who died in a single day for a bit of land no broader than a bean. It was also amusing to see how proud people were to possess, say, eight gold rings and four golden bowls – when the whole of Mount Pangaeus, gold-mines and all, was about the size of a millet-seed.

FRIEND: Oh, you *are* lucky, Menippus, to have seen things in such an unusual perspective! But how big did the towns look, for goodness' sake, and the people themselves?

MENIPPUS: Well, you know what an ant-hill looks like, with lots of ants crawling round it, some streaming off across country and some going back to town. One ant will be carrying out refuse, another racing in with a bean-pod or half a grain of corn. Then doubtless they have the ant-equivalents of architects, left-wing politicians, town councillors, literary men, and philosophers. Anyhow, the towns and the people in them looked exactly like that. If it seems to you rather a degrading comparison, you must investigate some of the ancient myths of Thessaly. You'll find that those famous militarists, the Myrmidons, were originally ants.

When I'd seen all I wanted to see, and had a good laugh over it, I started myself up again and took off for

'The palaces of aegis-bearing Zeus
And all the other gods.' [10]

But I'd hardly got up to six hundred feet, when I heard the Moon hailing me in a clear soprano.

'Menippus ahoy!' she called. 'Good luck to you – that is, if you'll do something for me.'

'Just tell me what it is,' I shouted back. 'I'll be only too glad to oblige – so long as I don't have to carry anything.'

'It's perfectly easy,' she assured me. 'I just want you to take a message, or rather a request to Zeus. The point is, Menippus, I'm sick and tired of hearing all the clever things that scientists say about me. They seem to have nothing to do but poke their noses into my affairs. They're always wanting to know who I am, what my measurements are, and why my figure keeps changing into a semicircle or a crescent. Some of them say I'm infested with living organisms, others that I'm a sort of mirror suspended over the sea – in fact they just pin on to me the first thing that comes into their heads. And it's really the last straw when they say that even my light isn't my own, that I've stolen it from the sun up there. You see, they never stop trying to make trouble between me and my brother.[11] As if they hadn't been rude enough about him already, calling him a stone, and a lump of red-hot iron!

'And yet what stories I could tell about the disgusting things they do at night – although they look so stern and manly in the daytime, behave in such a dignified manner, and are so much admired by ordinary people! Oh yes, I see it all, but I don't say anything about it. I think it would be most indelicate to throw light on these nocturnal activities of theirs and show what hypocrites they really are. So every time I see them committing adultery, or theft, or any other midnight crime, I immediately draw a cloud over my face. I've no wish to let the general public see old men playing the fool under cover of long white beards and long diatribes on virtue. But they never stop tearing *my* reputation to pieces and insulting me in every way. Eclipse me, if I haven't often thought of moving house to somewhere a long way off, just to get away from their gossip.

'So would you please remember to tell Zeus all about it? Tell him I simply can't stay here any longer if he doesn't rub out those scientists, put a gag on those logicians, demolish the Stoa, burn down the Academy, and stop those Peripatetics walking about all the time. Then I might be safe from their offensive calculations.'

'I won't forget,' I yelled, and started climbing steeply towards a part of the universe

'Where neither men nor oxen ever ploughed.' [12]

Soon the Moon herself looked quite small, and the earth was quite invisible beyond her. Keeping the sun to starboard I set a course between the stars, and two days later found myself on the outskirts of heaven. My first idea was to march straight in, just as I was. I thought no one was likely to notice me in my semi-aquiline condition, for I understood that the eagle was one of Zeus's oldest friends. But then I realized that my vulture-component was liable to make me conspicuous. It seemed wiser not to take any risks, so I went and knocked on the front door.

It was answered by Hermes, who took my name and hurried off to announce me. After a while I was asked to come in, which I did in much fear and trembling, and found the whole family sitting together. They weren't too happy about it either, for they were secretly rather upset by my sudden arrival, and expected to see practically the whole human race following my example and turning up on their doorstep. But Zeus gave me a piercing look – doubtless the sort of look he gave the Titans – and asked in a terrible voice:

'"Who and whence art thou? Name thy home and parents!"' [13]

When I heard these words, I nearly died of fright. I just stood there speechless, thunderstruck by the sheer volume of sound. But eventually I recovered, and told him the whole story clearly from the beginning – how I'd wanted to find out about celestial phenomena, how I'd consulted the scientists and got sick of being confused by their theories, and how I'd had my bright idea about wings. Then I described all my experiences, right up to my arrival in heaven, not forgetting to deliver the message from the Moon.

Zeus stopped frowning, and smiled.

'Well, talk about Otus and Ephialtes!' he exclaimed. 'Menippus has beaten them at their own game! Anyway, we'll put you up for the night, and tomorrow I'll answer your questions and send you home again.'

With these words he got up and walked to a part of heaven where reception from the earth was particularly good, for it was his time to listen to human prayers. On the way there he asked me various questions about things back home, first of all fairly easy ones like what was the current price of corn in Greece? Had we suffered much from the hard winter last year? Did we need more rain for the crops? Then he asked if we still had any sculptors left like Phidias. Why hadn't the Athenians celebrated the Festival of Zeus for so many years? Did they still plan to finish the temple[14] they'd started building for him? And had the burglars who broke into his shrine at Dodona been arrested yet? When I'd told him the answers, he went on:

'I say, Menippus, what do people really think of me these days?'

'How can you ask, Your Majesty?' I replied. 'Naturally they have the greatest possible respect for you, as the king of all the gods.'

'You will have your little joke,' he said. 'But I'm quite aware of the present craze for novelty, even if you won't admit it. There was a time when I was regarded as a prophet and healer, when I was everything to them,

'And all the streets and all the haunts of men
  Were filled with Zeus.' [15]

In those days my temples at Dodona and Pisa were beautifully decorated and much admired, and I got so many sacrifices that I could hardly see anything for smoke. But since Apollo set up an oracle at Delphi, Asclepius opened a surgery at Pergamum, Bendis acquired a temple in Thrace, Anubis in Egypt, and Artemis at Ephesus, everyone's been rushing off to them, holding national festivals in their honour and offering them enormous sacrifices. As for me, I'm just a thing of the past, and people seem to think they're doing me proud if they let me have a sacrifice once in every five years, at Olympia. The result is that my altars are about as much practical use as Plato's *Laws* or the syllogisms of Chrysippus!'

Having discussed various matters of this kind, we arrived at the place where he had to sit and listen to human prayers. There was a row of holes in the floor, like miniature wells. Each of them was fitted with a lid, and had a golden chair standing near it. Zeus sat down beside the first one, raised the lid, and prepared to receive supplications. Up came all sorts of different prayers from all over the world – for I squatted down beside him and listened in too. This is what they were like:

'O Zeus, please make me a king.'

'O Zeus, please give me a good crop of onions and garlic.'

'O Gods, please make my father hurry up and die.'

'Please make my wife leave all her money to me.'

'Please don't let it get about that I've been plotting against my brother.'

'Please let me win my lawsuit.'

'Please let me win a prize at Olympia.'

One sailor prayed for a North wind, another for a South

one. The farmers wanted more rain, and the fullers wanted more sunshine.

Zeus listened to them all, and having carefully considered each request, he didn't undertake to grant the lot,

'But now he nodded and now shook his head.' [16]

He allowed the good prayers to come right up through the hole, and filed them on his right-hand side, but the bad ones he returned unanswered by blowing them down again before they got anywhere near heaven.

In one case I could see that even he was rather at a loss. Two men were praying for diametrically opposite things, and offering precisely the same terms in the way of sacrifices. He didn't know which prayer to grant, and was so open-minded, he might have been a member of the Academy. In the end he had to take a Sceptical line and like Pyrrho suspended judgement.

When he dealt with the prayers, he moved on to the next chair, applied his ear to the second hole, and gave his attention to the swearers of oaths. Having dealt with them too, and wiped out Hermodorus the Epicurean for perjuring himself, he moved on again to keep in touch with current omens, signs, and portents. His next port of call was the sacrifice-intake, through which smoke came up to inform him of each sacrificer's identity. Finally he turned away, and started rapping out orders to the winds and the weather:

'Today I want some rain in Scythia, some lightning in Libya, and some snow in Greece. I want you, North Wind, to go and blow in Lydia. South Wind – you can have the day off. West Wind is to stir up the waves in the Adriatic, and I'd like about twelve thousand gallons of hail evenly dispersed over Cappadocia.'

He'd now completed most of his business for the day, so we went into the dining-room, as it was time for dinner.

Hermes directed me to a seat beside Pan, the Corybants, Attis, and Sabazius, who were aliens and rather doubtful characters, like me. I was given some bread by Demeter, some wine by Dionysus, some meat by Heracles, some myrtle-berries by Aphrodite, and some sardines by Poseidon. I also got a taste of ambrosia, and drank a little nectar on the side, for whenever Zeus wasn't looking, that splendid fellow Ganymede poured me out about half a pint of the stuff. The gods, of course, as Homer mentions somewhere[17] – presumably speaking from his own experience, as I do – never touch ordinary food or wine, but always have ambrosia served up to them and get tight exclusively on nectar. However, their favourite diet is the smoke that rises from sacrifices along with a smell of cooking, and the blood of slaughtered animals which is poured over their altars.

During the meal Apollo played the guitar, and Silenus danced the cancan, after which the Muses got up and recited Hesiod's *Theogony* and Pindar's First Olympian Ode. When one had had enough one just went to sleep on the table, for we were all quite adequately sozzled.

'So all night long the gods and men of war
Slept, but to me sweet sleep refused to come.'[18]

I lay awake trying to solve various problems, especially these two: why, after all that time, hadn't Apollo grown a beard? And how did it manage to get dark in heaven, when the Sun was invariably among those present? Finally I was just dropping off to sleep, when Zeus got up and called a general meeting. When everyone was assembled, he spoke as follows:

'The immediate reason for calling this meeting was the arrival of our friend here yesterday. But for some time I've been wanting to have a word with you about these philosophers and scientists, and especially in view of complaints made by the Moon, I've decided to take action without any further investigation.

'As we all know, that comparatively recent biological phenomenon known as the human race is lazy, quarrelsome, empty-headed, bad-tempered, rather greedy, rather stupid, with an inflated idea of itself, and a vast amount of arrogance. It is, to quote Homer,[19] 'a useless burden on the earth'. Well, these creatures have now split up into various schools of thought based on various tortuous arguments, and taken to calling themselves Stoics, Academics, Epicureans, Peripatetics, or even more ridiculous names. Their next step is to attach to themselves the grand word *virtue*, and go about with furrowed brows and flowing beards, concealing absolutely revolting characters beneath a veneer of respectability. They're exactly like actors in tragedy – take off the mask and the gold-embroidered costume, and all you have left is a funny little specimen of humanity that's been hired for that particular performance at a fee of seven drachmas.

'Although they're like that themselves, they despise everyone else and say all kinds of extraordinary things about the gods. They collect a lot of impressionable youngsters, and rant away to them on their favourite subject, virtue, claiming to know the answer to every conceivable problem. And of course, in front of their students, they're always praising such things as strong-mindedness and self-control. But when they're by themselves, you've no idea how much they eat, how often they copulate, or how willing they are to lick anyone's boots for the sake of a few coppers. Worst of all, they serve no useful purpose, public or private, but are utterly unproductive and redundant,

"Worthless alike in council and in war." [20]

But that doesn't stop them criticizing other people. On the contrary, they have a little collection of insults and sour remarks which they learn by heart and are constantly using against their neighbours. In fact the person they most admire is the one with the loudest voice and the most uninhibited power of abuse.

'But suppose you found one of them straining his lungs to shout accusations at other people, and asked him:

"Well, what exactly do *you* do? What contribution do you make, for heaven's sake, to the life of the community?"

'If he was honest, he'd have to reply:

'"I don't see any point in being a sailor, or a farmer, or a soldier, or following any other sort of trade. But I've made a great deal of noise in my time, I always keep myself scrupulously dirty, I never wash except in cold water, I go about without shoes in the winter, and spend my time like Momus, finding fault with everyone else. If a rich man orders an expensive dinner or keeps a mistress, I immediately make it my business and am most indignant about it. But if one of my own friends or acquaintances is ill in bed and needing care and attention, I'm quite unaware of it."

'Well, gods and goddesses, those are the sort of creatures that we're responsible for. Which reminds me that the ones who call themselves Epicureans are extremely rude about us, and are always pitching into us for taking no interest in human affairs, and never bothering to see what goes on. It's a point worth bearing in mind, for if this theory were to gain general acceptance, it would have a serious effect on your food supply. For who's going to offer you sacrifices, if he doesn't expect to get anything out of it? As for the complaints lodged by the Moon, you all heard them described in full by our visitor yesterday. So it's up to you to decided what course of action will be most beneficial to human beings and least dangerous to us.'

At this point the meeting got quite out of hand, for everyone started shouting:

'A clear case for a thunderbolt!'

'Total incineration!'

'Liquidate the philosophers!'

'Into the pit with them!'

'To hell with them, like the Giants!'

Zeus called the meeting to order, and then said:

'Resolution carried. All philosophical and scientific theories and theorists will be exploded. The only thing is, we can't carry out sentence immediately. As you know, there's another four months to go before the end of the vacation, and I've already sent round a circular announcing a general amnesty. Next year, however, the dread thunderbolt shall fall, and the guilty shall pay for their crimes!'

'He said, and nodded low his sable brows.' [21]

'As for Menippus,' he went on, 'my decision is as follows: his wings are to be confiscated, so that he doesn't come up here again, and Hermes is to take him down at once and replace him on the earth.'

With these words he dissolved the meeting, and Hermes picked me up by the right ear and deposited me yesterday evening in the suburbs of Athens. Well, that's the whole story, my dear fellow. That's all there is to tell you about heaven. So now I'll be off to the Stoa, to break the good news to the scientists and philosophers.

AN INTERVIEW WITH HESIOD

(Presumably recorded in the Elysian Fields)

LUCIAN: Well, Mr Hesiod, it's obvious from your works, which are very grand and inspired, that you've a real talent for poetry, and that you got it from the Muses when they made you Poet Laureate. I'm quite sure you did. But there's just one point that puzzles me. You say[1] the Muses gave you the divine gift of song, so that you could celebrate past events and prophesy future ones. Now, you've carried out the first of these assignments very thoroughly, in tracing the genealogy of the gods right back to Chaos, Earth, Sky, and Love. Then there are your biographies of famous women, and your manual of agriculture, which supplies useful information about the Pleiades, and the correct times for sowing, reaping, sailing, and so forth.

But you've never even begun to display your other qualification, though it's a far more valuable one, and far more the sort of thing you'd expect to get from a goddess – I mean your power of prophecy. You seem to have forgotten all about that part of it. Nowhere in your works do you attempt to emulate Calchas, or Telemus, or Polyidus, or Phineus. *They* weren't given any special powers by the Muses, but they prophesied just the same, and never hesitated to answer questions about the future.

So you've laid yourself open to one of three charges. Either – it's an unpleasant thing to say, but – either you were lying, when you said the Muses had promised you the gift of prophecy. Or else they kept their promise and gave it to you, but you've been too mean to use it, and kept it tucked away up your sleeve and refused to share it with anyone. Or else you've written lots of prophetic books and never published them, but are saving them up for some special occasion. For I hardly like to suggest that the Muses promised you those two things and then broke half of their promise – especially as prophecy is mentioned first in the actual text of your poem.

Well, sir, you're the best person to tell me the answer. The gods, we're told,[2] are the givers of all good things, and as you poets are their friends and disciples, it's only right that you should follow suit and give us all the benefit of your knowledge, and solve our problems for us.

HESIOD: The simplest answer I can give you, sir, is that none of my poetry is my own work. It's all composed by the Muses, and they're the only ones who can tell you why they've put in one thing and left out another. For the statements based on my personal knowledge – about sheep-farming, for instance, when to drive the animals out to pasture, when to milk them, and so on – I may reasonably be held responsible, but as for the rest, the Muses bestow their gifts on whom they please, and in whatever degree they think fit.

However, I'm quite prepared to defend myself on literary grounds as well. I don't think you should inquire too closely into a poet's work, or expect every syllable of it to be perfect. If he makes an occasional slip in the haste of composition, you mustn't judge it too harshly. You must remember that we often put things in for the sake of the scansion or the sound-effect, and the poem itself somehow manages to incorporate other things – they just seem to slide in. But you want to deprive us of our one great advantage, freedom of speech or poetic licence. You overlook all the beauties of a poem, and concentrate on finding hairs to split, and thorny problems to raise. All you really want is a handle against us. For you're not the only one to do it, nor am I the only sufferer. The same thing's happening to my colleague, Homer. Several critics have started tearing his works to pieces, by stressing equally minute and trivial details.

Still, if you want a straight answer to your question, my good man, you'd better read my *Works and Days*. You'll find that poem is full of prophetic passages, predicting the results of doing things in the right way and at the right time, and the penalties for leaving them undone. I mean bits like this:

'One basket will suffice to hold the grain,
And few will gaze in wonder at your harvest.' [3]

Similarly you'll find passages describing in advance the advantages to be gained by efficient methods of agriculture.

LUCIAN: Now, my dear sir, you're talking like a real country bumpkin! This certainly confirms your statement about being inspired by the Muses, for you're evidently quite incapable of defending your own poems. That isn't the sort of prophecy that we expected of you – or of the Muses either. In such matters any farmer's a better prophet than you. Any farmer can safely predict that, if there's plenty of rain, there'll be a good crop, but if there's a drought and the soil gets nothing to drink, the thirsty fields will inevitably generate hungry people – that you mustn't do your sowing in mid-summer, or the seed will be completely wasted – and that you mustn't reap when the ears are still green, or you'll find no grain inside them. Nor do we need a prophet to tell us that it's no use sowing seed unless you cover it up. You must have a farmhand coming along behind you with a spade and sprinkling soil on it – otherwise the birds will swoop down and gobble up all your hopes of harvest in advance. No one could go far wrong if he stuck to advice like that, but prophecy is surely something different. Its function is to predict events which are scientifically unpredictable – like telling Minos that his son will be suffocated in a jar of honey, or explaining to the Achaeans why Apollo is angry, or saying that Troy will fall in the tenth year of the war.[4]

That's the normal meaning of the term, but if you're going to use it in the sense you suggest, you can call *me* a prophet right away – for without any help from the Castalian Spring, the laurel of Apollo, or the tripod of Delphi, I hereby prophesy and prognosticate, that if you go round naked during a cold spell, especially if it's raining or hailing, you'll catch pneumonia. As an even more remarkable display of precognition, let me add that you'll probably run a high temperature. And I can prophesy various other things, too ludicrous to mention.

So you'd better abandon that line of defence, and I suppose I'll have to accept your original explanation, that you'd no idea what you were saying, and all your poetry was inspired by some divine agency – not a very reliable agency either, or it wouldn't have broken fifty per cent of its contract.

SOME AWKWARD QUESTIONS FOR ZEUS

Scene: The Terrestrial Communications room in heaven. It is prayer-time, so Zeus is sitting on a golden chair beside the hole in the floor marked PRAYERS. *He removes the lid, and applies his ear to the aperture. A cool, cynical voice is heard speaking at the other end.*

VOICE: Well, Zeus, I won't trouble you with the usual type of prayer. I won't ask you to make me a millionaire or a king. Such things can't be very easy for you to arrange – at any rate, you never seem to take much notice when people pray for them. But there's just one favour I'd like to ask – an extremely small one.

ZEUS [*graciously*]: And what is that? Your prayer shall be granted, especially if it's as moderate as you say.

VOICE: I'd just like you to answer a simple question.

ZEUS: Well, that sounds easy enough. Ask as many questions as you please.

VOICE: Look here then, Zeus – no doubt you've read Homer and Hesiod – well, is it true what they say[1] about Destiny and the Fates – that they determine the course of each man's life in advance, and there's no way out of it?

ZEUS: Perfectly true. Nothing is exempt from the Fates' control. Everything that happens is spun on their spindle, and turns out according to their original design. No alterations are allowed.

VOICE: Then when Homer himself says elsewhere,

'Lest you should die before your fated hour,' [2]

and that sort of thing, he's merely talking nonsense?

ZEUS: Certainly he is. There are no exceptions to the rule of the Fates, no kinks or flaws in their threads. You see, poets tell the truth when they're inspired by the Muses, but when they lose their inspiration and try to compose on their own, they're liable to make mistakes and contradict themselves. You can't really blame them for not getting their facts right when the divine afflatus has left them – after all, they're only human.

VOICE [*sounding unconvinced*]: Well, let's take it that that's the explanation. But tell me another thing – how many Fates are there? It's three, isn't it – Clotho, Lachesis, and Atropos?

ZEUS: Of course.

VOICE: And then there's a lot of talk about Destiny and Fortune. Who exactly are they, and how much power have they each got? The same as the Fates, or more? For people are always saying that Fortune and Destiny are the most powerful things in the world.

ZEUS [*indulgently*]: Little cynics mustn't expect to be told everything. But why do you ask?

VOICE: I'll explain that, Zeus, when you've answered another question – do the Fates control you too? Are you also suspended on one of their threads?

ZEUS: Obviously I must be.

[*A giggle is heard at the other end.*]

What's so funny about that?

VOICE: I was just thinking of that passage in Homer,[3] where you're making a speech in the House of Gods, and threatening to pull everything up on a golden chain. You say you'll let down this chain from heaven, and all the other gods can grab hold of it, if they like, and try to drag you down, but they won't be able to – whereas if you care to try, you can pull up the whole lot of them

'With sea and land and all that is therein.'

That line always used to give me a tremendous impression of your strength, and I got the shivers every time I read it.

But now you tell me that you yourself, chain, threats, and all, are hanging on a tiny thread! It seems to me that Clotho is really the one to boast, for she's got you dangling from her spindle like a fish on the end of a line.

ZEUS [*coldly*]: I don't quite see the point of all these questions.

VOICE: It's just this, Zeus – and for God's sake – I mean, for Fate's sake, don't take offence or be annoyed with me for speaking frankly. If that's how things are, if everything's controlled by the Fates and their decisions are quite unalterable, why do we make so many sacrifices to you? Why do we pray to you? I can't see what we hope to gain by it, if our prayers are incapable of influencing things one way or the other.

ZEUS: I know who's been putting all these clever ideas into your head. It's those blasted intellectuals[4] who say that we never do anything for human beings. They're always asking blasphemous question like that, and trying to stop people saying their prayers or making sacrifices, by telling them it's all a waste of time, because we never pay any attention to what goes on and haven't the slightest influence on human affairs. But they needn't think they'll get away with it!

VOICE: No, really, Zeus, cross my thread and hope to die, it's nothing to do with them. It just seemed to follow naturally from what we were saying that sacrifices must be quite superfluous. But if you like, I'll go briefly through the argument again. Don't be afraid to answer my questions, and mind you answer them carefully.

ZEUS: Very well – if you've really got time to waste on such nonsense.

VOICE: You say the Fates are responsible for everything that happens?

ZEUS: I do.

VOICE: And can you alter their arrangements or unspin their threads?

ZEUS: No, I can't.

VOICE: Well, do you want me to draw the logical conclusion, or is it clear enough without being stated?

ZEUS [*with dignity*]: It's perfectly clear, thank you. However, sacrifices aren't made for a utilitarian purpose, to buy favours from us, but as a mark of respect for a higher form of life.

VOICE: Right, that will do. You admit that sacrifices serve no useful purpose, and are merely offered out of the kindness of our hearts, to show respect for our superiors. But if one of those 'intellectuals' were here, he'd ask what's so superior about you anyway? On the face of it you're only our fellow-slaves, for you're just as much ordered about by the Fates as we are. And it isn't enough to say that you're immortal, as if that made your situation any better, for it actually makes it much worse. We, at least, get our freedom when we die, but your condition will be the same throughout all eternity, and you'll be slaves for ever, thread without end, Amen.

ZEUS: But it's great fun, this eternal life of ours. We have an extremely good time.

VOICE: Speak for yourself, Zeus. There are class distinctions in heaven just as there are down here, and plenty of social unrest. It's all very well for you – you're a king. You can always let down a rope if you want to, and pull up the whole earth and sea like a bucket out of a well. But what about Hephaestus? He's just a poor crippled blacksmith, a member of the working-classes. And Prometheus was once actually crucified. I need hardly mention your father, who's still doing time in Tartarus. I'm also told that you gods are liable to fall in love or get wounded, and occasionally have to work like slaves for human beings, as your brother did for Laomedon, and Apollo did for Admetus. That's not at all my idea of having a good time. The truth of the matter is, it seems to me, that some of you have all the luck and are very well off, while the rest are just the opposite – quite apart from the fact that you're always getting burgled by temple-thieves, and thus transformed at a moment's notice from plutocrats into paupers. In fact, several gold and silver divinities have actually had their precious persons melted down! No doubt it was fated to happen to them.

ZEUS [*reaching for a thunderbolt and poising it threateningly*]: Now look here, that's downright insulting. You're going to wish you hadn't said that.

VOICE: It's no use trying to scare me, Zeus. You know perfectly well you can't do anything to me without previous permission from Fate. Why you don't even punish all the people who rob your temples. As far as I can see, they generally get away with it. I suppose they're just fated not to be caught.

ZEUS: There, what did I say? You *are* one of those intellectuals who try to prove that there's no such thing as Providence!

VOICE: You've got quite a phobia about them, haven't you, Zeus? I wonder why. Everything I say you attribute to their influence. However, there is one thing I'd like to ask you – for what more reliable authority could I possibly consult? Just what, exactly, *is* this Providence of yours? Is it a sort of Fate, or something even higher up which gives the Fates their orders?

ZEUS: I've already told you, there are some things you're not meant to know. Anyway, you said at first that you'd only one question to ask me, so why do you keep pestering me with all these minor details? But I see what you're getting at. You're trying to prove that we don't have any effect on human life.

VOICE: *I'm* not trying to prove anything. It was you yourself who said a moment ago that the Fates were in complete control of everything. Or have you changed your mind now? Do you want to take it back and stand for the Government yourself – throw Destiny out of office?

ZEUS [*irritably*]: Of course not. But the point is, we are Fate's executives.

VOICE: Oh, now I understand. You're a sort of permanent Civil Service. But in that case it's the Fates that do the actual governing. You're merely tools of theirs.

ZEUS: What on earth do you mean?

VOICE: Well, take a carpenter's plane and drill. No doubt they're quite a help to him in his work, but you'd hardly call them carpenters themselves. Similarly, planes and drills can't actually make a boat – it takes a boat-builder to do that. In your case, Destiny seems to be the one that really does the job. You're just the planes and drills in Destiny's toolbox. So apparently what people ought to do is to sacrifice and pray to Destiny – instead of which they keep on presenting you with sacrifices and solemn processions. Come to that, though, there wouldn't be much point in worshipping Destiny either. For I don't suppose even the Fates can alter anything once it's been settled. I'm sure Atropos would never let anyone put her spindle into reverse and undo all Clotho's good work.

ZEUS: So now you don't want *anyone* to be treated with respect – not even the Fates! As far as I can make out, you're a complete anarchist! But surely we gods deserve some recognition, if only for supplying, through our oracles, advance information about the Fates' arrangements.

VOICE: The whole point is, Zeus, it's no use knowing something in advance if you can't do anything about it – unless you mean to suggest that if someone knows he's going to be killed by a steel spearhead, for instance, he can stay alive by locking himself up in his bedroom. But as a matter of fact he can't. Fate will lure him out on to the hunting-field, and station him well in range of that spearhead. Adrastus will throw his spear, miss the boar he's aiming at, and kill Croesus's young son instead, for the Fates will impel the weapon irresistibly towards him.[5]

Then there's that ridiculous oracle that was given to Laius:

> 'Sow not seed in female furrow:
> Do not flout the will of heaven.
> For a son of thee begotten
> Soon or late will surely kill thee.'[6]

To my mind the advice was quite superfluous, as things were bound to turn out like that anyway. Sure enough, the moment he heard the oracle he promptly started sowing, and his son duly killed him. So I don't see why you should expect to be paid for your advance information – quite apart from the fact that most of your oracles are deliberately obscure and ambiguous, failing, for instance, to specify whether by crossing the Halys Croesus will destroy Cyrus's kingdom or his own. For the oracle in question would bear either interpretation.

ZEUS: You must remember that Apollo was feeling very cross with Croesus for trying to catch him out by cooking that tortoise-and-lamb stew.

VOICE [*self-righteously*]: Gods oughtn't to lose their tempers. Though I dare say Croesus was fated to be taken in by the oracle. In other words, Destiny had already arranged that he shouldn't have accurate information about the future. So even your oracles are really produced by Destiny.

ZEUS [*with heavy sarcasm*]: That's right, take everything away from us! We serve no useful purpose, we have no influence on what goes on, we don't deserve any sacrifices, and we're nothing but a lot of planes and drills. Well, I must say you have every reason to despise me, considering that all this time I've had you covered with a thunderbolt, and yet I've let you go on being rude about us.

VOICE: Oh, have a shot at me by all means – that is, if I'm fated to be struck by a thunderbolt, in which case I shan't blame you for throwing it, any more than I'd blame the

thunderbolt itself for hurting me. I'll put all the blame on
Clotho for using you as an offensive weapon. Which reminds me of another thing I wanted to ask the pair of you,
you and Destiny, I mean. Perhaps you'll be kind enough to
answer for her as well. Why on earth do you let so many
people get away with sacrilege and burglary, perjury and
crimes of violence, and usually aim your thunderbolt at
something quite inoffensive like a tree, a stone, or a ship's
mast, or even at a perfectly innocent traveller?

[*Zeus tries to think up a suitable reply.*]

Why don't you say something, Zeus? Or aren't I 'meant'
to know the answer to that either?

ZEUS: No, you're not. You're altogether too inquisitive, and
I don't know what you mean by worrying me with all this
nonsense.

VOICE: Then I suppose I oughtn't to ask you this one either
– though I've always longed to know how you and Providence and Destiny would answer it – why should a good man
like Phocion, or Aristides before him, be so hard up and die
in abject poverty, whereas juvenile delinquents like Callias
and Alcibiades were simply rolling in money, and so were
lecherous types like Midias, and homosexuals like Charops
of Aegina, who starved his own mother to death? Then
again, why was Socrates executed, and Meletus allowed to
get away with it? Why was a pansy like Sardanapalus allowed to be a king and have all those decent Persians crucified, just because they disapproved of his goings-on – not to
mention all the current instances of criminals and profiteers
living in the lap of luxury, and excellent characters being
ruined and suffering every sort of misery from poverty and
disease?

ZEUS: But don't you realize what dreadful punishments the
wicked undergo in the next world, and what happiness
the righteous enjoy there?

VOICE: In Hades, you mean? Tityos, Tantalus and all that? Well, I shall doubtless know what truth there is in such stories, when I die. In the meanwhile, I'd rather spend whatever life I've got left in reasonable comfort, and have my liver torn to pieces by sixteen vultures when I'm dead, than suffer the torments of Tantalus in this world, and never get a drink until I reach the Islands of the Blest, or start lounging about with the Heroes in the Elysian Fields.

ZEUS: Why, don't you believe there really *is* any system of rewards and punishments – any legal inquiry into each person's behaviour during his lifetime?

VOICE: Well, I've been told that a Cretan called Minos deals with such things down there. Could you give me a few details about him? He's said to be a son of yours.

ZEUS: What do you want to know about him?

VOICE: Who exactly does he punish?

ZEUS: The wicked, of course. Murderers and temple-thieves, for instance.

VOICE: And who does he send off to live with the Heroes?

ZEUS [*unctuously*]: Good, pious people who have lived virtuous lives.

VOICE: And why does he do it, Zeus?

ZEUS: Because the former deserve to be punished and the latter to be rewarded.

VOICE: But suppose someone committed a crime involuntarily, would Minos consider it right to punish him?

ZEUS: Certainly not.

VOICE: Then presumably if someone did a good deed involuntarily, Minos wouldn't think fit to reward him either?

ZEUS: No, he wouldn't.

VOICE: In that case, Zeus, he has no business to reward or punish anyone at all.

ZEUS: Whyever not?

VOICE: Because we human beings don't do anything of our

own free will. We do everything under an irresistible compulsion – that is, if it's true what you admitted before, that Fate's responsible for everything, and if someone commits a murder, *she's* really the murderess, and if someone robs a temple, he's only carrying out her orders. So to be fair, Minos would have to punish Destiny instead of Sisyphus, and Fate instead of Tantalus. For neither of these men did anything wrong – they were merely obeying orders.

ZEUS: I really can't be bothered to answer any more of your questions. You're just an irresponsible intellectual. I refuse to listen to you. I'm going away.

[*He prepares to replace the lid*]

VOICE [*rather louder*]: Hold on! There's one more thing I want to ask you. Where do the Fates hang out? And how do they manage to keep track of even the smallest details, when they've so much to look after and only three of them to do it? It must be extremely hard work, and it doesn't sound to me a very happy fate to be a Fate, with all that business on one's hands. Apparently *they* weren't born under a lucky star either. I wouldn't be in their shoes for anything. I'd rather go on being as poor as I am, or even poorer if necessary, than sit slaving away at a spindle with so much depending on it, and have every single thing in the world to see to. But if these questions are too difficult for you, Zeus, I'll make do with what you've told me already. It's quite enough to give me a rough idea how Destiny and Providence work – and perhaps that's all I'm fated to know.

[*Zeus slams down the lid in a rage.*]

PHILOSOPHIES GOING CHEAP

Scene: A large auction-room with a platform at one end. The proprietors, Zeus and Hermes, and two of their employees are preparing for a sale.

ZEUS [*to one of the assistants*]: Here, you! Put out the chairs and get the place ready for the customers. [*Turning to the other.*] And you bring in the philosophers and line them up on the platform. Only do tidy them up a bit first, so that they look reasonably attractive. Try and give them as much sales-appeal as possible.

[*The assistants carry out his orders.*]

Hermes, would you act as auctioneer? Collect as many customers as you can, and ask them to step inside. Say we've got a wide selection of philosophical systems for sale, in fact all the brands available. If anyone can't pay cash, he can do it by instalments spread over the next twelve months – with suitable security, of course.

[*Hermes goes out into the street, and customers soon start streaming into the auction-room and sitting down on the chairs. Finally Hermes returns and closes the door.*]

HERMES [*quietly, to Zeus*]: Well, we've got a full house. We'd better not hang about and keep them waiting.

ZEUS: All right, let's start the sale.

HERMES: Who do you want put up first?

ZEUS: That long-haired type from Ionia. He's the most impressive to look at.

HERMES: Hey, you! Pythagoras! Come down and let the gentlemen take a look at you.

[*A lean, bearded man, badly in need of a hair-cut, steps down off the platform and starts parading slowly round the room.*]

ZEUS [*to Hermes*]: Go on, give them a little sales talk.

HERMES [*raising his voice*]: Now here's a first-rate philosophy, a really grand specimen! Any offers, gentlemen? Who wants to be superhuman? Who wants to hear the music of the spheres?

A CUSTOMER: He doesn't look too bad, but what's his speciality?

HERMES: Arithmetic, astronomy, tall stories, geometry, music, and confidence-tricks. You also see before you a top-notch fortune-teller.

CUSTOMER: May I ask him a few questions.

HERMES: By all means.

CUSTOMER: Where do you come from?

PYTHAGORAS: Samos.

CUSTOMER: And where were you educated?

PYTHAGORAS: In Egypt was I taught the wisdom of the East.

CUSTOMER: Well now, if I buy you, what'll you teach me?

PYTHAGORAS: Nothing. I will only bring things back from your unconscious.

CUSTOMER: How will you do that?

PYTHAGORAS: First, by purifying your psyche, and washing out your dirty mind.

CUSTOMER: All right, let's assume that it's no longer dirty. What's the next stage?

PYTHAGORAS: First, a long silence. You must not speak a word for five years.

CUSTOMER: My dear chap, you need a pupil who's a deaf mute! Personally I like talking, and I've no wish to turn myself into a statue. Still, what comes after the five-year period of silence?

PYTHAGORAS: You will be instructed in music and geometry.

CUSTOMER: It's a fine thing if I can't acquire a philosophy without taking music-lessons!

PYTHAGORAS: After that you must learn to count.

CUSTOMER: But I know how to count already.

PYTHAGORAS: Let me hear you count.

CUSTOMER: One, two, three, four –

PYTHAGORAS: What did I tell you? What you think is four, is actually ten[1] – an equilateral triangle,[2] and the oath by which we swear.[3]

CUSTOMER: By Four, then, I swear I've never heard anything so mysterious and holy in my life!

PYTHAGORAS: After that, my friend, you will learn the shapes and motions of earth, air, water, and fire.

CUSTOMER: But have fire, or air, or water *got* any shapes?

PYTHAGORAS: Clearly they have. For what does not exist in any shape or form is incapable of motion. Moreover you will learn that God is Arithmetic, Intelligence, Harmony.

CUSTOMER: That sounds marvellous.

PYTHAGORAS: Furthermore, in addition to what I have said, you will learn that you are not one person as you think, nor are you the same as you appear to be.

CUSTOMER: I'm not me, you mean? I'm not the person who's talking to you at this moment?

PYTHAGORAS: At this moment, yes, you are he. But once you had another body and another name.

CUSTOMER: Do you mean to say I'm going to live for ever, and keep changing bodies all the time? But never mind about that. What are your views on diet?

PYTHAGORAS: I am a vegetarian, except that I eat no Beans.

CUSTOMER: Whyever not? Do they turn you up or something?

PYTHAGORAS: No, but the Bean is holy, Its nature is truly wonderful. For first It is one hundred per cent reproductive. If you peel a Bean while It is still green, you will see that It closely resembles the male genital organs. If you boil It and expose It to the moon for precisely the right number of nights, It will turn to blood. What is more, Beans are used at Athens to register votes at elections.

CUSTOMER: That all sounds very fine and religious. But now

take off your clothes – I want to see what you're like stripped.

[*Pythagoras undresses.*]

Good Lord, he's got a golden thigh! He's not a human being at all – he's a god! I must certainly buy him. [*To Hermes.*] How much do you want for him?

HERMES: Ten minas.

CUSTOMER: I'll take him.

ZEUS [*to an assistant*]: Make a note of the buyer's name and address.

HERMES [*to Zeus*]: I think he's an Italian. Comes from Croton, or Tarentum, or somewhere in Magna Graecia. But he's not on his own. He represents a syndicate of three hundred members.

ZEUS: Well, they can have him. Bring down the next one.

HERMES: Which do you suggest? That filthy creature from Pontus?

ZEUS: Yes, he'll do.

HERMES: Hoy, you there! The half-naked one with the knapsack! Come and walk round the room.

[*Diogenes descends from the platform. He is dressed in a dirty old blanket, and carries a stick and a knapsack.*]

Now here's a good manly type, a noble type, a free type. What will you bid me?

A CUSTOMER: I say, what exactly do you mean by a free type? You're not selling a free man, are you?

HERMES: Certainly I am.

CUSTOMER: Aren't you afraid of being had up before the Areopagus for kidnapping?

HERMES: It's all right, he doesn't mind being sold. He thinks himself perfectly free whatever happens.

CUSTOMER: But what could one do with a dirty creature like that? Look what a wretched state he's in! Though I dare say one could use him for hedging and ditching, or carrying buckets of water.

HERMES: You could also employ him as a janitor. You'd find him a most reliable watch-dog. In fact he's called a Cynic, which is only another word for dog-like.

CUSTOMER: And where does he come from? What sort of life does he recommend?

HERMES: You'd better ask him that.

CUSTOMER: I hardly like to speak to him. He looks so sulky and bad-tempered that I'm afraid he might bark at me, or even bite me.

[*Diogenes shows signs of exasperation.*]

There you are, he's scowling at me and threatening me with his stick.

HERMES: Don't worry, he's perfectly tame.

CUSTOMER [*nervously*]: Well, first of all, my dear sir, where do you come from?

DIOGENES: Everywhere.

CUSTOMER: What do you mean?

DIOGENES [*irritably*]: Can't you see? I'm a citizen of the world.

CUSTOMER: And who's your favourite character?

DIOGENES: Heracles.

CUSTOMER: Then why aren't you wearing a lion-skin? You've got his club all right!

DIOGENES [*not amused*]: This old blanket's my lion-skin. Like Heracles I belong to the Anti-Pleasure Brigade. And I'm not a conscript either – I'm a volunteer. Cleaning things up – that's my line.

CUSTOMER: And a very good line too. But what exactly are you an expert at? What's your actual trade?

DIOGENES: I'm a Human Emancipator. I cure people of their feelings. In short, I aim to be the champion of truth and sincerity.

CUSTOMER: Good for you, Champ! But suppose I buy you, what course of treatment will you prescribe?

DIOGENES: Well, the first stage will be to eliminate all luxuries, reduce you to poverty, and make you wear a blanket. After that I'll order plenty of hard labour, sleeping on the ground, and a diet of water and any old food that happens to come along. If you have any money, I'll recommend you to go and throw it into the sea, and on my advice you'll lose all interest in your wife, your children, and your country, and regard all that sort of thing as a lot of nonsense. You'll leave your family residence and go and live in a tomb or a lonely tower, or even in a tub. You'll have a knapsack full of lupine seeds and dog-eared books, and with that amount of property you'll claim to be as happy as a king. And if you get flogged or tortured, you won't consider it at all unpleasant.

CUSTOMER: You say it won't hurt if I'm flogged? What do you think I am? A tortoise or a lobster?

DIOGENES: Don't you remember that line of Euripides?

'It was my mouth and not my mind that swore.'[4]

Well, that must be your motto – in a slightly adapted form, of course.

CUSTOMER: How do you mean?

DIOGENES: You'll mind it all right, but you'll keep your mouth shut. Otherwise, the chief requirements are as follows. You must have immense assurance and be rude to everybody, irrespective of rank. That's the way to make people admire you, and think you very brave. Then you must cultivate a hideous accent and speak in a grating voice, just like a dog snarling. You must pull a long face, and adopt the sort of walk that goes with it, and generally make yourself as savage and beastly as possible. To hell with all modesty, decency, and sense of proportion. Be barefaced and completely unblushing. Pick out the most crowded place you can find to be a recluse in, and refuse to have anything to do with either friends or strangers, for that's the way to bring down the government. Cheerfully do things in public that no decent person would do even in private, and specialize in the more ridiculous forms of sexual intercourse. Finally, if you feel like it, commit suicide by eating a raw octopus or squid. There! That's the sort of happiness I can give you.

CUSTOMER: Get away from me! Your programme's so inhuman it's quite disgusting.

DIOGENES: Ah, but a very easy one to follow, my good man. Anyone can do it. You don't need to have any training, or go to any lectures, or any nonsense of that sort. It's a real short cut to fame. Even if you're a perfectly ordinary person, a cobbler, a fishmonger, a carpenter, or a bank clerk, there's nothing to stop you being a huge success, so long as you're shameless enough, and learn the technique of vulgar abuse.

CUSTOMER: Well, I certainly don't want you for anything like that – but you might come in useful as a deck-hand or a gardener – that is, if this gentleman's not asking more than a couple of obols.

HERMES: He's all yours. We're only too glad to get rid of him. He's been a frightful nuisance, always shouting and jeering at everyone.

ZEUS [to Hermes]: Now let's have that character from Cyrene, the one in evening dress with the flowers round his neck.

[Hermes beckons to Aristippus, who staggers down from the platform, smiling and hiccuping in a drunken stupor, and zigzags unsteadily round the room.]

HERMES: Now listen, everybody. Here's a very expensive model – only millionaires need apply. Here's something really pleasant, really enjoyable. Who wants to live in the lap of luxury? What am I offered for this dainty creature?

A CUSTOMER [to Aristippus]: Come over here, my man, and

tell me what you can do. If you're any use to me, I'll buy
you.

HERMES: Oh, please don't worry him with questions, sir.
He's far too drunk to answer. He'd never get his tongue
round the words.

CUSTOMER: Well, I don't see much sense in buying a degener-
ate alcoholic like that. Phew! How he stinks of scent! And
just look at the way he's lurching about! However, perhaps
you can tell me what he's good at, Hermes, and what he
does with himself.

HERMES: Well, briefly, he's an experienced cohabiter, excellent at parties and nights out with girls, just the thing for a
highly-sexed and dissolute employer. Apart from that he
knows all about cooking and pastry-making, and is generally an expert at self-indulgence. He was educated at Athens,
and got his first job with a dictator in Sicily who gave him
a splendid reference. The main features of his doctrine are
despising everything, making use of everything, and extracting pleasure from everything.

CUSTOMER: You'd better try someone else – someone with
plenty of money to throw around. A gay life like that isn't
quite in my line.

HERMES [to Zeus]: It looks as if we're going to have him left
on our hands.

ZEUS: Well, send him away and bring down the next one –
or rather the next two, the man from Abdera and the man
from Ephesus, for I want them sold as a pair.

HERMES [beckoning to them]: Come down, you two, and take
the floor.

[Democritus and Heraclitus descend from the platform.]

Now here we have two real paragons of wisdom.

A CUSTOMER: Good Lord, what a contrast! One of them
never stops laughing, and the other must be in mourning
for someone – he's streaming with tears! [To Democritus.]

Well, my good man, what's the joke? Why are you laughing?

DEMOCRITUS: Why do you think? Because all your activities are so ridiculous, of course – and so are you.

CUSTOMER: What's that? You dare to make fun of *us* and the things we do?

DEMOCRITUS: That's right. It's not really a very serious subject, you know. Why the universe itself is merely a lot of empty space with a few atoms rushing about in it.

CUSTOMER: That description would be better applied to the contents of your head.

[*Democritus roars with laughter.*]

Oh, stop laughing, can't you? I never heard of such impudence!

[*Democritus goes on laughing.*]

[*Turning to Heraclitus.*] And why are you crying, my poor fellow? I'm sure I'll get more sense out of you.

HERACLITUS: I am in mourning, sir, for human life. It seems to me such a wretched and lamentable thing – all its goods are so very perishable. I feel so sorry for you that I can't help crying. I can't say much for your present situation, but your future prospects are absolutely appalling – nothing but conflagrations and universal catastrophe. That's why I'm in mourning – because nothing has any stability – everything gets thrown into the melting-pot, where pleasure is indistinguishable from pain, knowledge from ignorance, great from small, up from down. Everything keeps churning round and changing places with everything else, for they're all the playthings of Eternity.

CUSTOMER: Eternity? What's that?

HERACLITUS: A child playing with its toys, and flinging them about the nursery.

CUSTOMER: And what are human beings?

HERACLITUS: Dying gods.

CUSTOMER: And gods?

HERACLITUS: Undying human beings.

CUSTOMER: My good man, you're talking in riddles. Are you deliberately trying to muddle me? Why, you're as bad as an oracle – I can't make head or tail of you.

HERACLITUS: I don't much care if you can't.

CUSTOMER: Then nobody in his senses is going to buy you.

HERACLITUS: Whether you buy me or not, I strongly advise you all to spend your whole lives being miserable.

CUSTOMER [to the man sitting next him]: He must be a manic depressive. I'm not having either of them.

HERMES [to Zeus]: Now they're going to be left on our hands too.

ZEUS: Try another one.

HERMES: What about that Athenian over there who's always shooting his mouth off?

ZEUS: All right.

HERMES [beckoning]: Here, you!

[Socrates comes down from the platform. He has a squashed nose, thick lips, pop-eyes, and a very large stomach.]

Now here's a good sensible one. Any offers for this saintly specimen?

A CUSTOMER [to Socrates]: Tell me, what's your special subject?

SOCRATES: Sexology and homosexuality.

CUSTOMER: Then you're no use to me. I want a private tutor for my son – and he happens to be rather good-looking.

SOCRATES [licking his lips]: Private tutor to a good-looking boy? You won't find anyone better qualified for the job than I am. You see, I'm quite Platonic – it's only their minds I'm interested in. Why, even when I go to bed with them, they'll tell you nothing very terrible happens.

CUSTOMER: That's a bit much to believe – a homosexual who

only messes about with people's minds, even when he has a chance to go further!

SOCRATES: I swear to Dog and Plane-tree it's perfectly true.

CUSTOMER: What a very curious oath!

SOCRATES: Why, do you doubt the divinity of Dog? Haven't you ever heard of the great god Anubis in Egypt, or Sirius up in the sky, or Cerberus down below?

CUSTOMER: Quite right. My mistake. But what sort of life do you lead?

SOCRATES: I live in a strange *Republic* of my own invention, and abide by my own *Laws*.

CUSTOMER: Could you tell me one of them?

SOCRATES: The most important one is the Nationalization of Women Act, which abolished private ownership, and ensured that the Means of Reproduction were shared by all the males in the community.

CUSTOMER: Do you mean to say there's no law against adultery?

SOCRATES: Certainly not. We've done away with all nonsense of that sort.

CUSTOMER: And what are the regulations about attractive boys?

SOCRATES: They're reserved as special rewards for gallantry, or any type of social distinction.

CUSTOMER: Talk about a generous government! But what are the chief features of your philosophy?

SOCRATES: The Ideas, the prototypes of all objects in the Phenomenal world. Every visible object, like the earth, the things on the earth, the sky, the sea, has an invisible prototype outside the universe.

CUSTOMER: But where, exactly?

SOCRATES: Nowhere. For if they were anywhere, they wouldn't really exist.

CUSTOMER: I don't quite see the idea of these prototypes.

SOCRATES: Of course you don't. Your mind's eye isn't strong

enough. But I can see all the Ideas. I see another invisible You and another invisible Me – in fact, I see everything double.

CUSTOMER: You must be very clever and have remarkably good eyesight. You're obviously well worth buying. [*Turning to Hermes.*] Let's see, how much are you asking for him?

HERMES: Two talents.

CUSTOMER: I'll take him. Put it down on my account.

HERMES: What name, please?

CUSTOMER: Dion of Syracuse.

HERMES: Well, I wish you luck with him. Now you, Epicurus.

[*Epicurus steps down.*]

Any offers for this one? He's an ex-pupil of two previous items on the catalogue – the laughing one and the drunk one – and he gets higher marks than either of them for impiety. In other respects he's quite a pleasant character, and something of a gourmet.

A CUSTOMER: What's his price?

HERMES: Two minas.

CUSTOMER [*handing over the money*]: There you are. By the way, what sort of food does he like?

HERMES: Oh, anything sweet, like honey – and he's particularly fond of figs.

CUSTOMER: That's easy enough. I'll send for a packet of dried ones from Caria.

ZEUS [*to Hermes*]: Now let's have that Stoic, the one with the close-cropped hair and the gloomy look on his face.

HERMES: Good idea. As far as I can see, he's the one that most of the customers are waiting for.

[*He beckons to Chrysippus, who steps down.*]

Now here we have virtue itself – absolute perfection. Who wants to have a monopoly of knowledge?

A CUSTOMER: How do you mean?

HERMES: I mean, here we have the only person in the world who's really wise, just, and brave – the only genuine specimen extant of a king, an orator, a millionaire, a legislator, etc., etc.

CUSTOMER: Then presumably he's also the only genuine cook, cobbler, carpenter, etc., etc.?

HERMES: Presumably.

CUSTOMER [to Chrysippus]: Come here, my good fellow, and tell a prospective customer what sort of person you are. First of all, don't you mind being sold as a slave?

CHRYSIPPUS: Certainly not. A thing like that is quite beyond my control, and so a matter of complete Indifference to me.

CUSTOMER: I don't understand what you mean?

CHRYSIPPUS: Why, don't you understand that some things are Preferable, and others Non-Preferable?

CUSTOMER: No, I don't understand that either.

CHRYSIPPUS: That's probably because you're not used to our terminology, and have no Imaginative Grasp – whereas a serious student who has mastered Logical Theory not only knows about that, but can also explain the important distinction between a Primary and a Secondary Accident.

CUSTOMER: Oh, be a good philosopher and tell me what Primary and Secondary Accidents are. There's something so attractive about the rhythm of those words.

CHRYSIPPUS: I'll be only too glad to. Suppose someone has a gammy leg and accidentally bangs that gammy leg against a stone and cuts it open. Well, the gamminess is a Primary Accident, and the cut is a Secondary Accident.

CUSTOMER: What a clever example to think up on the spur of the moment! But what else are you good at?

CHRYSIPPUS: I'm very good at tying people in knots when they try to talk to me. I can put a gag on them which shuts them up and stops them saying another word. The secret of my power is the famous Syllogism.

CUSTOMER: My goodness, that must be a pretty deadly weapon!

CHRYSIPPUS: I'll just show you. Have you a baby?

CUSTOMER [*mystified already*]: Why do you want to know?

CHRYSIPPUS: Suppose that child was crawling about beside a river, and a crocodile got hold of it. Suppose the crocodile then promised to give it back provided you stated correctly whether the crocodile had decided to give the baby back or not. What would you say the crocodile had decided to do?

CUSTOMER: That's a very difficult question. I really can't think what would be the best thing to say in the circumstances. But for God's sake do tell me the right answer and save my baby's life, quick, before the crocodile gobbles it up!

CHRYSIPPUS: Don't you worry. I can teach you some far more remarkable things than that.

CUSTOMER: Such as?

CHRYSIPPUS: Oh, logical fallacies like the Reaper, the Master, and above all the Electra, and the Man Under The Sheet.

CUSTOMER: Tell me about the last two.

CHRYSIPPUS: Well, the Electra in question is the famous daughter of Agamemnon, and the point is that she's simultaneously in a state of ignorance and knowledge about the same subject. For when Orestes turns up in disguise,[5] she knows that Orestes is her brother, but she doesn't know that this stranger is Orestes. The Man Under The Sheet's a very good one too. Tell me, do you know your own father?

CUSTOMER: Yes.

CHRYSIPPUS: Well, suppose I put someone in front of you with a sheet all over him, and asked if you recognized him, what would you say?

CUSTOMER: That I didn't, of course.

CHRYSIPPUS: But the man under the sheet is your father. So if you don't recognize him, you obviously don't know your own father.

CUSTOMER: Maybe not. But I'd know him all right if I took

off the sheet. Anyway, what's the ultimate object of your system? What will you do when you've reached the top of the Hill of Virtue?

CHRYSIPPUS: I shall then concentrate on things like health and wealth, which are naturally of the first importance. But before that I'll have a lot of hard work to do, straining my eyes to read books in very small writing, collecting masses of footnotes, and filling myself up with ungrammatical paradoxes. And of course there's no hope of ever becoming a Wise Man, unless one takes three doses of hellebore.

CUSTOMER: What a splendid programme! It all sounds so terribly virile. But I gather you're also a bit of a skinflint and lend money at exorbitant interest. Is that quite the kind of thing one expects from a man who's had his three doses and perfected his moral character?

CHRYSIPPUS: Certainly it is. In fact the Wise Man is the obvious person to go in for moneylending. It's his business to be logical and it's only logical to be businesslike, therefore the Good Man has a good head for business. He's a man of many interests, and his interests are never simple, like other people's, but invariably compound – for, as you know, some interests are Primary and others Secondary. The former give birth, as it were, to the latter. You can put it in the form of a syllogism, if you like. Primary Interest gives rise to Secondary Interest. But the Wise Man charges Primary Interest. Therefore he charges Secondary Interest. Q.E.D.

CUSTOMER: I suppose the same argument would apply to the fees that you charge your students? Clearly the Good Man is the only person who makes virtue pay.

CHRYSIPPUS: You're getting the idea. You see, I don't charge fees for my own benefit, but for the benefit of my students. It's more blessed to give than to receive, so I force myself to do the receiving, and leave all the giving to my students.

CUSTOMER: Yet it really ought to be the other way round, because you're the only genuine millionaire.

CHRYSIPPUS: Oh, very funny – but mind I don't shoot you down with an Indemonstrable Syllogism.

CUSTOMER: Why, what harm would that do me?

CHRYSIPPUS: It would induce frustration and aphasia, and leave you with a permanent kink in the brain. What's more, if I care to, I can instantaneously turn you into stone.

CUSTOMER: My dear chap, how could you? You're hardly my idea of Perseus!

CHRYSIPPUS: Like this. A stone is a solid body, isn't it?

CUSTOMER: Yes.

CHRYSIPPUS: And what about a living creature? Isn't that a solid body?

CUSTOMER: Yes, it is.

CHRYSIPPUS: And are you a living creature?

CUSTOMER: I certainly thought I was.

CHRYSIPPUS: Then you're a solid body, and therefore a stone.

CUSTOMER: Oh, please don't say that! For God's sake give me some reductive analysis and turn me back into a human being!

CHRYSIPPUS: No difficulty about that. Just answer my questions. Is every solid body a living creature?

CUSTOMER: No.

CHRYSIPPUS: What about a stone? Is that a living creature?

CUSTOMER: No.

CHRYSIPPUS: But you're a solid body?

CUSTOMER: Yes.

CHRYSIPPUS: And you're a solid body which is also a living creature?

CUSTOMER: Yes.

CHRYSIPPUS: Then if you're a living creature, you're not a stone.

CUSTOMER: Oh, thanks awfully. My legs were beginning to feel all cold and stiff, like Niobe's. Well, I'll buy you. [To Hermes.] How much do I pay for him?

HERMES: Twelve minas.

CUSTOMER [*handing it over*]: There you are.

HERMES: Are you the only purchaser?

CUSTOMER: Good Lord, no! [*Waving his hand round the room.*] All these gentlemen are buying him too.

HERMES: Well, there are certainly enough of them, and they seem to have good strong arms – I should think the Reaper will be very glad of their help.

ZEUS [*to Hermes*]: Don't waste time. Let's have that Peripatetic now.

[*Hermes beckons to the Peripatetic, who affects not to know that he is wanted until he is properly addressed.*]

HERMES: Yes, I mean you, the rich, handsome one.

[*The Peripatetic comes down from the platform.*]

Now, gentlemen, here's a chance to buy supreme intelligence and universal knowledge.

A CUSTOMER: What sort of character can you give him?

HERMES: Oh, he's a very moderate, reasonable, adaptable type, and what's more, there are two of him.

CUSTOMER: What can you mean?

HERMES: Apparently his exterior is quite different from what he's like inside. So if you buy him, you must remember to call one of him Exoteric and the other Esoteric.

CUSTOMER: And what exactly does he know?

HERMES: That happiness depends on three things, one's mind, one's body, and one's circumstances.

CUSTOMER: Well, that sounds fairly sensible. How much is he?

HERMES: Twenty minas.

CUSTOMER: That's rather expensive.

HERMES: Oh no, it isn't, my dear sir, for it seems he's got private means of his own – so you'd better hurry up and buy him. Besides, he can tell you right away the life-span of a gnat, the depth to which sunlight penetrates into the sea, and all about the psychology of oysters.

CUSTOMER: Good Lord, what an eye for detail he must have!

HERMES: That's nothing. You should hear him on the subject of reproduction, and the development of the embryo in the womb – he goes into far more microscopic detail there. He can also tell you that Man is a risible animal, whereas donkeys are non-risible and incapable of carpentry or navigation.

CUSTOMER: How very impressive! Now that's what I call really useful information. Yes, I must certainly have him, even if he does cost twenty minas.

[*He pays over the money to Hermes.*]

HERMES: Right.

ZEUS [*to Hermes*]: Who have we got left?

HERMES: Only that Sceptic. Come on, Pyrrho, get a move on. Nearly all the customers seem to have left, and there isn't likely to be much demand for you.

[*Pyrrho steps down off the platform, carrying a pair of scales.*]

Still – does anybody want to buy this one?

A CUSTOMER: Yes, I do. But tell me first of all [*turning to Pyrrho*] what do you know about?

PYRRHO: I don't know about anything.

CUSTOMER: Why, what do you mean?

PYRRHO: I doubt if anything exists at all.

CUSTOMER: Then none of us are actually here?

PYRRHO: That I can't say.

CUSTOMER: Can't you even say if you exist yourself?

PYRRHO: No, that's even more problematical.

CUSTOMER: What an extraordinary state of indecision! But what are those scales for?

PYRRHO: I use them for weighing hypotheses and balancing them against one another. I make quite sure that the arguments on both sides have precisely the same weight, and then – I simply don't know what to believe.

CUSTOMER: But is there anything you're really good at?

PYRRHO: I'm good at everything except travelling.

CUSTOMER: What's so difficult about that?

PYRRHO: Well, sir, it's just that I never seem to get anywhere.

CUSTOMER: I'm not surprised. You don't look as if you could go very fast. But what exactly are you aiming at?

PYRRHO: A state of ignorance, hearing and seeing nothing.

CUSTOMER: Then to all intents and purposes you're blind and deaf?

PYRRHO: Also incapable of judgement or perception, and generally no better than a worm.

CUSTOMER: In that case I must certainly buy you. [*To Hermes.*] What's he supposed to be worth?

HERMES: One mina.

CUSTOMER [*handing over the money*]: There you are. [*To Pyrrho.*] Well, my man, have I bought you?

PYRRHO: I'm not quite sure.

CUSTOMER: Nonsense, of course I've bought you. I've actually handed over the money.

PYRRHO: I prefer to suspend judgement on that point.

CUSTOMER: Well anyway, come with me. You've got to, now you're my slave.

PYRRHO: Who knows if that's true or not?

CUSTOMER: The auctioneer knows. That mina knows. Everybody in the room knows.

PYRRHO: Is there anybody in the room?

CUSTOMER: Well, as a crude method of convincing you that I'm your master, I'm going to put you to work in my treadmill.

PYRRHO: Oh, do suspend judgement on that point!

CUSTOMER: Too late! I've already passed sentence.

HERMES [*to Pyrrho*]: Here, you, stop arguing and go along with your master. [*To the remaining customers.*] And may I invite you, gentlemen, to come back tomorrow? We'll be selling off our stock of ordinary, unenlightened common sense – just the thing for the man in the street.

FISHING FOR PHONIES
OR
THE PHILOSOPHERS' DAY OUT

Scene: A street in Athens. Lucian has just come face to face with a crowd of angry philosophers, heavily equipped with beards, sticks, and knapsacks. They advance threateningly towards him, and he starts backing away.

SOCRATES [*to the other philosophers*]: Go on, sling a few stones at him, the damned swine – lumps of earth – bits of broken tile – anything you can find! Beat him up with your sticks! Mind he doesn't get away! Go on, Plato, have a shot at him! You too, Chrysippus! And you!

[*The philosophers set up a heavy barrage.*]

Now let's all advance on him in a body,

'A serried mass of knapsacks, sticks, and beards,'[1]

for he's our common enemy. There's not one of us he hasn't insulted. Come on, Diogenes! Now's the time, if ever, to use that stick of yours.

[*Lucian starts running, and the philosophers gallop off in pursuit.*]

After him, everyone! Let him have it for all the disgusting things he's been saying about us!

[*Epicurus and Aristippus get out of breath and drop behind.*]

What, tired already, you two? You've got no right to be.

'Be men, philosophers, and call to mind
Your ancient valour and heroic rage.'[2]

[*The field has now spread out. Lucian is still in the lead, but Aristotle is close behind him. No doubt he is in good training, being a Peripatetic.*]

Just one more spurt, Aristotle!

[*Aristotle puts on speed and grabs hold of Lucian.*]

Oh, well done, sir!

[*Socrates comes panting up, and grabs hold of Lucian too. The other philosophers crowd round.*]

Got you at last, you brute! Now you'll know what it means to insult people like us. But how are we going to deal with him? We'd better think up some ingenious method of execution – something that will satisfy everyone, for he deserves to be killed separately by each of us.

A PHILOSOPHER: I vote we crucify him.

ANOTHER: I second that, provided he's flogged first.

ANOTHER: Gouge out his eyes!

ANOTHER: Cut out his tongue – that's much more to the point!

SOCRATES: What do you say, Empedocles?

EMPEDOCLES: I suggest throwing him into a volcano. That'll teach him to be disrespectful to his superiors.

PLATO: Wouldn't it be best to adopt the Pentheus- or Orpheus-procedure, and

'Dash him in countless pieces on the rocks?'[3]

Then we could each have a bit of him as a souvenir?

LUCIAN [*horrified*]: Oh, no! Not that! For God's sake spare my life!

SOCRATES: It's all settled. We're not letting you go. You know what Homer says:

'Expect not mercy from a ravening beast.'[4]

LUCIAN: Yes, but I can quote Homer right back at you. You

must have some respect for Poetry! You can't reject a plea
that actually scans!

'Oh, spare my life (I'm quite a decent type),
Accept a worthy ransom, boundless brass
And gold, dear even to philosophers.'[5]

PLATO: Do you think we don't know our Homer well enough
to answer that one?

'Think not, offensive rascal, to escape,
Now that we have thee in our hands, although
Thou hast made reference to ready cash.'[6]

LUCIAN: Oh dear! Now Homer's let me down – the one
person I was relying on! I'll have to fall back on Euripides.
Perhaps he'll do the trick.

'Slay not! To slay a suppliant is not right.'[7]

PLATO: Ah, but doesn't Euripides also say somewhere,

''Tis right that wrongdoers should suffer wrong?'[7]

LUCIAN: Do you really mean to kill me, simply because of a
few quotations?

PLATO: We certainly do – for according to your friend
Euripides,

'Tongues that will not bridled be,
Hearts that reverence no decree
End in utter misery.'[8]

LUCIAN: Well, if you're absolutely determined to kill me,
and there's no escape, you might at least tell me who you
are, and what this frightful thing *is* that I'm supposed to have
done. What have you got against me? What capital charge
have I been arrested on?

PLATO: What have you done? Ask yourself that, you wicked
man! Ask those fine literary efforts of yours, in which
you've been so rude about philosophy and us – actually

putting philosophers up for auction and treating free thinkers as if they were slaves! It made us all so angry that we applied to Pluto for twenty-four hours' leave and came up here to deal with you. As for who we are [*making appropriate gestures*], this is Chrysippus, this is Epicurus, I'm Plato, and that's Aristotle. The one who never opens his mouth is Pythagoras. And here we have Diogenes – and all the other philosophers that you've been making fun of in your books.

LUCIAN: Well, thank goodness for that! You aren't going to kill me after all – not when you've heard how I actually feel about you. So you can chuck those stones away – unless you'd like to keep them for the real criminals.

PLATO: Nonsense! We're going to kill you here and now, so get ready

'To wear, for punishment, a coat of stone.'[9]

LUCIAN: But, my dear sirs, you don't understand. If you kill me, you'll be killing the one person in the world that you ought to approve of – a devoted disciple who has been, to put it bluntly, your chief literary executor. You can't do this to me, after all the hard work I've put in on you. You don't want to be like *modern* philosophers, do you – bad-tempered and ungrateful towards your benefactors?

PLATO: Well, of all the nerve! So we're actually supposed to be grateful for the rude things you've said about us! Who do you think we are? A lot of slaves? You must do, or you'd hardly pretend you were conferring a kindness on us by holding us up to ridicule!

LUCIAN: But when or where have I ever been rude about you? I've always been a great admirer of philosophy. I've spent my whole life singing your praises and studying your surviving works. Why, all my ideas come from you. I'm merely a sort of bee – I just flit from flower to flower, picking out all the best ones, and then publish my findings.

People are very polite about it, but they know perfectly well who each flower belongs to, and exactly where I got it. They pretend to admire *me* for making such pretty bouquets, but what they really admire is the garden of your works, for growing so many flowers of different shapes and colours, just waiting to be picked by anyone who knows how to do it, and how to arrange them so that the colours don't clash. Now would anyone, after getting so much out of you, turn round and start insulting his own benefactors? Why, it would be like Thamyris challenging the Muses to a singing-competition, or Eurytus trying to beat Apollo at archery!

PLATO: That, my friend, is a rather unfortunate argument, for it goes completely against you, and shows you up in an even worse light. It shows that you're ungrateful as well as wicked, if we provided you with all your shafts of wit and you then aimed them straight back at us. So that's the reward we get for giving you the run of our garden, and letting you pick anything you liked and go off with whole armfuls of flowers! Such ingratitude is a capital offence in itself.

LUCIAN: There you go again – flying into a rage and refusing to listen to reason. I must say, I never expected to see Plato, or Chrysippus, or Aristotle, or any of the rest of you losing your tempers – I thought you were far above that sort of thing. But whatever you do, gentlemen, don't condemn me without a fair trial. You always took the line that nothing should be settled by force, but all differences should be equitably resolved, by giving both sides a hearing. So please choose a suitable judge, act as prosecutors yourselves, either collectively or through some single representative, and I will reply to the charges. If the judge finds me guilty, I shall naturally pay the penalty. But if, when I've given my account of the matter, the verdict is Not Guilty, I hope I shall leave the court without a stain on my character, and you will transfer your resentment to those who have misled you and prejudiced you against me.

PLATO: That would be asking for trouble. You'd just fool the jury and get away with it, for I'm told you're an expert barrister and can twist facts any way you like. Besides, what judge would you suggest? Unless you plan to bribe him, which is the usual practice with you people, what judge could be so unjust as to give a verdict in your favour?

LUCIAN: You needn't worry about that. I don't want any shady character on the bench, who'd be willing to sell his verdict. On the contrary, I suggest that the case should be tried by Philosophy herself, in collaboration with you gentlemen. There now!

PLATO: And who, may I ask, would be Prosecutor, if we were on the bench?

LUCIAN: You could be judges and prosecutors at the same time. Even then, I'd have no fears of the result. I feel that right is so overwhelmingly on my side, and there are so many things I can say in my own defence.

PLATO: Well, what about it, Pythagoras – Socrates? The fellow's proposal is not wholly unreasonable.

[*Pythagoras preserves a holy silence.*]

SOCRATES: There's really no alternative. We must obviously go to Court, co-opt Philosophy on to the bench, and hear what he has to say for himself. It's not our policy to refuse a fair hearing. That would be terribly unenlightened. It would look as if we'd lost our tempers and believed that Might was Right. We'd be laying ourselves wide open to hostile criticism, if we stoned a man to death without a hearing, when we're always saying how fond we are of justice. What possible grounds for complaint should we have against my own accusers, Anytus and Meletus, or the judges who heard my case, if we executed this fellow without letting him say a word in his own defence.

PLATO: You're absolutely right, Socrates. Let's go and ask Philosophy to adjudicate, and abide by her verdict.

LUCIAN: Congratulations, my learned friends! That's a far better plan – a far more constitutional procedure. But as I said, hang on to those stones – you'll be needing them later on.

Now, where are we likely to find Philosophy? I've no idea where she lives, though I've spent a lot of time wandering about, trying to locate her house, in the hope of having some intercourse with her. I was always meeting people in ragged cloaks and long flowing beards, who said they'd just been to see her. So thinking they must know where she lived, I asked them to tell me. But it turned out that they were even more in the dark than I was, and either refused to answer at all, for fear of betraying their ignorance, or else gave me a wrong address – and to this day I've never succeeded in finding the right one.

Relying on guesswork or information from official guides, I've knocked on any number of front doors, feeling firmly convinced each time that I'd found her at last – there were so many people going in and out, all looking very gloomy and thoughtful, and very soberly dressed. So I'd elbow my way in among them, and follow them into the house.

There I'd see a young lady who was very far from innocent, in spite of all her efforts to look plain and unadorned. It was obvious to me from the start that the apparent untidiness of her hair was by no means accidental, and the casual way she was dressed had been deliberately planned for effect. Such things were evidently part of her make-up, and neglect of appearances was just one more device for making herself attractive. I even detected traces of powder and lipstick. She talked just like a prostitute, enjoyed being paid compliments, and was only too glad to accept any presents that were offered. She made her wealthy admirers sit down close to her. As for the others, she never even glanced at them. Once or twice her dress slipped down a bit, and I caught sight of a great gold necklace as thick as a dog-collar. So I soon came away, feeling rather sorry for the poor souls who were letting her lead them by the nose, or rather by the beard, and were making love, like Ixion, to an imitation goddess.

PLATO: You're quite right. Her address is not generally known. But there's no need to go to her house. We can wait for her here, in the Ceramicos. She'll be coming back any moment now from the Academy, for her daily walk in the Stoa.

[*A group of ladies is seen approaching.*]

In fact, here she is now. Do you see that quiet-looking lady with the kind face, walking along deep in thought?

LUCIAN: I can see several ladies answering that description, all dressed alike – but there can't be more than one Philosophy.

PLATO: Very true. But you'll know which she is, as soon as she speaks.

PHILOSOPHY [*catching sight of them*]: Why, look who's here! Plato, Chrysippus, Aristotle, and all my leading exponents above ground again! What have you come back for? Didn't you like it down there? You look rather annoyed. And who's this man that you've arrested? What's he been doing? Robbing tombs, or committing murder or sacrilege?

PLATO: He certainly has, Philosophy, and the worst type of sacrilege too – he's actually blasphemed your sacred majesty, and insulted all of us who have handed down your teachings to posterity.

PHILOSOPHY: Is that all you're worrying about? A few rude remarks? You know the way Comedy talks about me at the Dionysia, but we're still the best of friends. I've never sued her for libel, or even complained to her about it. I just let her have her fun – it's all in the holiday-spirit. Besides, I know that ridicule never did anything any harm. On the contrary, if it's a good thing to start with, it's like gold – the more you hammer away at it, the cleaner it gets, the brighter it shines, and the more notice people take of it. But you seem to be very bad-tempered and irritable these days, I can't think why.

[*Lucian tries to say something, and Diogenes seizes him by the throat.*]

What are you throttling the man like that for?

PLATO [*refusing to be side-tracked*]: We're just up here for the day. We got special leave to come and see that he paid the penalty for his crimes. We'd been informed that he was spreading propaganda against us among the lower orders.

PHILOSOPHY: So you're going to execute him without a trial or a fair hearing? He's obviously got something he wants to say.

PLATO: No we've decided to refer the whole thing to you. We'd like you to give the final verdict, if you don't mind.

PHILOSOPHY [*to Lucian*]: What do you say to that?

[*Diogenes reluctantly releases his grip on Lucian's throat.*]

LUCIAN [*trying to get his breath back*]: I'm all for it – Your Majesty. You're the only one – who can discover the truth. In fact – I've worked very hard to get the case referred to you.

PLATO [*to Lucian*]: You damned fraud! So it's 'Your Majesty' now, is it? Only the other day you were holding Philosophy up to ridicule before a large audience, by selling off her various schools of thought at two obols each!

PHILOSOPHY: Are you quite sure his insults were aimed at Philosophy, not merely at the foul practices of impostors masquerading under our name?

LUCIAN: I can soon tell you that, if you'll only let me explain.

PHILOSOPHY: Then let's go off to the Areopagus, or better still the Acropolis – then we'll have a good view of everything that's going on in town. [*To the other ladies.*] Go and walk about in the Stoa, my dears. I'll join you there as soon as I've dealt with this case.

LUCIAN: Oh, before they go, Philosophy, would you mind introducing me to your friends? They look rather nice too.

PHILOSOPHY: Certainly. The one dressed like a man is Virtue, and that [*pointing*] is Wisdom, with Justice beside her. The one in front is Education, and that shadowy, transparent figure is Truth.

LUCIAN: Where is she? I can't see her.

PHILOSOPHY: Oh, surely you can. The one without any clothes on, who keeps avoiding your eye and trying to slip away.

LUCIAN: Yes, I can just see her now. But why don't you bring them all with you? Then we'll have a real Quorum. Besides, I want to call Truth as a witness.

PHILOSOPHY [*to her friends*]: All right, you come along too. It won't be much trouble – only one case to decide, and, anyway, we're all interested parties.

TRUTH: You others go. I don't need to hear the evidence – I've known all about it for ages.

PHILOSOPHY: Oh, but you'd be such a help to us on the Bench! You could keep us informed of all the relevant facts.

TRUTH: Well, can I bring these two maids of mine as well? [*She points to them.*] We're practically inseparable.

PHILOSOPHY: Of course. Bring anyone you like.

TRUTH [*to the maids*]: Come along then, Frankness and Candour, let's see if we can rescue this poor human lover of ours from the danger that so unjustly threatens him. [*To her footman.*] But you wait here, Conviction.

LUCIAN: Oh no, ma'am, do let him come too. We need him as much as anyone. You see, in this particular arena I shan't be fighting with ordinary wild beasts, but with dishonest human beings, who'll be very hard to convict, because they always find a way of wriggling out of things. So Conviction will be absolutely essential.

PHILOSOPHY: Yes, absolutely. And you'd better have Proof available as well.

TRUTH [*to her servants*]: Come along, then, the whole lot of you. [*With a smile.*] Apparently you're all 'absolutely essential' for this case.

ARISTOTLE: There you are, Philosophy! He's trying to win Truth over on to his side.

PHILOSOPHY: Why, are you afraid Truth might tell lies to help him?

PLATO: Not that exactly, but – he's so terribly clever, so good at flattering people, that he's liable to talk her round.

PHILOSOPHY: Don't you worry. Nothing's going to interfere with the course of justice – when Justice is here in person. So off we go to the Acropolis.

[*The whole party starts walking in that direction.*]

[*To Lucian.*] What's your name, by the way?

LUCIAN: Frank Truthson Prufrock.

PHILOSOPHY: Nationality?

LUCIAN: Syrian, Philosophy. I'm a poor foreigner from the banks of the Euphrates. But does it make any difference? I know several of my opponents were also born in foreign parts, but you'd never guess from their characters or their doctrines that they came from Soli, Cyprus, Babylon, or Stagira. And I can't believe that *you'd* think any less of a man for having a foreign accent, so long as his judgement was sound and reliable.

PHILOSOPHY: Quite right. My question was out of order. But what's your job? There's no harm in asking that.

LUCIAN: I'm an anti-cheatist, an anti-quackist, an anti-liarist, and an anti-inflated-egoist. I'm anti all revolting types like that – and there are plenty of them, as you know.

PHILOSOPHY [*smiling*]: Well, well! You're quite an antibody, aren't you?

LUCIAN: I certainly am. You can see why I've got myself so much disliked, and why I'm in such a dangerous situation. Not that I'm not an expert probody too. I'm a pro-truthist, a pro-beautician, a pro-sinceritist, and a pro-everything that's pro-worthy. But I don't find much scope for exercising my talents in that direction, whereas thousands of people are always queueing up for the anti-treatment. In fact I'm so out of practice as a probody, that I dare say I've lost the knack of it by now – but I'm a real expert at the other part of my profession.

PHILOSOPHY [*seriously*]: That's bad. They're opposite sides of a coin, as it were. So don't specialize in one at the expense of the other. They should merely be different aspects of the same fundamental attitude.

LUCIAN: Well, you know best, Philosophy. But I'm so constituted that I can't help hating bad types and liking good ones.

[*They have now reached the Acropolis, and stop in front of a temple, where a priestess is standing.*]

PHILOSOPHY: Right, here we are. Let's try the case here in the forecourt of Athena's-over-the-city. Perhaps the priestess will be kind enough to put out some chairs for us, while we say a short prayer to the goddess.

[*The priestess does as she is asked. The rest go down on their knees, and Lucian prays aloud.*]

LUCIAN: O Thou that watchest over the city, assist me in my campaign against impostors. Be mindful of all the oaths which Thou hearest them break every day, and of all the sins which Thou alone seest them commit, as Thou watchest over us. Now is the time to punish them. And if the voting seemeth to be going against me, do Thou use Thy casting vote, and get me off. Amen.

[*They all stand up again, and Philosophy and her colleagues sit down on the chairs provided.*]

PHILOSOPHY: Very well. The court is in session, and ready to hear the evidence. [*To the philosophers.*] Will you gentlemen choose the most suitable man among you to act as Prosecuting Counsel, and produce something coherent in the way of a charge – for you can't all speak at once. After that, Frank, will you make your speech for the Defence?

CHRYSIPPUS: Who could possibly do it better than you, Plato? You've got everything – a wonderful brain, a terribly good accent, a persuasive manner, any amount of charm, together with great shrewdness, an eye for detail, and a gift for special pleading, where necessary. So do act as our representative and say the right sort of thing for all of us. Try to remember the arguments you used against Gorgias, Polus, Hippias, and Prodicus, and roll them all into one – for this man's an even more slippery customer than they were. Sprinkle on a dash of your famous irony, keep asking him clever questions – and don't you think you might work in somewhere that bit about 'great Zeus, in his wingèd chariot on high'?[10] You could say that he'll be angry if they don't find the man Guilty.

PLATO: No, let's get one of our more violent friends to do it – Diogenes here, or Antisthenes, or Crates, or you yourself, Chrysippus. This is no time to worry about subtleties of style – what we want is someone who knows how to secure a conviction in a court of law. This Frank person is an experienced barrister, you know.

DIOGENES: All right, I'll take it on. I don't suppose I'll have to be very long-winded about it. Anyway, he's been ruder to me than anyone else. Two obols! That's what he knocked me down for the other day!

PLATO [*to Philosophy*]: Diogenes will state our case for us, Your Honour. [*To Diogenes.*] Now, don't forget, my dear chap, you're not bringing a private suit of your own – you must keep an eye on our common interests. So if there are any little disagreements between us, don't inquire into them now, or start saying which system is best. Just reserve your indignation for the outrageous insults that Philosophy herself has received from the prisoner. Ignore the questions on which we differ, and concentrate on what we all have in common. You're our sole champion, remember, and it's entirely up to you whether we're to preserve our splendid reputation, or be generally thought to be as he has described us.

DIOGENES: Don't worry, I won't leave anything out, and I'll speak for all of us. And even if Philosophy's touched by what he says – she's very soft-hearted – and considers letting him go, *I* won't fail you. I'll soon show him we don't carry sticks for nothing!

PHILOSOPHY [*overhearing*]: No, don't do that. Show us what you can do with words, not bits of wood. That's far more to the point. Hurry up, it's time for you to begin. The court is waiting for you.

LUCIAN: Let the other philosophers join you on the bench, Philosophy, and register their votes too. Diogenes can do all the prosecuting by himself.

PHILOSOPHY: Aren't you afraid they might vote against you?

LUCIAN: Not in the least – and I'd like to increase my majority.

PHILOSOPHY: That's a very fine gesture. [*To the philosophers.*] Sit down, then, gentlemen. Carry on, Diogenes.

DIOGENES: Well, I needn't say much about what we were like when we were alive, Philosophy. You know all that already. Everyone knows what great benefits Pythagoras here, Plato, Aristotle, Chrysippus, and the rest of them have conferred on the world – to say nothing of my own contribution.

Such being our characters, I shall now describe how we've

been treated by this damned scoundrel, Frank. He is, by his own account, an ex-barrister, who abandoned an honest career in the courts, and from then on devoted all his rhetorical skill to the one object of attacking us. He never stops abusing us, calling us frauds and impostors, and encouraging the masses to laugh at us and think nothing of us. In fact he's made us and you, Philosophy, thoroughly unpopular with the average man, by calling the serious truths that you've imparted to us a lot of silly nonsense, and expounding them only to make fun of them.

The result is that he gets clapped by his audiences, and we get abused. For most people are like that – they enjoy hearing destructive criticism, especially when the things being debunked are apparently very important, just as they doubtless enjoyed the comedies of Aristophanes and Eupolis in the old days, when Socrates was brought on to the stage as a figure of fun,[11] and made to go through all kinds of ridiculous adventures. But they at least never dared to attack more than one of us, and then only at the Dionysia, when such things are allowed. It was all part of the fun of the festival, and I dare say Dionysus quite enjoyed it, for he has a great sense of humour. But this chap, after long and careful thought, fills a great fat notebook with libellous remarks, collects a distinguished audience, and then proceeds at the top of his voice to insult Plato, Pythagoras, Aristotle, Chrysippus, me, and the rest of us – when there isn't even a festival going on, and none of us have done him any harm. For there might have been some excuse for it, if he'd been trying to get his own back – but he actually started it!

As if that weren't bad enough, he does it all under cover of your name, Philosophy, and has talked a friend of ours called Dialogue into joining him and delivering his diatribes against us. What's more, he's even persuaded one of our own number, Menippus, to take part in most of his performances. He's the only philosopher who's betrayed our common cause, and so isn't here to support the prosecution.

In view of all this, we demand that the prisoner shall pay the penalty. For how can he possibly justify making fun of such serious things, before so many witnesses? By the way, it would be a good idea if that audience of his could also witness his punishment. It might make them think twice before sneering at philosophy in future. For if we just keep quiet and swallow his insults, it won't be put down to tolerance, but to cowardice and stupidity – and quite right too, for his latest exploit is absolutely insufferable – bundling us into an auction-room as though we were slaves, putting us up for sale and selling us off, some, I'm told, for high prices, some for a mina, and me, damn his eyes, for two obols! And the audience roared with laughter.

That's why we're so angry and that's why we're here – to demand satisfaction for this unspeakable insult.

PHILOSOPHERS [*clapping*]: Oh, well done, Diogenes! You've said just what we all wanted you to say!

PHILOSOPHY: Silence in court! Now for the Defence. Come on, Frank, it's your turn to speak. You have the floor, so don't waste any time.

LUCIAN: The case for the Prosecution has not been adequately stated, Philosophy. For some reason or other, Diogenes has failed to mention some of the most shocking things I've done. But I've no wish to deny them, nor have I thought up any ingenious way of refuting the charges. On the contrary, what I want to do is to fill in the gaps in his accusations and in my own previous statements. I thus hope to show you who the people actually were that I put up for auction and insulted by calling cheats and impostors. All I ask of you is to decide whether I'm right about them or not. If my language seems unduly harsh, don't blame me. Blame the men whose behaviour I'm trying to expose. I think they deserve it more than I do.

As soon as I realized what a career at the bar involved,

lying, cheating, shouting, thrusting oneself forward, and various unpleasant things like that, I naturally turned my back on it and set off in search of you, Philosophy. Like a sailor returning to port after a stormy voyage, I asked for nothing better than to spend the rest of my life under your protection. Needless to say, one glance at your doctrines was enough to fill me with admiration both for you and for all these gentlemen who had defined the Good Life and held out a helping hand to those of us who were struggling towards it. I realized their advice was quite invaluable, so long as one followed it closely without backsliding, so long as one kept one's eyes fixed on the principles that you've laid down, and governed one's whole life by them – a thing that has rarely been done, even in your day, gentlemen.

However, I soon saw that most philosophers had no real love of philosophy, but only of the prestige that went with it. In mere externals, which were easy enough to copy, beards, clothes, deportment, and so on, they were exactly like good men. But their lives and actions completely contradicted their appearance, and went dead against your teaching. In fact they were a disgrace to their profession, and it made me very angry. It was like seeing a pansy acting the part of Achilles, or Theseus, or even Heracles, and instead of moving and speaking in a suitably heroic manner, actually waggling his hips below that awe-inspiring mask, and generally behaving in a way that even Helen or Polyxena would have found intolerably effeminate, and as for Heracles – I should think he'd have smashed him and his mask to pieces with one blow of his club, for making such a womanish creature of him!

Well, that's what they seemed to be doing to you, and I couldn't stand it. They were like a lot of silly apes dressed up as supermen – or like that donkey at Cumae who put on a lion-skin and pretended to be a lion, terrifying the ignorant natives with ear-splitting brays, until a passing traveller who'd had some experience of both donkeys and lions finally showed him up and gave him a good beating.

The really dreadful thing, it seemed to me, was this. Whenever one of them was caught doing something wicked, or improper, or indecent, everyone immediately put the blame on Philosophy and Chrysippus, Plato, or Pythagoras, according to the school that the man belonged to, and his bad behaviour encouraged them to attribute the same type of thing to you gentlemen, although you'd been dead for ages. You see, such cases didn't come on during your lifetime, so you were tried *in absentia*. And as it was perfectly clear that the man in question had been behaving in a most disgraceful manner, you were convicted along with him – just because you weren't there to defend yourselves.

When I realized the situation, it seemed to me so intolerable that I started trying to expose them, and to differentiate between them and you – and instead of being grateful, as you should be, you drag me into court! Suppose I'd caught an initiate betraying the secrets of the Mysteries, and indignantly denounced him, would you have regarded *me* as the criminal? It's not fair. If an actor gives a bad or undignified performance as Athene, or Zeus, or Poseidon, the festival-organizers normally have him thrashed – but I don't suppose the gods are angry with them for daring to punish a man who's been dressed up as a god. On the contrary, I should think they're only too pleased that he *is* thrashed! For though it doesn't matter much if a servant or a messenger is badly played, it's really abominable to give the audience an unworthy impression of Zeus or Heracles.

The ridiculous thing is that most of them know your published work backwards, but from the way they live, you'd think their only reason for studying you was to practise the reverse of what you preach. It's all very fine, what they say about despising money and fame, and thinking nothing worth having but virtue – never losing one's temper, and treating millionaires as equals or inferiors. But for teaching you to despise money they charge a high fee. They gaze in wonder at rich people, and grab all the money they can. They snarl like dogs, cringe like hares, fawn like apes, rut like stags, steal like cats, and quarrel like fighting-cocks. They make laughing-stocks of themselves by elbowing each other out of the way to get to a rich man's door, or going to big dinner-parties and crudely flattering their hosts, eating more than is good for them, grumbling, and preaching off-key sermons on morality in their cups, and finally passing out from a surfeit of neat alcohol. Naturally their unenlightened fellow-guests roar with laughter, and don't think much of philosophy, if that's the sort of scum it produces.

Even more disgraceful is the way they claim to be self-sufficient, and keep dinning it into your ears that 'Only the Wise Man is really rich' – and a few minutes later come and ask you for money and get very cross if you don't give them any. It's as if a man in royal robes, with a crown and diadem and all the usual kingly attributes, were to go round begging for charity from his subjects.

When they want to get something out of you, there's always a lot of talk about one's duty to the community, the unimportance of wealth and – 'What are silver and gold? No more than pebbles on a beach!' But the moment a friend in need comes and asks them for a small loan, immediately there's silence, complete inability to oblige, great philosophic calm, and a total reversal of principles. All those fine speeches about Friendship, Virtue, and Goodness have become literally 'wingéd words' and flown off into the blue. They were merely academic exercises.

A philosopher is always very friendly, so long as there isn't any money about. But the moment he catches sight of an obol, the armistice is over, it's war to the knife, everything he's written is rubbed out, and Virtue has fled. The same thing happens with dogs. If you throw them a bone, they all jump up and start biting one another, and barking at the one who grabs it first. There's a story that a certain king of Egypt once taught some monkeys to dance the sword-dance. Monkeys are very good mimics, and before long they were doing it splendidly, complete with masks and purple robes. The show was a great success, until a frivolous member of the audience who happened to have some nuts in his pocket threw them on to the stage. As soon as the monkeys saw them, they forgot about the dance and reverted to normal – that is, they became monkeys instead of ballet stars. They all started fighting for the nuts, smashing their masks, and tearing their costumes to pieces in the process. The performance ended in chaos, and the audience shrieked with laughter.

Well, that's how these philosophers behave, and that's why I was so rude about them. What's more, I mean to go on exposing them, and holding them up to ridicule. But as for you, or anyone like you – for there still are some people who really love Philosophy and abide by her laws – I hope I'd never be crazy enough to say anything disrespectful about you or them. How could I, anyway? *You* never behaved like that when you were alive. No, what I hate are these god-damned charlatans, and I think I'm quite right to do so. Let's have your opinion, Pythagoras – Plato – Chrysippus – Aristotle. Have you really anything in common with people like that? I should say about as much as Heracles has with a monkey! Can one really compare them with you, just because they wear beards, look very solemn, and call themselves philosophers? I shouldn't mind so much if their performance were even convincing – but as it is, they're no more like philosophers than vultures are like nightingales.

There! I've said what I had to say. Now, Truth, will you please confirm my statements?

PHILOSOPHY: Would you mind leaving us for a minute or two, Frank?

[*Lucian withdraws, and Philosophy consults with her colleagues on the bench.*]

Well, what shall we do? What did you think of his speech?

TRUTH: Personally, Philosophy, it made me want to sink into the ground. It was all so true. I recognized the people he described, and while he was listing the various things they did, I was associating each type of behaviour with a definite individual. Yes, I thought, So-and-so does that – and Such-and-such does *that*. Altogether, the picture he drew was not only vivid, but also accurate down to the smallest detail, psychological as well as physical.

MODESTY: I quite agree, Truth. It made me blush to hear it.

PHILOSOPHY [*to the philosophers*]: And what's your opinion?

PHILOSOPHERS [*in chorus*]: There's no question about it. We'll have to acquit him, and register him as a friend and benefactor. We're like those Trojans who asked a poet to recite to them, and found themselves listening to *The Fall of Troy*. Good luck to him, anyway! The ruder he is about those god-damned charlatans the better!

DIOGENES: I must say, Philosophy, I've quite come round to the man myself. I take back all my accusations, and in future I'll regard him as my friend. He's a splendid fellow.

[*At a sign from Philosophy, Lucian approaches.*]

PHILOSOPHY: Congratulations, Frank! We find you Not Guilty. You've been unanimously acquitted, and from now on you shall be one of us.

LUCIAN: Well, thank goodness for that! I've won the first round anyway. Or perhaps I ought to say it in verse – it might sound better.

'Hail, Victory! Be with me all my days,
And crown my temples with unfading bays!'[12]

VIRTUE: Right, now let's open the second bottle – I mean, let's summons those impostors, and make them answer for their crimes. Frank can do the prosecuting this time.

LUCIAN: That's a good idea, Virtue. Here, boy! Syllogism! Just poke your head over the edge and call up the philosophers, will you?

[*Syllogism runs to the edge of the rock, leans over precariously, and shouts down into the town.*]

SYLLOGISM: Calling all philosophers! Calling all philosophers! Come up to the Acropolis and stand your trial before Virtue, Philosophy, and Justice!

[*A few solitary figures start climbing up the hill.*]

LUCIAN: They got the message all right, but look how few are showing up. You see, they're afraid of Justice. Besides, most of them are far too busy buttering up millionaires. But if you want them all to come, I suggest that you draft the message like this, Syllogism –

PHILOSOPHY: No, do it yourself, Frank, just as you think best.

LUCIAN: All right, it won't be very difficult.

[*He goes to the edge and shouts.*]

Calling all who pretend to be philosophers! Calling all who pretend to be philosophers! All who think this description applies to them should report to the Acropolis for their unemployment benefit, which will be at the rate of two minas plus two seed-cakes per head. And anyone who can show a long beard will be eligible for a supplementary allowance of dried figs. No need to bring any modesty, fairness, or self-control. They're not essential, if you don't happen to have any. But every applicant must produce at least five syllogisms, for according to the regulations you can't be Wise without them.

'And in the midst two golden talents lie,
A prize for whatseover man excels
All others at the art of bickering.'[13]

[*Hundreds of bearded figures start converging on the Acropolis.*]

My goodness, look at them all pushing and shoving their way up here! It only needed those two minas to fetch them.

[*He strolls about, reconnoitring.*]

And there are crowds more coming up the other side of the hill – and another lot streaming past the temple of Asclepius – and an even larger party crossing over from the Areopagus – and some others hurrying past Talus's Tomb – and just look, they're actually putting ladders against the temple of Castor and Pollux and clambering up that way! Why, they're like a great swarm of insects buzzing towards us, or to adapt Homer,

'They're pouring in from this side and from that,
Unnumbered as the leaves and flowers of Spring.'[14]

[*The bearded figures reach the top of the hill.*]

There! That didn't take long, did it? The whole Acropolis is a mass of yelling figures, and there's nothing to be seen for miles but beards, sticks, knapsacks, syllogisms, brazen faces, mealy mouths, greedy guts, and close fists. The few that answered the first summons are completely lost in the crowd – they're all dressed so much alike, one can't tell them apart. That's the trouble, Philosophy. That's where we've got a legitimate grievance against you. Why don't you give your people some sort of identity-card? As it is, these impostors are sometimes more convincing than the genuine article.

PHILOSOPHY: We'll see to all that in a moment. But first let's entertain our guests.

[*The bearded figures start shouting even louder.*]

PLATONICS: Us first! Platonics first!

PYTHAGOREANS: No, Pythagoreans first! Pythagoras came before Plato!

STOICS: Nonsense! We're better than anyone!

PERIPATETICS: No, you're not. Peripatetics are far better at making money!

EPICUREANS: Give us our seed-cakes and figs right away! We don't mind waiting for the two minas, even if we don't get paid till the end!

ACADEMICIANS: Where are those two talents? Nobody can bicker like we can! We'll soon win the prize!

STOICS: Oh no, you won't! Not while *we're* about!

PHILOSOPHY [*with immense authority*]: Stop squabbling.

[*There is a dead silence.*]

And will you Cynics please stop pushing and banging one another with your sticks? Now I'll explain what you're really here for. My name is Philosophy, and this lady is Virtue, and that is Truth. We intend to discover which of you are genuine philosophers. Those who turn out to be living in accordance with our laws will have the happiness of being judged to be good men. The impostors, on the other hand, will meet the fate they deserve, for pretending to be better than they are.

[*The crowd disperses rapidly, except for a very few.*]

What's happening? Why are you running away? Good Lord, they're practically throwing themselves down the hill! The Acropolis is suddenly deserted – except for these few who aren't afraid to face investigation. [*Pointing.*] Will someone fetch me that knapsack? One of the Cynics was in too much of a hurry to take it with him.

[*Lucian picks it up and brings it over to her.*]

Let's see, what has he got inside it? Lupine-seeds, presumably, or books, or crusts of bread.

LUCIAN: Not a bit of it.

[*He takes out the contents one by one and drops them on the ground.*]

Here's some money – a bottle of scent – a carving-knife – a mirror – and some dice.

[*He throws the empty knapsack over the edge of the rock.*]

PHILOSOPHY: Congratulations, my fine friend! So that was your equipment for a life of asceticism, was it? That was what entitled you to abuse the rest of the world and tell other people how they ought to live?

LUCIAN: Yes, that's the sort of person you're up against. And you must arrange some method of making it generally known, so that people can tell at a glance which are the good ones, and which are the other kind. Can't you think of anything, Truth? After all, your interests are at stake. We want to make sure that you don't get beaten by Falsehood, and that Ignorance doesn't let bad men appear to be good ones in spite of you.

TRUTH: Well, if you all agree, I suggest we give the job to Frank. We know he's a sound type and completely on our side, and he obviously has a great admiration for you, Philosophy. So let's send him off with Conviction to investigate all the people who call themselves philosophers. When he finds someone who's really one of the family, he can give him an olive-wreath and arrange for him to have free meals at the Town Hall. But when he comes across one of these wretched creatures – and there seem to be plenty of them – who are merely play-acting, he can rip off their cloaks, give them a close shave with a pair of goat-shears, and brand either a fox or a monkey on their foreheads.

PHILOSOPHY: Yes, that will do splendidly, Truth. And you'd better have some way of testing them, Frank – something like the famous ordeal by sunlight that eagles are supposed to use. Only instead of making them stare at the sun, you might test their reactions by showing them a bit of money, or fame, or pleasure. If they take no notice of it and show no signs of being drawn towards it, you can give them an olive-wreath. But if they can't take their eyes off it, or actually make a grab at it, you can safely take them away to be branded – though not, of course, until you've trimmed their beards.

LUCIAN: Just as you say, Philosophy. The Fox and Monkey Brigade will soon be well up to strength, but you won't see many olive-wreaths about. If you like, though, I'll do some of my investigating up here.

PHILOSOPHY: What do you mean? They've all run away. How are you going to get them back?

LUCIAN: Oh, quite easily – if the priestess will lend me that hook and line for a moment.

[*He points to a votive offering hung up on the wall of the temple.*]

It was presented by a fisherman from the Piraeus, I seem to remember.

PRIESTESS [*taking it down and handing it to him*]: There you are. I'll get you the rod that goes with it. You might as well have the lot.

[*She takes the rod down too and gives it to him.*]

LUCIAN: And now could I have a few dried figs – quick as you can – and a gold coin?

[*The priestess goes and fetches them.*]

PRIESTESS [*handing them over*]: There you are.

[*Lucian hurries off towards a low wall on the edge of the rock, where there is a sheer drop.*]

PHILOSOPHY: What on earth is he going to do?

[*The priestess follows him, and calls back a running commentary.*]

PRIESTESS: He's baiting the hook with a dried fig – and the gold coin as well. Now he's sitting on top of the wall and casting into the town.

[*The rest of the party go over and join him.*]

PHILOSOPHY: What's the idea, Frank? Are you planning to fish up some of those stones down there?

LUCIAN: Sh! Wait until I get a bite. O dear Poseidon, please send me a good catch! Ah, there's something now. It looks like a huge shark – unless perhaps it's a goldfish.

CONVICTION [*leaning over the wall and peering down*]: No, it's a dogfish. It's coming towards the hook with its mouth wide open. It's smelt the money – it's getting closer – it's touched it – it's caught! Let's pull it up.

LUCIAN: Yes, give me a hand with the line, will you, Conviction? That's it. Up we come.

[*They haul up their catch and land it.*]

Now let's see what you are, my fine fishy friend. Oh, it's a Cynic. My word, look at those teeth! So, my beauty, we've caught you nosing round the rocks, looking for titbits. You thought nobody could see you, but now you're going to be hung up by the gills in full view of everyone. Let's take out the hook.

[*They do so.*]

Why, there's nothing on it! The fig and the money must be firmly imbedded in his stomach!

DIOGENES: Then he'd jolly well better sick them up again. We need bait for the others.

[*The Cynic obliges.*]

LUCIAN: That's the idea.

[*He replaces the bait on the hook.*]

Well, Diogenes, do you know who this fellow is? Is he anything to do with you?

DIOGENES: Certainly not.

LUCIAN: How much would you say he's worth? Two obols was my own estimate the other day.

DIOGENES: Far too high. He's no good to eat – he looks most unappetizing and is obviously very tough – in fact he's absolutely worthless. Chuck him back and cast again.

[*The Cynic is thrown over the wall, and Lucian casts again.*]

There's just one thing, though, Frank. Mind you don't put too much strain on that rod and break it.

LUCIAN: Don't you worry, Diogenes. They're as light as a feather.

DIOGENES: Well, they're feather-brained, all right. Anyway, carry on.

LUCIAN: Oh, look! What's that flat fish coming up to the hook with its mouth open? It looks as though it had been sliced in half[15] – it must be a plaice or something. It's swallowed the bait – it's caught. Pull it up.

[*They land it and remove the hook and bait.*]

DIOGENES: What on earth is it?

CONVICTION: A so-called Platonic.

PLATO [*shocked*]: And yet you were interested in money, you wretched creature?

LUCIAN: Well, Plato, what shall we do with him?

PLATO: Over the wall with him too.

[*The Platonic is disposed of.*]

DIOGENES: Cast again.

LUCIAN [*having done so*]: Ah, there's a real beauty coming along now. It's a long way down still, but as far as I can see, it's got a skin all the colours of the rainbow, with gold stripes across its back. Do you see it, Conviction? It looks like an Aristotelian. It's coming nearer – now it's swum away again. It's glancing cautiously round – it's coming back – it's opening its mouth – it's caught! Haul it up.

[*They land it, remove the hook and bait, and then look inquiringly at Aristotle.*]

ARISTOTLE: Don't ask me, Frank. I've no idea who he is.
LUCIAN: All right, over the wall he goes then.

[*They heave him over.*]

Oh, look now! I can see a whole shoal of fish all the same colour, with rough skins as prickly as a hedgehog's. We really need a net to catch all those – but we haven't got one. Oh well, I suppose we'll have to make do with a single specimen. No doubt one of the bolder ones will get himself hooked.
CONVICTION: Have a try, if you like. But I'd recommend using wire instead of line – otherwise they're liable to gnaw it through with their teeth, once they've swallowed the money.
LUCIAN: Too late, I'm afraid – I've already let it down. Oh please Poseidon, send me a catch quickly! Good Lord, look how they're fighting for the bait! Lots of them are nibbling at the fig, and the rest are clinging on to the money. That's right – one of the big ones has got the spike through him.

[*They pull him up and remove the hook.*]

Now let's see, what do *you* call yourself?

[*No reply.*]

What an idiot I am, expecting a dumb fish like you to talk! You'll have to answer for him, Conviction.
CONVICTION: He's a Stoic.
LUCIAN: I see. I suppose that's why he's so keen on stowing things away. But for the love of Athens, do tell me,

Chrysippus – are these people friends of yours, or shall we adopt the usual procedure?

CHRYSIPPUS: I consider that a most insulting question. How dare you suggest that people like that have anything to do with me!

LUCIAN: Well done, Chrysippus! That's the right attitude. Well, he'd better go over the wall and join the others. He's so prickly that one would probably cut one's throat if one tried to eat him.

[*The Stoic is thrown back.*]

PHILOSOPHY: That's enough fishing for today, Frank. You never know, one of them might pull the money off the hook and keep it. Then you'd have to pay the priestess back. So we'll go off for our walk, and it's time you gentlemen [*to the philosophers*] returned to your quarters. You don't want to overstay your leave. And you, Frank, can start going round with Conviction, handing out olive-wreaths or branding foreheads, as the case may be.

LUCIAN: I'll do just that, Philosophy. [*To the philosophers.*] Good-bye, my dear sirs. Come along, Conviction, let's get on with our job. But where had we better begin – the Academy, the Stoa, or the Lyceum?

CONVICTION: It really doesn't matter. All I know is, wherever we go, we'll have very little wreathing and a hell of a lot of branding to do!

THE PATHOLOGICAL LIAR

OR

THE UNBELIEVER

Scene: A street in Athens. A young man called Tychiades is on his way home from paying a social call, when he runs into his friend, Philocles. They walk along together.

TYCHIADES: Can you tell me something, Philocles? Why do some people have such a passion for lying? They actually seem to enjoy talking nonsense, and listen most attentively when anyone else is doing so.

PHILOCLES: Well, there are any number of possible reasons for lying, if one's out for what one can get.

TYCHIADES: Oh, but that's quite a different story. I didn't mean the ones who tell lies when there's something to be gained by it. That's quite forgivable, and may even be praiseworthy – for instance, when it's a case of deceiving the enemy, or a matter of life and death – the kind of thing Odysseus was always doing,

'To save his life and bring his comrades home.'[1]

No, the people I'm talking about, my dear chap, are the ones with a purely disinterested love of lies, who lie for the sheer pleasure of lying, even when they don't need to. And what I want to know is, why on earth do they do it?

PHILOCLES: But have you ever actually known any people like that?

TYCHIADES: Certainly I have – dozens of them.

PHILOCLES: Well, if they've really got such a distorted sense of values that they prefer lies to truth, I can only suppose they're mentally deficient.

TYCHIADES: No, it's not that. I could show you lots of highly intelligent people, with excellent judgement in other respects, who have somehow succumbed to this morbid passion for lying. In fact, it makes me very angry to see talented men like that so fond of deceiving themselves and everyone else. To quote some examples from rather before my time, you've doubtless heard of Herodotus and Ctesias of Cnidos, and earlier still there were famous poets like Homer, who, not content with deceiving their contemporaries, actually put their lies in writing and bequeathed them to posterity, enshrined in the most beautiful poetry. Personally I blush for them when they start describing the castration of Uranus, the torture of Prometheus, the rebellion of the Giants, and the melodramatic set-up in Hell – when they talk about Zeus transforming himself for erotic purposes into a bull or a swan, and women being turned into birds and bears – not to mention Pegasus, the Chimaera, the Gorgons, the Cyclops, or all the other fabulous creatures which no doubt are very fascinating to children who still believe in the Bogy-man.

Well, that sort of thing may be all right in poetry, but when whole towns and nations tell lies as a matter of policy, isn't it really getting a bit ridiculous? For instance, the Cretans calmly point out to tourists the Grave of Zeus, the Athenians claim that Erichthonius and the first human beings grew out of the soil like vegetables, and the Thebans have an even more undignified story about so-called Plant-men, who germinated from the teeth of a snake. And if anyone questions the truth of these absurd traditions, and after scientific investigation fails to understand how any sane person could possibly believe that Triptolemus drove through the air in a chariot drawn by winged dragons, or that Pan turned up from Arcadia to help the Athenians at the battle of Marathon, or that Orithyia was carried off by the North Wind, he's regarded as a blasphemous idiot for daring to disbelieve such obvious facts. Which only goes to show how powerful lies can be.

PHILOCLES: There's some excuse for the poets and the inventors of national myths, Tychiades. Poets have to include a certain amount of fiction in their works, because of its entertainment value and audience appeal. And people like the Thebans and the Athenians tell such stories from patriotic motives. Besides, if you abolished mythology throughout Greece, all the official guides would starve to death, for foreign tourists have no wish to hear the truth about anything, even when they're not paying for it. But to enjoy telling lies without any such justification is merely absurd.

TYCHIADES: How right you are! I've just been paying a call on Eucrates, and listening to some absolutely incredible yarns – in fact I came away before he'd finished. I really couldn't stand it. He was talking such fantastic nonsense that I felt I was going crazy, and simply had to get away.

PHILOCLES: But surely Eucrates is a fairly reliable type! I can hardly believe that a man with a beard like that – he must be at least sixty, and spends most of his time studying philosophy – would be willing even to hear lies told in his presence, let alone tell them himself.

TYCHIADES: My dear chap, you should have heard the things he said. He kept assuring us that it was all true, and actually took his oath on most of it. Once he even swore by his own children! In fact, as I watched him, I was forming various theories in my mind. One moment I thought he'd gone schizoid and developed a completely new personality. The next, I decided that all this time he'd been an utter fraud without my realizing – a funny little monkey dressed up as a lion. The stories he told us were so ridiculous.

PHILOCLES: Oh, do tell me what they were, Tychiades! I'd love to know what he had tucked away behind that great beard of his.

TYCHIADES: Well, I often go and see him when I've nothing

better to do, and today I also wanted a word with Leontichus – he's a friend of mine, you know, and his servant said
he'd gone off early this morning to visit Eucrates, who was
ill in bed. So for both these reasons, to contact Leontichus
and to ask after Eucrates – for it was the first I'd heard of his
illness – I turned up at his house. I didn't see Leontichus –
apparently he'd left a few minutes before – but several other
people were there, including Cleodemus the Peripatetic,
Dinomachus the Stoic, and Ion – you know him, don't you?
He prides himself on being the only man in the world who
really understands Plato and can interpret his works correctly. So you see the sort of people they were, all paragons
of wisdom and virtue, and what's more, they belonged to
different schools of thought. They looked extremely vener-
able, in fact almost frighteningly so. Another member of
the company was Dr Antigonus – I suppose he'd been
called in professionally, and Eucrates seemed to be feeling
better already. It was one of his chronic ailments, by the
way – an attack of gout.

As soon as he saw me, he beckoned me over to him, and
started talking in a feeble whisper, though he'd been arguing
at the top of his voice when I came in. So taking great care
not to touch his feet, I sat down beside him on the bed, and
made the usual excuses for not coming before – that I hadn't
known he was ill, but the moment I'd heard I'd come dashing
round to see him.

They'd been discussing his complaint before I arrived, and
they went on doing so, with everyone suggesting a different
form of treatment.

'Get someone to kill a field-mouse by that method,'
Cleodemus was saying. 'Then tell him to pick one of its
teeth off the ground with his left hand, and tie it on to the
skin of a freshly flayed lion. Wrap that round your legs, and
the pain will stop at once.'

'Not a lion-skin, surely?' objected Dinomachus. 'I was

always told it should be the skin of an unmated female deer. It certainly seems more reasonable, for deer can run very fast and all their strength is in their legs. Lions are very powerful, I admit, and you can do wonders with their fat, or their right fore-paws, or the straight hairs in their manes, provided you know the right spell to use in each case – but a lion-skin doesn't sound much good for curing a disease of the foot!'

'Yes, that's what I used to think myself,' replied Cleodemus. 'I thought it had to be a deer-skin, because deers are so nippy on their feet. But a Libyan expert recently explained to me that lions actually run much faster than deer. After all, as he said, a lion can always catch a deer if it wants to.'

Everyone agreed that the Libyan had made a good point.

'But do you really believe', I asked, 'that these things can be put right by spells or external applications, when the root of the trouble is internal?'

At this they burst out laughing. They obviously thought I must be a frightful fool not to understand plain facts which every sensible person took for granted. However, Dr Antigonus seemed to be rather pleased. No doubt he'd been trying for ages to cure Eucrates by scientific methods, telling him to keep off alcohol, become a vegetarian, and generally try to reduce his blood-pressure – but no one had paid any attention to him.

'My dear Tychiades, what an odd thing to say!' said Cleodemus with a pitying smile. 'So you find it quite incredible that this type of treatment should have any effect?'

'I certainly do,' I replied. 'In fact I'd be a drivelling idiot if I seriously believed that something purely external, quite unconnected with the internal cause of disease, plus a few magic words could possibly bring about a cure. You could tie sixteen whole field-mice on to the skin of the Nemean Lion himself, and it still wouldn't work! Why, I've often

seen actual lions limping with pain, in spite of having perfectly good lion-skins of their own!'

'You must have very little scientific curiosity,' said
Dinomachus, 'if you've never bothered to find out how
effective such treatments are. I suppose you also refuse to
accept the evidence for well-known phenomena like snake-
charming, the cure of inguinal hernia, and intermittent
fever, and various other things that any old woman can do.
For if these methods do in fact work, why shouldn't they
work now?'

'But that argument's not valid, Dinomachus,' I said.
'You're begging the whole question. For it's not at all clear
that the phenomena you mention *are* brought about by
magic. Until you can show me how it's physically possible
for a fever to be frightened, or a swelling to be scared away
from the groin by a holy name or a word in some foreign
language, the cases you quote are still only old wives' tales.'

'So you don't believe a holy name could ever cure a
disease?' asked Dinomachus. 'That sounds as if you're an
atheist.'

'Oh, don't say that, my dear sir,' I answered. 'There's
nothing to stop those stories from being a pack of lies, even
if the gods do exist. Personally, I have every respect for the
gods, and I know they often cure people who are ill and
restore them to perfect health – but only by means of drugs
and proper medical treatment. When Asclepius and his sons
were nursing the sick, they "laid on soothing drugs"[2]
remember – not lion-skins and field-mice!'

'Oh, never mind him,' said Ion. 'I want to tell you something really amazing that happened when I was about fourteen. My father got a message that an extremely tough,
hard-working servant of his called Midas, who looked after
the vines, had been bitten by an adder at about half past
eleven, with the result that he was completely laid out, and
his leg had already begun to mortify. Apparently he'd been

staking up the vines, when the creature came gliding up and bit him on the big toe. It then nipped back into its hole, leaving the poor man screaming with pain. Well, that was the message, and the next moment Midas himself was brought in by his fellow-servants on a stretcher. His skin was all black and swollen and dripping with sweat, and he was practically at his last gasp. My father was terribly upset, until one of his friends said to him:

'"Don't worry, I know a Babylonian astrologer who'll be able to cure him. I'll go and fetch him."

'To cut a long story short, the Babylonian came and put Midas right at once. He expelled the poison from his body, partly by pronouncing a certain spell, and partly by attaching to the patient's foot a piece of stone chipped off the tombstone of a recently deceased virgin. Well, you may not think there was very much in that – though Midas immediately picked up the stretcher and went straight back to work, which shows how effective that spell and that bit of tombstone must have been – but the other thing the Babylonian did was really sensational.

'Early next morning he went out on to the estate, and after reading seven mysterious words aloud from an ancient scroll, made three complete circuits of the area, purifying it with fire and sulphur, and thus got rid of all the reptiles on our land. Out they came in tremendous numbers, as though irresistibly drawn by the spell, snakes, asps, adders, vipers, lizards, frogs, and toads. But one old python stayed behind – I suppose he must have been bedridden, or else he was hard of hearing and so missed the summons. Realizing that they weren't all there, the magician appointed the youngest snake to act as a sort of ambassador, and sent him off to fetch the python, who eventually showed up. When they were all assembled, the Babylonian just breathed over them, and they instantly vanished in a sheet of flame.'

'Do tell me something, Ion,' I said. 'Did the young snake

who acted as ambassador give the python his arm to lean on, or had the old gentleman got a walking-stick?'

'You can laugh if you like,' said Cleodemus. 'I was once just as sceptical about such things as you are. I thought they were quite incredible. But when I saw that mysterious foreigner flying – he said he was a Hyperborean – I finally had to give in and admit that they were true. What else could I do, when I saw him floating through the air in broad daylight, walking on water, and calmly strolling through the middle of a fire?'

'You actually saw this Hyperborean flying and walking on water?' I asked.

'Certainly I did,' he replied. 'What's more, he was wearing thick brogues at the time. Hyperboreans generally do. I needn't mention all his minor exploits, like making people fall in love, calling up spirits, resuscitating rotting corpses, materializing Hecate, and dragging down the moon from the sky, but I'd just like to tell you what I saw him do at the house of a young man called Glaucias.

'This young man's father, Alexicles, had just died, leaving him all his property, and Glaucias had fallen in love with a girl called Chrysis, the daughter of Demaenetus. I'd been coaching him in science and philosophy, and if this love affair hadn't taken up so much of his time, he'd have mastered the whole Aristotelian system by now, for before he was eighteen he'd got right to the end of the *Physics*, and was half-way through the *Analytics*. Anyway, he was so desperately in love that he finally told me all about it. As his director of studies, I felt the least I could do was to put him in touch with my Hyperborean magician, whose terms were four minas cash down – he needed a deposit to cover the sacrificial expenses – and sixteen more, payable on delivery of the girl.

'He waited until the moon was in the first quarter – that's usually the best time to do these things – and then, at midnight, he dug a trench in the courtyard, and began by calling up the ghost of Glaucias's father, who'd died seven months before. The old man disapproved of the match and flew into a rage, but eventually gave his consent. The Hyperborean then summoned Hecate, who arrived with Cerberus on a leash, and drew down the Moon from the sky. She, by the way, was quite a variety show in herself, never looking the same for two minutes on end. First she appeared as a woman, then she turned into a very handsome cow, and then into a puppy.

'Finally the Hyperborean moulded a little Cupid out of clay, and said to it: "Go and fetch Chrysis." Off flew the clay figure, and a few seconds later Chrysis was knocking at the front door. The moment she came in, she flung her arms round Glaucias's neck, as if she was madly in love with him, and slept, with him until we heard the cocks start crowing. The Moon then flew back into the sky, Hecate dived into the ground, all the other apparitions vanished, and we packed Chrysis off home just as it was beginning to get light. If you'd seen all that, Tychiades, you'd soon stop disbelieving in magic!'

'You're quite right,' I said. 'If I'd seen it, I'd certainly believe it – but in the meanwhile, I'm sure you'll forgive me for not having such good eyesight as you. Besides, I know that girl Chrysis. She's a nymphomaniac, and extremely easy to get. In fact I don't see why you had to go to all that trouble with the Moon, the clay carrier-pigeon, and the Hyperborean magician, merely to fetch a girl who'd have gone to Hyperborea itself for twenty drachmas. For money has a magic that she simply can't resist, and in one respect her reactions are quite the opposite of a ghost's. According to people like you, ghosts run away if they hear the chink of metal, but if Chrysis hears the faintest jingle of coins, she goes rushing towards it. However, what really puzzles me is the behaviour of the magician. If he could make all the richest women in the world fall in love with him, and make vast sums of money out of them, why did he take on the job of giving Glaucias sex-appeal, for such chickenfeed as four minas?'

'But this is ridiculous!' said Ion. 'You can't refuse to believe everybody. What about those people who exorcize ghosts and cure victims of demonic possession? There's no need to quote individual instances, for everyone knows about that Syrian in Palestine who specializes in such cases. His patients are the sort who throw fits at the new moon, rolling their eyes and foaming at the mouth. Yet he always manages to cure them, and sends them home perfectly sane, charging a large fee for his services. When he finds them lying on the ground, the first question he asks is: "What are you doing in there?" The patient makes no reply but the devil explains, either in Greek or in some foreign language, who it is, where it comes from, and how it got into the man. Then the Syrian starts swearing at the devil and, if necessary, threatening it until it goes away. I've actually seen one coming out myself. It was all black and smoky.'

'I'm not in the least surprised to hear that you can see things like that, Ion,' I said. 'After all, you can see the point of Plato's Ideas, which is more than most of us can do.'

'But Ion can't be the only one who's had such an experience,' said Eucrates. 'There must be lots of people who have seen a ghost, for instance, at some hour of the day or night. I know I have, not once but thousands of times. It used to upset me at first, but now I've got so used to it that I take if for granted – expecially since that Arab gave me an iron ring made from a nail of the cross, and taught me a long spell to repeat on such occasions. But perhaps you'll refuse to believe me either, Tychiades?'

'How could I possibly doubt the word of a sensible person like you, Eucrates?' I asked. 'I'm sure you'll say exactly what you think in your own house, as you've every right to do.'

'Well, there was that statue, for instance,' said Eucrates. 'Everybody in the house, old and young, saw it every single night. So you needn't take my word for it – you can ask the whole household.'

'Which statue would that be?' I asked.

'Oh, didn't you notice it as you came into the courtyard?' said Eucrates. 'It's a very fine piece of work, by Demetrius.'

'You don't mean that man with the discus, do you?' I asked. 'The one who's bending forward as if he's just about to throw it, with his head turned back towards the throwing arm, one leg slightly bent, and his whole body preparing to straighten up as he lets fly?'

'No, not that one,' he said. 'That's the Discobolus, by Myron. And I don't mean the one beside it either, that lovely one of the boy putting a wreath on his head. That's by Polyclitus. And you can forget about the statues on your right as you come in, which include the group by Critias and Nesiotus called The Tyrannicides. But just beside the fountain you may have noticed a statue of a bald man with a large stomach, his cloak half slipping off, a few hairs in his beard being blown about by the wind, the veins on his forehead clearly visible – in fact extraordinarily lifelike altogether. Well, that's the one I mean. It's said to be a portrait of Pellichus, the Corinthian general.'

'Oh, good Lord, yes,' I said. 'It's just to the right of Cronus, with lots of ribbons and withered flowers hanging on it – and there's some gold leaf stuck on its chest.'

'I put it there myself,' said Eucrates, 'when I nearly died of pneumonia, and he cured me in two days.'

'Why, was our friend Pellichus a doctor as well?' I asked.

'He still is,' said Eucrates. 'And you'd better not make fun of him, or he'll soon be after you. You may laugh, but I know what that statue can do. If he can cure pneumonia, he can probably also give it to anyone he likes, don't you think?'

'Statue be merciful unto me a sinner!' I exclaimed, 'if

it's as powerful as all that! But what else has "the whole household" seen him doing?'

'Every night, as soon as it gets dark, he descends from his pedestal and goes the round of the house. People are always meeting him in corridors – he's usually humming quietly to himself, and never does anyone any harm. All you have to do is step aside, and he just walks past without giving the slightest trouble. Oh, and he also does a good deal of bathing. You can often hear him splashing about in the water all night long.'

'You're quite sure it's a statue of Pellichus?' I asked. 'It sounds more like Talus, the son of Minos. He was also made of bronze, you remember, and he was employed as a night-watchman too – only his beat was Crete. And are you sure the statue's by Demetrius? Apart from the fact that it's made of bronze, not wood, there's no reason why it shouldn't be by Daedalus. His statues didn't stay on their pedestals either.'

'You'd better be careful, Tychiades,' he said, 'or you'll be laughing on the other side of your face. I know what happened to the man who stole the obols that we offer Pellichus every full moon.'

'For such an act of sacrilege,' said Ion, 'the punishment must have been terrible indeed. But what exactly was it, Eucrates? I'd very much like to know, however sceptical Tychiades may be.'

'Well, there was this pile of obols beside his feet,' said Eucrates, 'and he also had various silver coins and pieces of silver foil stuck to his thigh with wax. They were either votive offerings or thankofferings from people that he'd cured of pneumonia. One night the whole lot was stolen by a wretched Libyan stableboy of mine. He waited until the statue had got down, and then just helped himself. But Pellichus discovered the theft the moment he came back, and this is how he detected and punished the criminal. He kept the poor devil walking round and round the courtyard all night, as if he was trapped in a maze and couldn't find the way out – until finally it grew light, and he was caught with the stolen money in his possession. He was soundly whipped on the spot, and came to a bad end shortly afterwards. He said he got a thrashing every single night – and certainly every morning there were new weals on his body. So go ahead and make fun of Pellichus, Tychiades! Call me a relic of the Minoan Age, and say I'm getting weak in the head, if you like!'

'My dear Eucrates,' I said, 'so long as bronze is bronze, and the figure remains the work of Demetrius, whose sitters were human beings, not gods, I refuse to be intimidated by a statue. Besides, I never thought much of Pellichus, even when he was alive.'

At this point Dr Antigonus chipped in.

'I have a statue like that too, Eucrates,' he said. 'Or rather a statuette, about eighteen inches high, of Hippocrates. Every night, as soon as the lights are out, he goes wandering round the house, knocking over bottles, mixing up drugs, and slamming doors – especially when we've forgotten to give him his annual sacrifice.'

'So even doctors expect regular sacrifices nowadays,' I said, 'and get cross if you don't produce them exactly on time. They ought to make do with a wreath and a little honey and water at their funerals, like anyone else.'

'Now let me describe an experience I had five years ago,' said Eucrates, 'in front of witnesses, too! It was about midday, during the vintage season. I'd left my farmhands busy picking grapes, and wandered off into the wood by myself. I had something on my mind, and wanted to think it over. As I strolled along beneath the roof of leaves, I heard some hounds giving tongue, and assumed that my son Mnason was out hunting as usual with his friends. But it was something very different. A few seconds later there was an earthquake. I heard a voice like thunder, and saw a dreadful woman coming towards me, who must have been nearly three hundred feet tall. In her left hand she held a flaming torch, in her right, a thirty-foot sword. Down below she had legs like serpents, and up above she was exactly like a Gorgon – in the way she looked at me, I mean, and her generally horrifying appearance. Instead of hair she had great ringlets of snakes, some wriggling round her neck and some falling down over her shoulders. You can see what it does to me even to speak of it,' he added, pointing to the hair on his forearm, which, sure enough, was standing on end.

Ion, Dinomachus, Cleodemus, and the rest gazed at him open-mouthed. Apparently they were still not old enough to know when they were having their legs pulled, but sat contemplating in awestruck silence that incredible colossus, that hundred yards of female, that gigantic terror of the nursery! So these, I thought, are the people we admire so much – the people who teach wisdom to the young! Why, apart from their beards and white hair they're indistinguishable from babies – except that no normal baby would be so absurdly gullible!

'Do tell me, Eucrates,' said Dinomachus, 'how big were the hell-hounds?'

'Slightly larger than Indian elephants,' he replied, 'pitch-black and shaggy, with filthy matted coats. Luckily I was wearing a magic ring that an Arab once gave me, so I twisted it round on my finger until the signet was inside. Hecate promptly stamped on the ground with her serpent-foot, and made a hole in it, almost the size of Tartarus. She then leapt into it and disappeared. I plucked up enough courage to peep over the edge, holding on to a convenient tree, in case I got dizzy and fell in. I found I had a splendid view of Hell, including the River of Fire, the Infernal Lake, Cerberus, and the souls of the dead, some of whom I could actually recognize. I distinctly saw my father, still wearing his shroud.'

'And what were the souls doing, Eucrates?' asked Ion.

'Oh, just lying about in groups on fields of asphodel, chatting away to their friends and relations, of course.'

'So much for the Epicureans!' said Ion. 'Now let's hear them try to refute our divine Plato's arguments for the immortality of the soul. But you didn't actually notice Plato or Socrates down there?'

'I saw Socrates all right,' he answered. 'Not very clearly, but I could tell it was him by his bald head and his huge stomach. As for Plato, I'll be quite honest with you – I couldn't really identify him. Anyway, just as I'd taken all this in, the hole started closing – but some servants who'd come to look for me, including Pyrrhias here, arrived on the spot before it had closed completely. Isn't that so, Pyrrhias?'

'Yes, indeed, sir,' said Pyrrhias. 'What's more, I heard a bark or two coming from the hole, and caught a glimpse of flame from that torch of hers.'

I was much amused to hear the witness throw in these two items for good measure.

'But lots of people have seen things like that,' said Cleodemus. 'I had a similar experience myself not long ago, when I was ill. Antigonus here was looking after me and trying to put me right. For a week on end I'd been running a high temperature – I felt as if I was on fire. I was all alone in the room. Everyone had gone out and left me, shutting the door behind them. Those were your orders, Antigonus – you wanted me to try and get some sleep. Just then, while I was still wide awake, a beautiful youth in a white robe appeared beside me. He told me to get up, and led me through a sort of underground passage into Hades, where I immediately recognized Tantalus, Tityus, and Sisyphus. There's no point in going into details, but eventually I arrived at a law court, where I saw not only Aeacus, Charon, the Fates, and the Furies, but also a kinglike person whom I assumed to be Pluto. He sat reading out the names of people who'd completed their allotted span of life, and were due to die. But when the young man produced me, Pluto was most annoyed.

'"This one's got plenty of time to go yet," he told him. "Take him away, and bring Demylus the blacksmith instead. He's considerably overdue."

'Of course I was delighted, and nipped back here to find that my temperature was down to normal. I told everyone that Demylus was going to die – for he was a neighbour of mine, who was also reported to be ill. And sure enough, a few minutes later we heard them mourning for him.'

'That's nothing,' said Antigonus. 'I know a man who came back to life three weeks after his funeral. I was his medical adviser, both before and after it happened.'

'If he was dead for three weeks,' I asked, 'why hadn't the body putrefied? And why didn't he die of starvation? Or was your patient called Epimenides,[3] by any chance?'

At this point in the conversation Eucrates's sons came back from school. One of them was almost grown up, and the other was about fifteen. They said 'How do you do?' to us, and took my place on the bed beside their father – I was fetched a chair instead. The sight of them apparently reminded Eucrates of something else.

'Now here's a story that really is true, Tychiades,' he said, 'as true as it is that I love these two lads here.' And he laid a hand on each of them as he spoke. 'You all know how fond I was of my late wife, their mother. It was obvious from the way I treated her, not only during her lifetime but also after her death – for I had all her favourite clothes and jewellery cremated with her. Well, a week after she died, I was lying on this bed here, trying to comfort myself by quietly reading Plato on the immortality of the soul, when in came Demaenete herself, and sat down beside me, just where Eucratides is sitting.' Here he pointed to his younger son, who gave a shudder, as any child would do in the circumstances. He'd turned very pale the moment his father began the story.

'I threw my arms round her,' Eucrates went on, 'and burst into tears. But instead of letting me cry, she started grumbling at me for not having burnt one of her gold slippers along with the rest of her things at the funeral. She said it had fallen down behind the chest-of-drawers. That's why we failed to find it, and only burnt the other one. While we were talking, a blasted little spaniel that was lying under the bed started barking, and she immediately disappeared. However, we found the missing slipper behind the chest-of-drawers, and it was duly cremated. Now I ask you, Tychiades, is it really right to disbelieve such obvious, everyday facts as these?'

'Certainly not,' I replied. 'Anyone who dares to question the truth of a story like that deserves to have his little bottom smacked with a gold slipper.'

We were now joined by Arignotus the Pythagorean, a gentleman of imposing appearance with very long hair. You must know him – he's got a tremendous reputation for wisdom. They call him the Holy Man. As soon as I saw him, I breathed a sigh of relief.

'Here comes a pair of scissors', I thought, 'to snip through their tissue of lies. He'll soon shut them up, if they start talking any more nonsense.'

In fact I regarded him as a *deus ex machina* specially organized by Fate.

Cleodemus gave him his seat, and having sat down, he began by asking after his host's health. Eucrates replied that he was feeling much better.

'Well then,' said Arignotus, 'what's the subject under discussion? From what I could hear as I came in, you're having quite an argument about something.'

'Oh, we're just trying to convince this obstinate character here', said Eucrates, pointing at me, 'that there are such things as ghosts, and that dead people do in fact wander about the earth and show themselves to anyone they like.'

Such was my reverence for Arignotus that I blushed and hung my head in shame.

'You're quite sure', he asked, 'that Tychiades isn't merely excluding those who die natural deaths? Perhaps he means that no one returns from the dead unless he's been hanged, or beheaded, or crucified, or something like that? If so, there may be a great deal in what he says.'

'On the contrary,' said Dinomachus. 'He denies that ghosts exist at all, or are ever seen by anybody.'

'What on earth do you mean?' asked Arignotus, giving me a very stern look. 'You don't believe in ghosts, when people are seeing them practically all the time?'

'My only excuse', I said, 'is that I'm an exceptional case – I've never seen one. Of course, if I had, I'd believe in them just as much as you do.'

'Well,' he said, 'if you ever go to Corinth, get someone to tell you where Eubatides lives. When you've found the house – it's just beside the Cranium – knock on the door and ask to see the place where Arignotus dug up an evil spirit, and so made it possible to live there.'

'Why, what exactly happened, Arignotus?' asked Eucrates.

'The house in question', he answered, 'had been empty for some time, on account of being haunted. Every prospective tenant had been promptly evicted by a terrifying ghost. So the place was practically dropping to pieces, the roof was falling in, and no one had the courage to set foot in it. As soon as I heard about it, I equipped myself with the necessary volumes – for I possess a good deal of Egyptian literature on the subject – and set off for the house late one night. When my host heard where I was going, he tried to dissuade me, in fact he almost refused to let me go, for he thought it meant certain death. However, I got him to lend me a lamp, and entered the house alone.

'I put the lamp down in the largest room I could find, seated myself on the floor, and quietly started reading. The ghost appeared, as a filthy, long-haired creature, black as night, and thinking he'd got an ordinary person to deal with, expected me to be frightened like the others. He tried several different methods of attack, and became in swift succession a dog, a bull, and a lion. But having provided myself in advance with a really horrifying spell, I recited it in a perfect Egyptian accent, until I'd driven him into a dark corner. I noted the point at which he disappeared into the ground, and then went to sleep for the rest of the night.

'Next morning, when everyone had given up hope, and expected to find me dead like all the others, to everybody's great surprise I strolled out of the front door, went straight up to Eubatides, and told him the good news that his house was now free from ghosts, and could move in as soon as he liked. I then took him and a crowd of astonished bystanders back into the house, showed them the place where the ghost disappeared into the ground, and told them to fetch some spades and start digging. They did so, and about six feet down they discovered a dead body – or rather, it was so rotted away that there was nothing left but a few bones, arranged in the shape of a human figure. We took him out and gave him a proper burial, and they've had no trouble with ghosts ever since.'

And this from a much respected, highly intelligent person like Arignotus! Of course, everyone present thought I must be crazy not to believe in ghosts after Arignotus had told a story like that, but I refused to be daunted by his reputation or his length of hair.

'I'm disappointed in you, Arignotus,' I said. 'You were our only hope as a champion of truth, and all we get is a lot of hot air. Well, you certainly have let us down with a bump!'

'Very well,' said Arignotus. 'If you won't listen to me, or Dinomachus, or Cleodemus here, or even Eucrates, may I ask what more reliable authority you can quote against us?'

'Certainly,' I said. 'That splendid character, Democritus

of Abdera. He was such a convinced materialist that he shut himself up in a tomb outside the town, and stayed there day and night, so that he could get on with his writing. One night some youngsters thought it would be fun to give him a fright. They made themselves up as corpses, with black shrouds and masks that were meant to look like skulls, and started dancing round him, stamping their feet, and jumping up and down. But he wasn't a bit afraid. He didn't even look up. He just went on writing, and said: "Oh, do stop playing about!" He was so absolutely certain that souls couldn't exist apart from bodies.'

'If he thought that,' said Eucrates, 'he must have been a very silly fellow. But now I'm going to tell you something that actually happened to me – I didn't just hear it from someone else. And perhaps it may serve to convince even you, Tychiades. In my youth, when I was living in Egypt – my father sent me there to finish my education – I thought it would be nice to sail up the Nile as far as Coptus, travel on from there to the statue of Memnon, and hear the strange sound that it makes at sunrise. Well, I heard it all right, but it wasn't just the meaningless noise that most people hear. On the contrary, Memnon actually opened his mouth and gave me a seven-line oracle in verse, which I could repeat to you word for word, if there were any point in doing so. On the voyage back, one of my fellow-passengers was a holy scribe from Memphis, an incredibly wise man who'd mastered all the mystic lore of Egypt. He was said to have lived for twenty-three years in an underground shrine, receiving instruction in magic from Isis.'

'Why that sounds like the man that taught me!' exclaimed Arignotus. 'Pancrates, his name was – a very holy man, clean-shaven, always wore linen, highly intelligent, spoke rather bad Greek, tallish, snub nose, thick lips, and rather thin legs.'

'Yes, Pancrates! That's exactly who it was,' said Eucrates. 'I'd never heard of him before, but when I saw the amazing things he did every time we landed, like riding about on crocodiles and going for swims with them – when I saw the great brutes crouching at his feet and wagging their tails, I realized that he must be a Holy Man. Very gradually, by various small acts of courtesy, I managed to make friends with him and he told me all his secrets. Finally he persuaded me to leave my own employees at Memphis, and go off with him. He said there wouldn't be any problem about servants. So off we went.

'Whenever we stopped at an inn, he used to take a broom, or a rolling-pin, or the bolt off the door, dress it up, and then, by saying a spell, make it walk about just like a human being. It went and fetched us hot water, did all the shopping and the cooking, and generally acted as a most efficient domestic servant. When there was nothing more for it to do, he'd say another spell, which turned it back into a broom, or a rolling-pin, as the case might be. Much as I wanted to, I could never get him to show me how he did it, for he was very jealous of this particular accomplishment, though he was quite prepared to tell me everything else.

'However, one day I hid in a dark corner while he was doing it, and overheard the spell – it was only three syllables long. Having told the rolling-pin what he wanted done, he went off into the town. So next day, when he again had business in town, I seized the rolling-pin, dressed it up, pronounced the three syllables, and told it to fetch some water. When it came back with a bucketful, I said: "That'll do. Don't fetch any more water, but turn back into a rolling-pin." This time it refused to obey me, but went on fetching bucket after bucket of water, until the whole house was flooded. I couldn't think what to do, for I was afraid Pancrates would be rather annoyed when he got back – as indeed he was. In despair, I seized an axe and chopped the rolling-pin in two – whereupon each half grabbed a bucket and went on fetching water, so now I had twice as much water coming in! At this point Pancrates turned up, and realizing what had happened, turned both halves back into wood again. He then abandoned me in disgust, and mysteriously disappeared.'

'So you still know how to turn a rolling-pin into a human being?' asked Dinomachus.

'I certainly do,' answered Eucrates. 'Or rather, I know half of it. For once I'd got it fetching water, I'd never be able to reverse the process, and before you knew where you were, the whole house would be awash.'

'Oh, do stop talking such nonsense, you silly old men!' I burst out. 'Or at least postpone such weird and frightening stories until later, if only for the sake of these two boys here. You don't want to fill them up with a lot of irrational fears. You really might show some consideration for the young, and not keep telling them things that will stick in their minds and worry them all their lives, making them nervous at the slightest sound and a prey to all sorts of ungodly superstitions!'

'I'm glad you used that word "ungodly",' said Eucrates. 'It reminds me of something I wanted to ask you. What about the oracles given by certain gods – either through the mouths of their prophets, or spoken from their inmost shrines, or recited in verse by virgins inspired with knowledge of the future? Presumably you don't believe in them either? I'd better not mention the fact that I possess a holy ring, engraved with a tiny Pythian Apollo, who frequently talks to me. If I did, you'd only think I was boasting. But I do want to tell you about my visit to the temple of Amphilochus at Mallus, where the demigod actually granted me a personal interview and gave me advice on my problems. And then I'd like to describe what I saw at Pergamum, and what I heard at Patara.

'The first I heard of this oracle at Mallus was on the voyage home from Egypt. I was told that it was famous for its accuracy. You just wrote your question on a piece of paper and handed it to the interpreter, and he gave you a plain answer. So I thought I might as well stop off at Mallus, and as an experiment consult the oracle about my future.'

I could see how it was going to end. He hadn't produced that pompous preamble about oracles for nothing. I didn't see much point in arguing with a roomful of opponents, so I abandoned him in mid-ocean, half-way between Egypt and Mallus. I knew they'd be only too glad to get rid of me, because I was always spoiling their best stories.

'Well, I'll be off,' I said. 'I must try and find Leontichus. There's something I want to tell him. Besides, the conversation's getting rather above my head. Apparently human beings are no longer good enough for you, and you mean to talk exclusively about gods.'

With these words I left them, and they doubtless took advantage of my absence to indulge in a real orgy of lies.

Well, Philocles, that's the sort of stuff I've been listening to, and my goodness – you know what it's like when you've drunk a lot of very new wine? Your stomach seems all blown up and you want to be sick. That's just about how I feel. I'd give anything for a wonder drug to make me forget what I've heard. I don't want it to become a permanent resident, and give me some sort of trauma. Why, I've started seeing things already – ghosts, miracles, Hecates wherever I look!

PHILOCLES: Same here, Tychiades. They say if you're bitten by a mad dog, you don't just go mad and catch hydrophobia yourself – you're liable to go round biting other people, and they catch hydrophobia too. That must be what's happened to us. Eucrates & Co. have infected you with various phobias, and you seem to have passed them on to me – for I feel absolutely sick of psychic phenomena!

TYCHIADES: Cheer up, old man. There's always the great antidote of truth and common sense. If we take a dose of that, none of their lies will do us any harm.

STORIES

ALEXANDER

OR

THE BOGUS ORACLE

My dear Celsus, I dare say you thought you were giving me quite an easy job, when you asked me to write and tell you about Alexander of Abonoteichos, listing all his various swindles. But if I did it properly, it would be like writing a biography of Alexander the Great – for this Alexander was equally great in his way. Still, if you're prepared to make allowances, and fill in the gaps for yourself, I'll have a shot at it. I won't attempt to clean out the whole of the Augean Stable, but at least I'll do enough muck-raking to give you some idea what an incredible amount of filth those three thousand cows managed to produce over a large number of years.

Mind you, I think we both ought to be ashamed of ourselves – you for wanting such disgusting behaviour committed to writing, and I for taking great pains to compile a biography of a man that no decent person would want to read about – someone who's only fit to be shown as a low turn at the circus, being torn to pieces by apes or foxes. We can, of course, reply to any such criticism by quoting the example of Arrian, the disciple of Epictetus, for there you have a distinguished Roman who devoted his whole life to culture, and yet thought fit to do something that may serve as an excuse for us – he wrote the life of a bandit called Tilloborus. But we're planning to immortalize a far more dangerous type of criminal, who operated in large towns, not merely in the woods or on the mountains, and instead of confining himself to Bithynia, Mount Ida, and the more deserted parts of Asia Minor, extended his activities over almost the whole of the Roman Empire.

First, I'll give you a brief sketch of the man himself, getting as good a likeness as I can, though portrait-painting isn't really in my line. To start with his body; he was 'divinely tall and most divinely fair', with a white skin and a not too bushy beard. Some of his hair was his own, and his *toupet* was such a perfect match that most people didn't realize he was wearing one. He had piercing eyes, with an almost inspired look about them, and a pleasant but powerful voice. Physically, in fact, he was above criticism.

As for his mental and moral qualities – heaven help anyone who gets involved with a man like that! Personally, I'd rather become a prisoner of war any day. He was extraordinarily shrewd, quick-witted, and intelligent. He would have made a very good scientist, for he had an inquiring mind, an excellent memory, and a great capacity for absorbing knowlege. But he put all his brilliant gifts to the worst possible use, and became a master-criminal, far in advance of such notorious characters as the Cercopes, Eurybatus, Phrynondas, Aristodemus, and Sostratus.

In a letter to his son-in-law, Rutilianus, he once made the modest boast that he was like Pythagoras. Well, with all respect to that great genius, if Pythagoras had ever come up against Alexander, he'd have seemed a mere child beside him. For goodness' sake don't think I'm being rude about Pythagoras, or suggesting any comparison between their actual behaviour. But if you collected all the most libellous stories that have ever been told about Pythagoras – which I don't believe for a moment – they'd represent only a tiny fraction of Alexander's worldly wisdom.

To sum up, picture to yourself a mixture of deceit, cunning, and general wickedness, reckless audacity and executive ability, combined with a plausible manner that always made him seem better than he was, and completely contradicted his real intentions. For the first time one met him, one got the impression that he was the most decent, honest fellow in the world, and what's more, the most straightforward and unaffected. On top of all this he was extremely enterprising, and never attempted anything on a small scale, but always went in for something really big.

In his youth, he was very attractive – or so I've been informed, and I'd have guessed as much from the traces of beauty that remained in later life. So he became a regular prostitute, and slept with anyone who was willing to pay him. Among his clients was a certain magician – the type of person who undertakes to make you successful in love, put a spell on your enemies, discover buried treasure, or get you left a fortune. Realizing the boy's talents – for Alexander was just as much in love with the old man's wickedness as the old man was with Alexander's beauty – he took him on as an apprentice, and finally made him his personal assistant. Ostensibly he practised as a doctor, and like the wife of the Egyptian Thon

Knew many healing drugs and many poisons,[1]

all which medical knowledge Alexander inherited. His learned lover came from Tyana, where he had studied under Apollonius, and become an expert in his particular brand of pretentious nonsense. So now you know how our hero was educated.

Just as Alexander was beginning to grow a beard, his master died and left him without any means of support – for he couldn't live on his looks any more. However, he now had more ambitious plans, so he teamed up with an even lower type, a ballet-dancer from Byzantium – I think he was called Cocconas – and the two of them went round cheating and fleecing 'fatheads' – a technical term used by magicians to denote people with money. While they were so engaged, they came across a Macedonian heiress who was past her prime but still liked to be thought attractive. They lived on her for some time, and when she went back to Macedonia, they went too. She came from a place called Pella, which had been very prosperous in the old days, when the Kings of Macedonia lived there, but now had only a tiny population.

There they saw some enormous snakes, which were so tame and domesticated that women used to keep them as pets, and children even took them to bed with them. They didn't mind being pinched or trodden on, and would actually take milk from the breast like babies. These creatures are very common in those parts – which is doubtless the origin of that story about Olympias, the mother of Alexander the Great. I suppose she must have been seen with a pet snake in her bed.

Anyway, they bought a magnificent specimen for a few coppers, and that, as Thucydides would say,[2] was how it all started. For those two unscrupulous adventurers put their heads together, and decided that human life is ruled by a pair of tyrants called Hope and Fear, and if you treat them right, you can make a lot of money out of them. They saw that the one thing people want, the one thing they must have, when they're oppressed by either Hope or Fear, is information about the future. That was why places like Delphi, Delos, Claros, and Branchidae had become so fabulously wealthy – because the tyrants I mentioned made people keep going there and paying exorbitant prices, in cattle or in gold, for any sort of prophecy. Having turned these facts over in their minds, they finally cooked up a plan to establish an oracle of their own. If all went well, they expected it to show an immediate profit – and in fact the results surpassed their wildest dreams.

The next question was, where was it to be? And after that, how was it to be started, and how was it to operate? Cocconas suggested locating it at Chalcedon, as this was a commercial centre readily accessible from Thrace and Bithynia, and not too far from any part of Asia Minor. But Alexander voted for his own home-town, making the very sound point that in the initial stages of such an enterprise you needed plenty of fat-heads from whom to build up a clientele, and that the Paphla-gonians who lived at Abonoteichos mostly fell into this category. They were so superstitious and silly that you'd only to appear with someone playing the flute, the drum, or the cymbals, and start producing prophecies out of a hat, and they'd all gaze at you open-mouthed, as though you were something quite out of this world.

After a good deal of argument, Alexander finally won. But they still thought something could be made of Chalcedon, so they went there first, and in the temple of Apollo, which is the oldest one in the town, they buried a brass plate inscribed with the information that Asclepius and his father, Apollo, would shortly be leaving for Pontus, where they would take up residence at Abonoteichos. They then arranged for the brass plate to be found, with the result that the news soon spread all over Bithynia and Pontus, especially among the citizens of Abonoteichos – who promptly decided to build a temple for the gods in question, and started digging the foundations right away.

Cocconas was then left at Chalcedon, to compose some suitably obscure and ambiguous responses, but died a few weeks later – I believe he was bitten by an adder. Alexander, however, made a triumphal entrance into Abonoteichos. He had let his hair grow in the meantime, so he now had long flowing locks. He wore a purple-and-white robe with a white mantle on top of it, and brandished a sickle of the type used by Perseus, from whom he claimed descent on his mother's side. And those hopeless Paphlagonians, who knew perfectly well that his parents were both obscure and humble people, immediately accepted the truth of the following solemn pronouncement:

> See the godlike Alexander!
> See the darling of Apollo!
> Scion of the line of Perseus!
> Progeny of Podalirius!

I can only think that Podalirius must have been very highly

sexed – if his reactions to Alexander's mother were powerful enough to reach all the way from Tricce to Phaphlagonia!

A prophecy had also been discovered, purporting to be by the Sibyl. It went like this:

> By the shores of Euxine Pontus,
> By the city of Sinope,
> There shall live, not far from Tyrsis,
> Under Roman sway, a prophet.
> And his first is first of letters,
> And his second is the twelfth one,
> And his third is fifth of letters,
> And his fourth, the four-and-twentieth,
> And his whole a four-wheeled wonder
> Running back from Rednaxela.

Having staged this dramatic come-back into his home-town, he still further increased his reputation by pretending to be insane, and occasionally foaming at the mouth. This was quite easily done by chewing the root of a herb called soap-wort, which is used in the dyeing trade, but it seemed to them a fearful manifestation of divinity. Another piece of equipment that he'd already prepared for their benefit was a semi-human snake-head made of linen. It was painted to look quite lifelike, with a mouth that could be made to open and shut by means of horse-hairs, and a forked black tongue sticking out, which was similarly operated. And then, of course, there was the snake from Pella, which had been kept at his house for some time, waiting for its cue to appear and take part in the performance – or rather, to play the lead.

It was now time to begin, and this is how he set about it. He went off one night to the place where they'd been digging the foundations of the new temple. A certain amount of water had collected on the site – I suppose it had seeped up out of the ground, or it may have been rainwater. In it he deposited a goose-egg, the contents of which had been emptied out and replaced by a newly-hatched snake. He tucked it away under the mud, and went back home.

Next morning he leapt into the market-place stark naked, except for a loin-cloth – needless to say, a gold one. He was carrying the same old sickle and whirling his long hair about, like those people who go round making collections in aid of the Mighty Mother, and having fits of divine inspiration. He climbed on to a high altar and did a bit of tub-thumping, congratulating the town on the fact that it would soon see the god in bodily form. Everyone present – and by this time practically the whole population, irrespective of age or sex, had come rushing to the spot – everyone was struck with awe, and knelt down and prayed. Alexander then uttered some unintelligible sounds, which might have been either Hebrew or Phoenician, thus impressing his audience even more – for they had no idea what he was saying, except that it included frequent references to Apollo and Asclepius.

He then ran off at full speed to the site of the new temple. He made straight for the excavations which contained the pre-arranged source of the oracle, stepped into the water and sang a loud hymn to Asclepius and Apollo, concluding with the prayer: 'O God, be graciously pleased to enter our town!' Next he asked for a bowl, which was duly produced, plunged it below the surface, and promptly fished out, along with a good deal of muddy water, the egg in which the deity was enclosed. He'd stuck the two halves of the shell together with a mixture of wax and white lead. Taking the egg into his hands, he solemnly intoned the words: 'Asclepius is here!'

Everyone was watching intently to see what would happen next, for the mere discovery of the egg had already caused a big sensation. But when he broke the shell, and dropped the baby snake into the palm of his hand, so that people could see it moving about and wriggling round his fingers, they immediately let out a yell, and started celebrating the advent of the god, congratulating one another on their good fortune, and gabbling off prayers for health, wealth, and happiness. Alexander then dashed off home again, taking with him the new-born Asclepius. You see, unlike ordinary mortals, who are only born once, he'd just been born for the second time, and on this occasion his mother wasn't Coronis. She wasn't even a Crow. She was just a plain goose. And yet all the people went pouring after him, mad with enthusiasm.

Alexander stayed at home for a few days after that, rightly anticipating that when the story got round, vast numbers of Paphlagonians would come flocking in from all directions. At last, when the town was absolutely packed with mental defectives, who resembled *homo sapiens* only in their appearance and were otherwise indistinguishable from sheep, he gave a reception in a small room of his house. Having got himself up to look quite divine, he seated himself on a couch with Asclepius of Pella in his lap. This snake was, as I said, a very large and beautiful specimen, and he wound it round his neck with its tail hanging down. There was so much of it, that part of it overflowed his lap and trailed along the ground. The only bit that he didn't show them was its head. This he kept well up his sleeve – for the snake didn't mind what you did to it – and poked out the linen head from behind his beard, as though it belonged to the body that they could see.

Well, you can just imagine what it was like. There was this tiny room, with a surging mass of excited people outside it, all in a highly impressionable state and expecting something fantastic. In they came, and there was this huge snake, instead of the tiny creature that they'd seen a few days before. Naturally it seemed like a miracle, especially as the snake looked so tame and had an almost human face. The next moment they were being hustled towards the exit by the queue of people behind them, before they'd got a chance to examine anything closely. You see, he'd had another door knocked through the far wall, just as they did at Babylon, when

Alexander the Great was dying and the palace was besieged by Macedonians wanting to pay their last respects.

They say he often repeated this exhibition, especially when any rich young men arrived in town. And frankly, my dear Celsus, I think those poor stupid, ignorant types in Paphlagonia and Pontus had every excuse for being taken in on these occasions – when they were actually allowed to touch the snake themselves, and saw what looked in the dim light like its mouth, opening and shutting. In fact the whole thing was so well organized that only a Democritus, an Epicurus, a Metrodorus, or someone with equally strong views about such matters would have been capable of detecting the fraud, or of remaining convinced that it could not possibly be genuine, in spite of some doubt about the precise methods used.

So gradually more and more people started pouring in from all over Bithynia, Galatia, and Thrace, as each original eyewitness spread the story of how he'd seen the god being born, and had actually touched Him a few days later, by which time He'd grown enormous and developed a human face. Soon icons, images, and bronze or silver statuettes of the new god were on sale everywhere, and a name had been found for Him, Glycon. This was based on a special announcement from heaven, intoned by Alexander:

> I am Glycon, light of mortals,
> Zeus's offspring, third begotten.

At last preparations were completed, and the moment came to put the oracle into full production. At this point Alexander adopted the procedure used by Amphilochus in Cilicia. After the death, or rather the disappearance, of his father Amphiaraus at Thebes, Amphilochus was thrown out of his country. But when he got to Cilicia, he didn't do too badly, for he supplied the local inhabitants with information about the future, at a charge of two obols per question.

Well, Alexander copied his methods, and informed all visitors that, as from a certain date, the god would be prepared to answer questions. He told each client to write his question on a piece of paper, fold it up, and seal it with wax, or clay, or something like that. He then took the pieces of paper into the Holy of Holies – for by this time the temple had been built, and a suitable scene was set for the performance – and told an assistant prophet-cum-receptionist to call up the inquirers one by one. After consulting the god, he would hand each paper back, still sealed, but with the god's answer written inside it, immediately below the question.

How this was done would have been clear enough to an intelligent person like you – or me, if I may say so – but these people were such drivelling idiots that they found it almost incredibly wonderful. Of course, he'd merely thought up various methods of removing the seals, so that he could read the questions, write down appropriate answers, seal the papers up again and hand them back to their astonished owners. 'How on earth can he know what I asked?' they kept saying. 'I sealed it most carefully, and my seal would be impossible to copy. He really must be a god, and know everything!'

What were these various methods, you may ask? I'll tell you, so that you can spot them if they're ever tried on you. Well, Method No. 1 was to melt the wax underneath the seal with a red-hot needle, and take it off like that. Then, when he'd read and answered the question, he used the same needle to warm the underside of the wax, and simply stuck it on again. Another method was to use stuff called collyrium, which is made out of Bruttian pitch, bitumen, powdered quartz, wax, and resin. Having mixed this compound, he applied it hot to the seal, which he'd previously smeared with grease, and thus took an impression of it. As soon as the collyrium had set, he just opened the paper in the normal way and read it, after which he replaced the wax, stamped it with the collyrium cast, which was now as hard as a rock, and left it looking exactly the same as before.

And here's a third method. He made a waxlike substance by adding chalk to the glue used for bookbinding. While it was still pliable, he applied it to the seal and immediately took it off again – for it set very quickly, and became like Odysseus's eyes 'harder than horn or iron'.[3] He was then able to duplicate the original seal. There are lots of other ways of doing it, but I needn't mention them all. I'd only be boring you, especially as you've already listed quite enough tricks like that in your book debunking magicians – a very fine book too, I may say, and a very useful one, well calculated to make its readers a bit more sensible.

In deciding what answers to give, he relied upon common sense, combined with a certain amount of imagination and guesswork. Sometimes his responses were rather obscure and ambiguous, and sometimes they were downright unintelligible – which he considered in line with the best traditions of his trade. He encouraged or discouraged people's plans, according to what seemed wisest in the circumstances. He also gave advice on diet and medical treatment, for as I said before, he knew quite a lot about medicine. His favourite prescription was a Cytmis – which was a name he'd invented for a sort of pick-me-up concocted out of goat-fat. But legacies and all forms of good fortune or success he invariably postponed to a later date, adding a note to the effect that 'all such things will come in my own good time, when my prophet, Alexander, has made intercession for you'.

For each consultation he charged a fee of one and two.[4] But my dear chap, don't get the idea that because his prices were low, he couldn't have made much out of it. On the contrary, he knocked up an annual income of seven or eight thousand, for his clients were so insatiable that they consulted him ten to fifteen times a year. However, it wasn't all clear profit and he couldn't accumulate any capital, as he had a large number of employees – attendants, detectives, script-writers, librarians, copying-clerks, seal-experts, and interpreters – who had to be paid appropriate salaries.

He now started sending out foreign representatives to advertise the oracle, and tell people how good he was at predicting the future, locating runaway slaves, detecting burglars, discovering buried treasure, and in some cases resurrecting the dead. The result was a mad rush of new customers. Gifts and offerings came pouring in, and the holy prophet doubled his fees – for the following instructions had been issued by the god:

> Honour ye my holy servant,
> Honour, I command, the prophet.
> For your precious gifts I care not,
> But I care for him, my prophet.

At this point the more intelligent members of the community began to turn against him. It was as though they'd been dead drunk, but were now sobering up. The movement was led by the Epicureans, who were fairly numerous, and in the big towns information started leaking out about his various theatrical devices. To scare them off, he produced an oracle declaring that Pontus was full of atheists and Christians who had most wickedly blasphemed against him, and must be stoned and driven out of the land, if his people wished to find favour in his sight. He also made a special statement about Epicurus. Someone had asked what Epicurus was doing in hell, to which the answer was:

> In the mud he sits for ever,
> Leaden fetters on his ankles.

No wonder the oracle was such a success, if its patrons were silly enough to ask questions like that.

He was, in fact, permanently at war with Epicurus, and very reasonably so – for what more suitable opponent could be found for a professional liar than the one person who's really understood the truth about things? He was quite friendly towards the Stoics, the Platonics, and the Pythagoreans, with whom he pursued a policy of peaceful co-existence. But 'that invincibly ignorant Epicurus', as he used to call him, was his natural enemy, because he made fun of everything that Alexander stood for. That's why Amastris, where Lepidus and several other Epicureans lived, was his least favourite town in Pontus, and he never gave a response to anyone who came from there.

However, he did once take the risk of prescribing for a certain Senator's brother, and made rather a fool of himself in the process, because he got stuck with the versification, and had no one available at the time to do it for him. The patient had complained of stomach-ache, and Alexander wanted to tell him to eat pig's trotters prepared with mallow. This was the best he could manage:

> Salt and pepper from the holy
> Cruet swinish mallow hooflets.

As I said before, he often put the snake on show – not the whole of it, of course, but only the tail and body. The head he kept well out of sight underneath his clothes. Then, wishing to astonish the multitude even more, he promised to let them see the god actually talking, and delivering oracles in person. It wasn't very difficult to arrange. He just made a long tube by joining together the wind-pipes of several cranes, and attached one end of it to the mechanical snake-head. He then made the god answer questions by getting someone in the next room to shout down the far end of the tube, so that the voice seemed to come from the linen mouth of Asclepius. Such responses were officially described as Autophones, and were not granted indiscriminately to everyone, but only to the well-dressed few who were prepared to pay highly for the privilege.

One of these Autophones was given to Severianus before

the Armenian War. It encouraged him to go ahead with the
invasion, and ran as follows:

> Lo! the Parthians and Armenians
> Bow beneath thy conquering spearhead.
> Back to Rome and Tiber's waters
> Thou shalt come, a crown of triumph
> Flashing splendour on thy temples.

The silly Celt believed it, and invaded Armenia, with the
result that he and his entire army were cut to pieces by
Othryades. The response was therefore deleted from the
records, and replaced by the following:

> Wage not war against Armenia.
> Such a war is best avoided,
> Lest a man in female clothing
> Shoot from bowstring fate disastrous,
> Stop thy breath and quench the sunlight.

You see, he'd just had another brainwave, which was to doctor
the text of unfulfilled prophecies, so as to make them prophesy
what had actually happened. For instance, he often told inva-
lids that they'd recover, but if one of them died, a revised
version of the response would be added to the records:

> Seek no more to cure thy sickness.
> See, thy fate is hanging o'er thee,
> And thou canst not now escape it.

He also tried to ingratiate himself with his famous colleagues at Claros, Didyma, and Mallus, by recommending his
own clients to consult them, in some such terms as these:

> Hasten, hasten now to Claros,
> Hear the wisdom of my father.

Or else:

> Seek the Didymaean temple,
> Listen humbly to Apollo.

Or perhaps:

> Go to Mallus, pray for succour
> To Amphilochus the prophet.

So far, he was only catering for the home market, i.e. for Asia Minor. But when his fame spread to Italy and reached the capital itself, there was soon great competition, especially in high society, for the privilege of consulting the new oracle, either in person or by proxy. The chief enthusiast was Rutilianus, an excellent person who'd done very well in public life, but was crazy about religion and had the most extraordinary beliefs. He'd only to see a bit of stone with a wreath on it, or some oil poured over it, and down he'd go on his knees and pray to it for hours. So of course, when he heard of this oracle, he very nearly threw up his job and went flying off to Abonoteichos the same day.

He kept sending people to consult it, and as these people were only ignorant servants, they were easily taken in. So back they came, and told him what they'd seen and heard, what they thought they'd seen and heard, and whatever else they thought he'd like to hear. The result was that they added fuel to the flames, and sent the poor old chap quite mad. He knew practically all the most important people in Rome, and he went round telling them what his servants had told him, adding one or two improvements of his own, until the whole town was full of it, everyone at Court was quite unbalanced on the subject, and several gentlemen went rushing off to have their fortunes told too.

When they arrived, Alexander received them most politely, gave them expensive presents to ensure their goodwill, and sent them back prepared not only to repeat the answers to their questions, but to sing the god's praises generally, and tell fantastic lies about the oracle and its proprietor. He also thought of a rather clever trick that would never have occurred to an ordinary criminal. If he found anything politically dangerous in the questions that were sent to him, he held on to the papers and refused to give them back, so that he could blackmail the writers and make them practically his slaves – for you can imagine the type of question that important people at Rome were liable to ask. He thus contrived to make a lot of money out of them, for they knew that he'd got the whip hand.

Oh, and I must tell you some of the oracles he gave Rutilianus. This gentleman had a son by a previous marriage, who was old enough to go to school, and the father had asked for advice on where to send him. The answer was:

> Let Pythagoras instruct him,
> And the bard that sings of battles.

A few days later the boy died. It made the oracle look so silly, that Alexander was completely baffled, and couldn't think what to reply to his critics. But that splendid fellow Rutilianus immediately sprang to his defence, and explained that the god had virtually prophesied his son's death, by not mentioning any living schoolmasters but only Pythagoras and Homer, who'd been dead for ages, and were now presumably giving the boy private coaching in Hades. Which just shows how well Alexander picked his friends!

On another occasion Rutilianus asked whose soul he'd inherited, and was told:

> First thou wast the son of Peleus,
> After that thou wast Menander,
> Now thou art the man thou seemest,
> Later thou shalt be a sunbeam,
> But before that thou shalt number
> Four-score years beyond a hundred.

In point of fact he died of a bilious attack at seventy, so he didn't stay around long enough for the god to keep his promise – although he gave it personally, by Autophone.

On the subject of matrimony, Rutilianus received some very definite advice:

> Thou must take to wife the daughter
> Of the Moon and Alexander.

Alexander had previously put it about that his daughter was the offspring of the Moon, who'd seen him asleep one night and fallen in love with him. She was always doing that kind of thing, you know. So the silly ass went straight off and proposed to the girl, became a bridegroom at the age of sixty, and after making large-scale sacrifices to please his mother-in-law, actually consummated the marriage, thus transforming himself, as he thought, into a heavenly body.

Once Alexander started doing business in Italy, he got even bigger ideas. He sent missionaries all over the Roman Empire, warning every town to look out for plagues, earthquakes, and conflagrations, and offering to protect them against such disasters. During the great epidemic[5] he sent each country a copy of the following oracle, which originated as an Autophone:

> Phoebus, lord of unshorn tresses,
> Will not let the plague come nigh thee.

Soon you could see these words scribbled on front doors everywhere, as a form of immunization. In most cases it had precisely the opposite effect, for as it happened, the first households to go down were the ones with these inscriptions. I don't mean to suggest that the words had anything to do with it – doubtless it was pure coincidence. Or perhaps their faith in the oracle made people careless about taking other precautions. So they did nothing to avoid infection, but relied on the prophylactic effect of the trochaic tetrameter, and just waited for the lord of unshorn tresses to shoot down the germs with his bow and arrow.

He stationed a large number of private detectives in Rome,

to report what his clients were like, what questions they were going to ask, and what they particularly wanted, so that he could work out his answers in advance. To whip up trade in Italy, he also established a three-day festival there, complete with torchlight services and initiation ceremonies. On the first day, as at Athens, there was a proclamation: 'If any atheist, Christian, or Epicurean has come to spy upon our sacred mysteries, let him begone! But let all true believers be made holy before the god!' This was immediately followed by an expulsion ceremony. Alexander led off with the words: 'Out with all Christians!' to which the congregation made the response: 'Out with all Epicureans!'

After that there was a Nativity Play, in which Leto gave birth to Apollo, who then married Coronis and begat Asclepius. On the second day the Birth and Epiphany of Glycon was celebrated, and on the third there was a Mystic Marriage between Podalirius and Alexander's mother. She was called The Lady with the Torch, and torches were lighted in her honour. Finally there was the Passion of the Moon, and the Conception of Mrs Rutilianus. Alexander was now the Gentleman with the Torch, and played the part of Endymion. He lay down in full view of the congregation and pretended to go to sleep. Then down from heaven, or rather from the ceiling, descended, not the Moon, but a most attractive girl called Rutilia, the wife of a Civil Servant. The love-making was extremely realistic. In full view of everyone, including her wretched husband, they lay there kissing and fondling one another, and if it hadn't been for all those torches, things would probably have gone even further. A few minutes later Alexander reappeared in priestly robes, and amid deep silence loudly intoned the words: 'Hail Glycon!' Immediately from his holy acolytes – Paphlagonians in hob-nailed boots – came the response, accompanied by a strong smell of garlic: 'Hail Alexander!'

In the course of a mystic torch-dance, he frequently man-

aged to lay bare a golden thigh. No doubt he was wearing a
gold stocking, which glittered in the torchlight. So a couple
of solemn idiots raised the question whether he was a reincarna-
tion of Pythagoras, or someone like that. The problem was
referred to Alexander himself, who produced the following
solution:

> Now Pythagoras's spirit
> Wanes, and now again it waxes.
> Prophecy is but an offshoot
> From the mind of Zeus the Father.
> Zeus has sent it forth to succour
> Righteous men, till hence departing
> In a flash of Zeus's lightning
> It returns to Zeus the Father.

He was always holding forth on the wickedness of homosexuality, but just listen to how that exemplary character
behaved himself. He instructed all the towns in Pontus and
Paphlagonia to send young priests to him for a three-year
course in theology. Candidates had to be specially selected,
and have the highest qualifications in the way of birth, beauty,
and physical charm. When they arrived, he locked them up
in his house and treated them as his personal property, going
to bed with them and committing various other acts of in-
decency. He also made it a rule never to let anyone over the
age of eighteen touch his lips, but just held out his hand for
them to kiss. The only ones he kissed properly were teenagers,
who were therefore known as Children of the Kiss.

And so he went on enjoying himself at those silly people's
expense, freely seducing their wives and sexually assaulting
their children. In fact it was generally regarded as a consum-
mation devoutly to be wished, for one's wife to catch Alexander's eye. If he actually deigned to kiss her, one expected a
shower of blessings to descend on one's household, and many
women even boasted of having had children by him, a claim
which their husbands were only too proud to confirm.

But I'd like to report a conversation that took place between Glycon and a certain priest from Tios, whose IQ can be deduced from his questions. I found it all inscribed in letters of gold on the man's own house.

'Tell me, O Lord Glycon,' began the priest, 'who art thou?'

'I am the new Asclepius,' replied Glycon.

'Art thou then different from the old Asclepius, or what meanest thou?'

'That is a Mystery. Seek not to understand it.'

'For how many years wilt thou remain with us?'

'For a thousand years and three.'

'And where wilt thou go then?'

'To Bactra or thereabouts, for the heathen also must enjoy the privilege of my presence.'

'And what about the other oracles, Lord, at Didyma, Claros, and Delphi? Are they still inspired by thy forefather Apollo, or have they ceased to prophesy the truth?'

'Seek not to know that either, for it is a Mystery.'

'And what shall I be, Lord, after this life?'

'First a camel, then a horse, then a great prophet like Alexander.'

Here the conversation ended with two lines of verse, doubtless suggested by the fact that the priest was a friend of Lepidus:

> Trust not Lepidus, for he is
> Bound to come to a bad ending,

– because, as I said, he was terrified of Epicurus, and regarded his school as a sort of rival firm which was always trying to undermine his business. And when an Epicurean attempted to show him up in front of a large audience, Alexander practically had him lynched.

The man walked up to him and said in a loud voice:

'Alexander, do you remember once advising a Paphlagonian to hand his slaves over to the authorities for execution, on a

charge of murdering his son, while he was a student at Alexandria? Well, the boy's still alive. He's just this moment come
home – after you've had those slaves thrown to the lions!'

What had happened was this. The young man had gone for
a sail up the Nile to Clysma, where he happened to find a
boat just sailing for India. He was persuaded to go on board,
and stayed away so long that his wretched slaves thought he
must have been drowned on his way up the river, or killed
by bandits – for there were lots of them about. So they went
home and reported his disappearance. Then the oracle was
consulted, the slaves were sentenced to death, and finally the
young man turned up and told the story of his travels.

The justice of the criticism was more than Alexander could
bear, and he lost his temper. He ordered everyone present
to stone the Epicurean, unless they wanted to be excom-
municated as Epicureans themselves. The stones had already
begun to fly, when a visitor from Pontus called Demostratus
made the first move to save the man's life, by running up to
him and putting an arm round his shoulders. Another moment,
and he would have been dead – and quite right too, for why
should he remain sane when everyone else had gone mad?
How dared he make fun of Paphlagonian stupidity?

Occasionally, when a client reached the head of the queue
– which formed the day before the responses were given out
– and the receptionist asked if this man's question would be
answered, a voice from within would cry: 'To hell with him!'
This meant that he was to be refused shelter, fire, and water,
hounded from one country to another, and generally treated
as an outcast, an atheist, an Epicurean – for that was the ultimate term of abuse.

In this connexion, Alexander did one rather silly thing. He
got hold of a copy of Epicurus's *First Principles*, which is, as
you know, his finest work and sums up his whole philosophy,
took it into the middle of the market-place, and solemnly
burnt it on a bonfire of fig-wood, as though it was the man

himself. He then threw the ashes into the sea, and concluded the operation with yet another oracle:

> Burn with fire, I command you,
> Burn with fire the dotard's doctrines.

A person of his type couldn't be expected to understand how much good that book has done, by giving people peace of mind, freeing them from superstitious fears, irrational hopes, and exaggerated emotions, forcing them to face facts, and literally purifying their minds, not by any idiotic ritual, but by reason, truth, and plain speaking.

To return to that unpleasant character, Alexander – let me tell you about his biggest piece of effrontery. Through Rutilianus, whose reputation stood very high at Court, he now had access to the Emperor. So at a critical point in the war with Germany, when his late majesty Marcus Aurelius was actually in contact with the forces of the Quadi and the Marcomanni, Alexander sent him an oracle recommending that two live lions should be thrown into the Ister, plus plenty of spices, and all that was necessary to make a really splendid sacrifice. But I'd better give you the original text:

> Cast, I bid you, on the waters,
> Cast upon the river Ister,
> Two that serve the Mighty Mother,
> Two wild beasts that roam the mountains,
> Garlanded with fragrant herbage
> Such as Indian breezes foster.
> Straightway victory will follow,
> Glory great and peace delightful.

His instructions were duly carried out. The lions swam across the river and landed on enemy territory, where the Huns beat them to death with sticks, under the impression that they were merely some strange variety of dog or wolf. And 'straightway' the Roman forces suffered a crushing defeat, in which they lost about two thousand men at one go. Then came the disaster at Aquileia, which was very nearly taken by storm. Alexander dealt with the situation by rather feebly plagiarizing the Delphic oracle, and saying that the god had foretold a victory, but had not specified whether the Romans or the Germans would win it.

Meanwhile people kept pouring into the town to consult the oracle, until the place was so overcrowded that food supplies began to run short, So Alexander started working night-shifts. He went to sleep with the questions under his pillow – that was his story, anyway – and the god told him the answers in dreams. Most of these answers were not very clear, in fact they were extremely muddled and obscure, especially if the paper appeared to have been sealed with more than usual care. In such cases he took no risks, but just scribbled down the first thing that came into his head – which seemed to him perfectly normal procedure for an oracle. There was also an interpretation department, which charged a high fee for trying to make sense of these responses. Needless to say, he got his rake-off too, for each interpreter had to pay him the sum of one talent, Attic currency.

Occasionally, without any question being asked, or any message sent – in fact without any justification at all – he produced something like this, to impress the weaker-minded brethren:

> Who, thou askest, hath been bouncing
> Calligenia, thy consort,
> Up and down among the bedclothes,
> All unknown to thee, her husband?
> 'Tis Protogenes, thy slave-boy,
> 'Tis the boy that thou hast trusted.
> For one night thou didst seduce him,
> So thy wife he now seduceth,
> Paying thee in thine own coinage.
> What is more, a deadly poison
> Hath been purchased by the lovers,
> That henceforward thou mayst never
> See or hear what they are up to.

> Thou shalt find it 'neath thy bedstead,
> By the wall thy pillow toucheth,
> And thy parlour-maid, Calypso,
> Is their dastardly accomplice.

At first sight, all that detailed information might seem enough to startle Democritus himself. But once he knew the trick of it, he wouldn't have given it a second thought.

He sometimes answered questions in foreign languages like Syrian or Celtic, but this meant finding some tourist of the right nationality to act as interpreter, which wasn't always easy. So these questions usually remained unanswered for some time, as the practical difficulties of translation tended to slow up production. One such response was in Scythian, and went like this:

> Morfu bargolis ischia
> Anche nechi psida osda.

Another inquirer, who was not there at the time – nor anywhere else either – was instructed in prose to go home at once, 'For he that sent thee hath just been slain by his neighbour Diocles, at the hands of three hired assassins called Magnus, Celer, and Bubalus, who have already been arrested and taken to prison.'

And now you must hear some of the oracles that I was given myself. First of all I asked: 'Is Alexander bald?', sealing up the paper with particular care, and making it quite obvious that I'd done so. Back came the midnight prophecy:

> Malach, son of Sabadálach,
> Was an Attis, not the same one.

On another occasion I sent in two papers under different names, each containing the question: 'Where was Homer born?' When the boy who delivered the first one was asked what he'd come about, he said:

'Oh, my master wants some treatment for a pain in his side.' On the strength of this, I received the following reply:

> Rub on Cytmis, I command you,
> Sprinkled with the dew of horses.

In the second case Alexander was told that I wanted to know whether to take the sea route or the land route to Italy. So again his answer had very little bearing on Homer:

> Do not sail upon the ocean.
> Journey rather by the highroad.

I laid several other such traps for him. For instance, I sent in a paper containing the usual one question, but with the words 'Eight questions from So-and-so' (giving a false name) written on the outside. I also sent along the eight drachmas odd that would be charged for that number of consultations. The statement of contents, and the amount of the remittance had the desired effect. To my one question ('When will Alexander's tricks be found out?') he gave me eight different answers, which had no reference to anything in this world or the next, being all quite unintelligent and unintelligible.

When he found out about it later, and also heard that I'd tried to stop Rutilianus's marriage and undermine his faith in the oracle, Alexander was naturally furious, and regarded me from then on as his deadliest enemy. So one day, when Rutilianus asked a question about me, the reply was:

> All he careth for is dalliance,
> Beds of lust and midnight orgies.

As a matter of fact I *was* his deadliest enemy, and with very good reason. When he first heard that the famous Lucian had arrived in town – complete with a two-man bodyguard provided by the Governor of Cappadocia, who was a friend of mine, to escort me to the coast – he most politely invited me to come and see him. When I arrived, I found him surrounded by servants, so it was just as well I'd brought my bodyguard with me. He held out his right hand for me to kiss, as he normally did when receiving visitors, and I grabbed hold of it, as if to kiss it – instead of which I gave it a jolly good bite, and practically crippled it for life. His servants promptly started beating me up, and trying to twist my head off, for I'd already annoyed them by saying 'Good morning, Alexander!' instead of 'Hail, mighty Prophet!' However, by a noble effort of self-control, he called them off.

'I'll soon make him tame,' he told them. 'I'll show him that Glycon has power to soothe the most savage breast.'

He then sent them all out of the room, and started trying to reason with me, saying he knew perfectly well who I was, and what I'd been saying to Rutilianus.

'Now, why should you treat me like that,' he asked, 'when I can use my influence with Rutilianus to get you rapid promotion?'

In view of my dangerous situation, I was only too glad to accept this kind offer, and by the time I left, I was his dearest friend – a transformation which struck the people outside as little short of miraculous.

Later, when I was just leaving for Amastris – I'd sent my father on ahead, with all the rest of my party except Xenophon – Alexander not only gave me several parting gifts, but even offered to charter a special boat for my benefit. This I took to be a perfectly innocent and friendly gesture. But when we were half-way across, I noticed that the man at the helm was showing signs of distress, and arguing hotly with the other members of the crew. I began to feel rather anxious about my future prospects, and sure enough, it turned out that Alexander had told them to throw us overboard – in which case his war against me would very soon have been over. However, the steersman begged them with tears in his eyes not to do such a dreadful thing and they finally decided they wouldn't.

'You see,' he said, turning to me, 'I've led a decent life for sixty years, and I don't want a murder on my conscience now, when I've a wife and children to think of.'

He then explained the purpose of the voyage, as laid down

in Alexander's sailing-orders, after which he landed us at Aegialus, the place that good old Homer talks about,[6] and sailed back home. At Aegialus we met some people who were coasting along from the Bosporus to Bithynia. King Eupator had sent them to pay his income-tax. I told them about our narrow escape, and finding them sympathetic, cadged a lift in their boat, and arrived safe and sound at Amastris.

From then on it was total war between us, and I strained every nerve to get my revenge. I hadn't liked him much, even before he tried to murder me, for he always struck me as a most unpleasant character, but now I really set about exposing him. I had plenty of support, especially from scientists of the school of Timocrates. But Anectus, who was then the Governor of Bithynia and Pontus, practically implored me to call it off. He said his friendship with Rutilianus would make it impossible for him to punish Alexander, even if his guilt were publicly established. This put a stopper on the enterprise, and I gave it up. It was obviously not the moment to stick my neck out, when I had to contend with so much prejudice on the bench.

I mustn't forget Alexander's two great acts of bravado – his request to the Emperor for Abonoteichos to be renamed Glyconopolis, and his issue of a new coinage to the following specification: obverse, head of Glycon, reverse, portrait of Alexander, complete with fillets of paternal grandpapa Asclepius, and sickle of maternal ditto, Perseus.

Having announced in a special bulletin that he was destined to live for a hundred and fifty years, and then be struck by lightning, he came to a miserable end before he was even seventy. He died of *delirium* – or perhaps I should say, *Podalirium* – *tremens*, complicated by gangrene of the foot, which spread right up to the groin, and made his leg a seething mass of worms. His baldness was not discovered until he got the doctors to put cold compresses on his head to lessen the pain, which could not be done without removing the *toupet*.

Thus ended the tragic history of Alexander, with a dénouement so appropriate as to seem almost providential, though it was doubtless quite fortuitous. His obsequies were equally worthy of him, for they included a curious Funeral Game in which his chief accomplices competed for the control of the oracle. Finally they appealed to the umpire, Rutilianus, and asked him to decide which of them should inherit the organization and win the Prophecy Championship. One of the competitors was a white-haired doctor called Paetus, whose behaviour was as unsuitable to his age as it was to his profession. But the umpire disqualified them all. He ruled that Alexander still retained his world title, even after his departure from this world.

Well, my dear fellow, I've made this representative selection from the material available, partly as a favour to a friend I love and admire more than anyone else in the world, for his wisdom, his passion for truth, his kindness, his fairness, his calm attitude to life, and his genius for personal relations, but still more – and you'll find this part less embarrassing – as a tribute to Epicurus, a really great man who perceived, as no one else has done, the beauty of truth, and by passing that insight on to his followers, has given them a wonderful sense of freedom. And I hope what I've written may also be some use to the general reader, by shattering a few of his illusions, and confirming any sensible ideas that he may have.

Yours ever,

Lucian

THE TRUE HISTORY

PREFACE

IF you were training to be an athlete, you would not spend all your time doing exercises: you would also have to learn when and how to relax, for relaxation is generally regarded as one of the most important elements in physical training. To my mind it is equally important for intellectuals. When you have been doing a lot of serious reading, it is a good idea to give your mind a rest and so build up energy for another bout of hard work.

For this purpose the best sort of book to read is one that is not merely witty and entertaining but also has something interesting to say. I am sure you will agree that this story of mine falls into that category, for its charm consists not only in the remarkable nature of its subject-matter and the beauty of its style, not only in the plausibility of its various flights of fancy, but also in its satirical intention – since every episode is a subtle parody of some fantastic 'historical fact' recorded by an ancient poet, historian, or philosopher.

There is no need to tell you their names, for you will recognize them soon enough; but I might just mention Ctesias of Cnidos, who made a number of statements in his history of India for which he had no evidence whatsoever, either at first or second hand. Then there was Iambulus, who told us a lot of surprising things about the Atlantic Ocean. They were obviously quite untrue, but no one could deny that they made a very good story, so hundreds of people followed his example and wrote so-called histories of their travels describing all the huge monsters, and savage tribes, and extraordinary ways of life that they had come across in foreign parts.

Of course, the real pioneer in this type of tomfoolery was Homer's Odysseus, who told Alcinous and his court an extremely tall story about bags full of wind, and one-eyed giants, and cannibals, and other unpleasant characters, not to speak of many-headed monsters and magic potions that turned human beings into animals. He evidently thought the Phaeacians were fools enough to believe anything.

I do not feel particularly shocked by this kind of thing, on moral grounds, for I have found that a similar disregard for truth is quite common even among professional philosophers. My chief reaction is astonishment – that anyone should tell such lies and expect to get away with it. But if other people can do it, why should not I? For I too am vain enough to wish to leave some record of myself to posterity, and as no interesting experiences have ever come my way in real life, I have nothing true to write about.

In one respect, however, I shall be a more honest liar than my predecessors, for I am telling you frankly, here and now, that I have no intention whatever of telling the truth. Let this voluntary confession forestall any future criticism: I am writing about things entirely outside my own experience or anyone else's, things that have no reality whatever and never could have. So mind you do not believe a word I say.

I

I once set sail from the Pillars of Heracles[1] with a brisk wind behind me and steered westward into the Atlantic. My reason for doing so? Mere curiosity. I just felt I needed a change, and wanted to find out what happened on the other side of the Ocean, and what sort of people lived there. With this object in view I had taken on board an enormous supply of food and water, and collected fifty other young men who felt the same way as I did to keep me company. I had also provided all the weapons that we could possibly need, hired the best steersman available (at an exorbitant wage), and had our ship, which was only a light craft, specially reinforced to withstand the stresses and strains of a long voyage.

After sailing along at a moderate speed for twenty-four hours, we were still within sight of land; but at dawn the following day the wind increased to gale-force, the waves rose mountain-high, the sky grew black as night, and it became impossible even to take in sail. There was nothing we could do but let her run before the wind and hope for the best.

The storm went on for seventy-nine days, but on the eightieth the sun suddenly shone through and revealed an island not far off. It was hilly and covered with trees, and now that the worst of the storm was over, the roar of the waves breaking against the shore had died down to a soft murmur. So we landed and threw ourselves down, utterly exhausted, on the sand. After all we had been through, you can imagine how long we lay there; but eventually we got up, and leaving thirty men to guard the ship, I and the other twenty went off to explore the island.

We started walking inland through the woods, and when we had gone about six hundred yards we came across a bronze tablet with a Greek inscription on it. The letters were almost worn away, but we just managed to make out the words: 'Heracles and Dionysus got this far.' We also spotted a couple of footprints on a rock nearby, one about a hundred feet long, and the other, I should say, about ninety-nine. Presumably Heracles has somewhat larger feet than Dionysus.

We sank reverently to our knees and said a prayer. Then we went on a bit farther and came to a river of wine, which tasted exactly like Chian. It was deep enough in places to float a battleship, and any doubts we might have had about the authenticity of the inscription were immediately dispelled. Dionysus had been there all right!

I was curious to know where the river came from, so I walked up-stream until I arrived at the source, which was of a most unusual kind. It consisted of a group of giant vines, loaded with enormous grapes. From the root of each plant trickled sparkling drops of wine, which eventually converged to form the river. There were lots of wine-coloured fish swimming about in it, and they tasted like wine too, for we caught and ate some, and they made us extremely drunk. Needless to say, when we cut them open we found they were full of wine-lees. Later, we hit on the idea of diluting them with ordinary water-fish and thus reducing the alcoholic content of our food.

After lunch we waded across the river at one of the shallower spots, and came upon some specimens of a very rare type of vine. They had good thick trunks growing out of the ground in the normal manner, but apart from that they were women, complete in every detail from the waist upwards. In fact they were exactly like those pictures you see of Daphne being turned into a tree just as Apollo is about to catch her. From the tips of their fingers sprouted vine-shoots loaded with grapes, and their hair consisted of vine-leaves and tendrils.

When we went up to them, they shook us warmly by the hand and said they were delighted to see us, some saying it in Lydian, some in Hindustani, but most of them in Greek. Then they wanted us to kiss them, and every man who put his lips to theirs got very drunk and started lurching about. They would not allow us to pick their fruit, and shrieked with pain when anyone tried to do so; but they were more than willing to be deflowered, and two of us who volunteered to oblige them found it quite impossible to withdraw from their engagements afterwards. They became literally rooted to the spot, their fingers turning into vine-shoots and their hair into tendrils, and looked like having little grapes of their own at any moment.

So we left them to their fate and ran back to the ship, where we told the others what we had seen and described the results of the experiment in cross-fertilization. Then we went off again with buckets to replenish our water-supply, and while we were about it to restock our cellar from the river. After that we spent the night on the beach beside our ship, and next morning put to sea with a gentle breeze behind us.

About midday, when we had already lost sight of the island, we were suddenly hit by a typhoon, which whirled the ship round at an appalling speed and lifted it to a height of approximately 1,800,000 feet. While we were up there, a powerful wind caught our sails and bellied them out, so instead of falling back on to the sea we continued to sail through the air for the next seven days – and, of course, an equal number of nights. On the eighth day we sighted what looked like a big island hanging in mid air, white and round and brilliantly illuminated, so we steered towards it, dropped anchor, and disembarked.

A brief reconnaissance was enough to tell us that the country was inhabited and under cultivation, and so long as it was light that was all we could discover about our situation; but as soon as it got dark we noticed several other flame-coloured islands of various sizes in the vicinity, and far below us we could see a place full of towns and rivers and seas and forests and mountains, which we took to be the Earth.

We decided to do some more exploring, but we had not gone far before we were stopped and arrested by the local police. They are known in those parts as the Flying Squad, because they fly about on vultures, which they ride and control like horses. I should explain that the vultures in question are unusually large and generally have three heads. To give you some idea of their size, each of their feathers is considerably longer and thicker than the mast of a fairly large merchant-ship.

Now, one of the Flying Squad's duties is to fly about the country looking for undesirable aliens, and if it sees any to take them before the King. So that is what they did with us.

One glance at our clothes was enough to tell the King our nationality.

'Why, you're Greek, aren't you?' he said.

'Certainly we are,' I replied.

'Then how on earth did you get here?' he asked. 'How did you manage to come all that way through the air?'

So I told him the whole story, after which he told us his. It turned out that he came from Greece too, and was called Endymion. For some reason or other he had been whisked up here in his sleep and made King of the country, which was, he informed us, the Moon.

'But don't you worry,' he went on. 'I'll see you have everything you need. And if I win this war with Phaethon, you can settle down here quite comfortably for the rest of your lives.'

'What's the war about?' I asked.

'Oh, it's been going on for ages,' he answered. 'Phaethon's my opposite number on the Sun, you know. It all started like this. I thought it would be a good idea to collect some of the poorer members of the community and send them off to form a colony on Lucifer, for it's completely uninhabited. Phaethon got jealous and despatched a contingent of airborne troops, mounted on flying ants, to intercept us when we were half-way there. We were hopelessly outnumbered and had to retreat, but now I'm going to have another shot at founding that colony, this time with full military support. If you'd care to join the expedition, I'd be only too glad to supply you with vultures from the royal stables, and all other necessary equipment. We start first thing tomorrow morning.'

'Thanks very much,' I said. 'We'd love to come.'

So he gave us an excellent meal and put us up for the night, and early next morning assembled all his troops in battle-formation, for the enemy were reported to be not far off. The expeditionary force numbered a hundred thousand, exclusive of transport, engineers, infantry, and foreign auxiliaries, eight thousand being mounted on vultures, and the other twenty on saladfowls. Saladfowls, incidentally, are like very large birds, except that they are fledged with vegetables instead of feathers and have wings composed of enormous lettuce-leaves.

The main force was supported by a battery of Pea-shooters and a corps of Garlic-gassers, and also by a large contingent of allies from the Great Bear, consisting of thirty thousand Flea-shooters and fifty thousand Wind-jammers. Flea-shooters are archers mounted on fleas – hence their name – the fleas in question being approximately twelve times the size of elephants. Wind-jammers are also airborne troops, but they are not mounted on anything, nor do they have any wings of their own. Their method of propulsion is as follows: they wear extremely long nightshirts, which belly out like sails in the wind and send them scudding along like miniature ships through the air. Needless to say, their equipment is usually very light.

In addition to all these, seventy thousand Sparrowballs and fifty thousand Crane Cavalry were supposed to be arriving from the stars that shine over Cappadocia, but I did not see any of them, for they never turned up. In the circumstances I shall not attempt to describe what they were like – though I heard some stories about them which were really quite incredible.

All Endymion's troops wore the same type of equipment. Their helmets were made of beans, which grow very large and tough up there, and their bodies were protected by lupine seed-pods, stitched together to form a sort of armour-plate; for on the Moon these pods are composed of a horny substance which is practically impenetrable. As for their shields and swords, they were of the normal Greek pattern.

Our battle-formation was as follows. On the right wing were the troops mounted on vultures; among them was the King, surrounded by the pick of his fighting men, which included us. On the left wing were the troops mounted on saladfowls, and in the centre were the various allied contingents.

The infantry numbered approximately sixty million, and special steps had to be taken before they could be suitably deployed. There are, you must understand, large numbers of spiders on the Moon, each considerably larger than the average island in the Archipelago, and their services were requisitioned to construct a continuous cobweb between the Moon and Lucifer. As soon as the job had been done and the infantry had thus been placed on a firm footing, Knightley, the youngest son of Setfair, led them out on to the field of battle.

On the enemy's left wing was stationed the Royal Ant Force with Phaethon himself among them. These creatures looked exactly like ordinary flying ants, except for their enormous size, being anything up to two hundred feet long. They carried armed men on their backs, but with their huge antennae they did just as much of the fighting as their riders. They were believed to number about fifty thousand.

On the right wing were placed an equal number of Gnat-shooters, who were archers mounted on giant gnats. Behind them was a body of mercenaries from outer space. These were only light-armed infantry, but were very effective long-range fighters, for they bombarded us with colossal radishes, which inflicted foul-smelling wounds and caused instantaneous death. The explanation was said to be that the projectiles were smeared with a powerful antiseptic.

Next to the mercenaries were about ten thousand Mushroom Commandos, heavy-armed troops trained for hand-to-hand fighting who used mushrooms as shields and asparagus stalks as spears; and next to them again were five thousand Bow-wows from Sirius. These were dog-faced human beings mounted on flying chestnuts.

It was reported that Phaethon too had been let down by some of his allies, for an army of slingers was supposed to be coming from the Milky Way, and the Cloud-Centaurs had also promised their support. But the latter arrived too late for the battle (though far too soon for my comfort, I may add) and the slingers never turned up at all. Phaethon, I heard, was so cross about it that he went and burnt their milk for them shortly afterwards.

Eventually the signal-flags went up, there was a loud braying of donkeys on both sides – for donkeys are employed as trumpeters up there – and the battle began. The enemy's left-wing immediately turned tail and fled, long before our vulture-riders had got anywhere near them, so we set off in pursuit and killed as many as we could. Their right wing, however, managed to break through our left one, and the Gnat-shooters came pouring through the gap until they were stopped by our infantry, who promptly made a counter-attack and forced them to retreat. Finally, when they realized that their left wing had already been beaten, the retreat became an absolute rout. We took vast numbers of prisoners, and killed so many men that the blood splashed all over the clouds and made them as red as a sunset. Quite a lot of it dripped right down on to the earth, and made me wonder if something of the sort had happened before, which would account for that extraordinary statement in Homer that Zeus rained down tears of blood at the thought of Sarpedon's death.[2]

In the end we got tired of chasing them, so we stopped and erected two trophies, one in the middle of the cobweb to commemorate the prowess of the infantry, and one in the clouds to mark the success of our airborne forces. Just as we were doing so, a report came through that Phaethon's unpunctual allies, the Cloud-Centaurs, were rapidly approaching. When they finally appeared they were a most astonishing sight, for they were a cross between winged horses and human beings. The human part was about as big as the Colossus at Rhodes, and the horse-part was roughly the size of a large merchant-ship. I had better not tell you how many there were of them, for you would never believe me if I did, but you may as well know that they were led by Sagittarius, the archer in the Zodiac.

Hearing that their allies had been defeated, they sent a message to Phaethon telling him to rally his forces and make a counter-attack. In the meantime they set the example by promptly spreading out in line and charging the Moon-people before they had time to organize themselves – for they had broken ranks as soon as the rout began, and now they were scattered about all over the place in search of loot. The result was that our entire army was put to flight, the King himself was chased all the way back to his capital, and most of his birds lost their lives.

The Cloud-Centaurs pulled down the trophies and devastated the whole cobweb, capturing me and two of my friends in the process. By this time Phaethon had returned to the scene of action and erected some trophies of his own, after which we were carried off to the Sun as prisoners of war, our hands securely lashed behind our backs with pieces of cobweb.

The victors decided not to besiege Endymion's capital, but merely to cut off his light-supply by building a wall in the middle of the air. The wall in question was composed of a double thickness of cloud, and was so effective that the Moon was totally eclipsed and condemned to a permanent state of darkness. Eventually Endymion was reduced to a policy of appeasement, and sent a message to Phaethon humbly begging him to take down the wall and not make them spend the rest of their lives in the dark, volunteering to pay a war-indemnity and conclude a pact of non-aggression with the Sun, and offering hostages as a guarantee of his good faith.

Phaethon's Parliament met twice to consider these proposals. At the first meeting they passed a resolution rejecting them out of hand; at the second they reversed this decision, and agreed to make peace on terms which were ultimately incorporated in the following document:

AN AGREEMENT made this day between the Sun-people and their allies (hereinafter called *The Victors*) of the one part and the Moon-people and their allies (hereinafter called *The Vanquished*) of the other part

1. The Victors agree to demolish the wall, to refrain in future from invading the Moon, and to return their prisoners of war at a fixed charge per head.

2. The Vanquished agree not to violate the sovereign rights of other

stars, and not to make war in future upon the Victors, but to assist them in case of attack by a third party, such assistance to be reciprocal.

3. The Vanquished undertake to pay to the Victors annually in advance ten thousand bottles of dew, and to commit ten thousand hostages to their keeping.

4. The colony on Lucifer shall be established jointly by both parties, other stars being free to participate if they so wish.

5. The terms of this agreement shall be inscribed on a column of amber, to be erected in the middle of the air on the frontier between the two kingdoms.

SIGNED for and on behalf of the Sun-people
and their allies

RUFUS T. FIREMAN
for and on behalf of the Moon-people
and their allies

P. M. LOONY

As soon as peace was declared, the wall was taken down and we three prisoners were released. When we got back to the Moon, we were greeted with tears of joy not only by the rest of our party but even by Endymion himself. He was very anxious for me to stay and help him with the colony, and actually offered to let me marry his son – for there are no such things as women on the Moon – but I was intent on getting down to the sea again, and as soon as he realized that I had made up my mind, he gave up trying to keep me. So off we went, after a farewell dinner which lasted for a week.

At this point I should like to tell you some of the odd things I noticed during my stay on the Moon. First of all, their methods of reproduction: as they have never even heard of women up there, the men just marry other men, and these other men have the babies. The system is that up to the age of twenty-five one acts as a wife, and from then on as a husband.

When a man is pregnant, he carries the child not in his stomach but in the calf of his leg, which grows extremely fat on these occasions. In due course they do a Caesarean, and the baby is taken out dead; but it is then brought to life by being placed in a high wind with its mouth wide open. Incidentally, it seems to me that these curious facts of lunar physiology may throw some light on a problem of etymology, for have we not here the missing link between the two apparently unconnected senses of the word *calf*?

Even more surprising is the method of propagating what are known as Tree-men. This is how it is done: you cut off the father's right testicle and plant it in the ground, where it grows into a large fleshy tree rather like a phallus, except that it has leaves and branches and bears fruit in the form of acorns, which are about eighteen inches long. When the fruit is ripe, it is picked and the babies inside are hatched out.

It is not uncommon up there to have artificial private parts, which apparently work quite well. If you are rich, you have them made of ivory, but the poorer classes have to rub along with wooden ones.

When Moon-people grow old, they do not die. They just vanish into thin air, like smoke – and talking of smoke, I must tell you about their diet, which is precisely the same for everyone. When they feel hungry, they light a fire and roast some frogs on it – for there are lots of these creatures flying about in the air. Then, while the frogs are roasting, they draw up chairs round the fire, as if it were a sort of dining-room table, and gobble up the smoke.

That is all they ever eat, and to quench their thirst they just squeeze some air into a glass and drink that: the liquid produced is rather like dew. They never make water in the other sense, nor do they ever evacuate their bowels, having no hole in that part of their anatomy; and if this makes you wonder what they do with their wives, the answer is that they have a hole in the crook of the knee, conveniently situated immediately above the calf.

Bald men are considered very handsome on the Moon, and long hair is thought absolutely revolting; but on young stars like the comets, which have not yet lost their hair, it is just the other way round – or so at least I was told by a Comet-dweller who was having a holiday on the Moon when I was there.

I forgot to mention that they wear their beards a little above the knee; and they have not any toe-nails, for the very good reason that they have not any toes. What they have got, however, is a large cabbage growing just above the buttocks like a tail. It is always in flower, and never gets broken, even if they fall flat on their backs.

When they blow their noses, what comes out is extremely sour honey, and when they have been working hard or taking strenuous exercise, they sweat milk at every pore. Occasionally they turn it into cheese, by adding a few drops of the honey. They also make olive-oil out of onions, and the resulting fluid is extremely rich and has a very delicate perfume.

They have any number of vines, which produce not wine but water, for the grapes are made of ice; and there, in my view, you have the scientific explanation of hail-storms, which occur whenever the wind is strong enough to blow the fruit off those vines.

They use their stomachs as handbags for carrying things around in, for they can open and shut them at will. If you look inside one, there is nothing to be seen in the way of digestive organs, but the whole interior is lined with fur so that it can also be used as a centrally-heated pram for babies in cold weather.

The upper classes wear clothes made of flexible glass, but this material is rather expensive, so most people have to be content with copper textiles – for there is any amount of copper in the soil, which becomes as soft as wool when soaked in water.

I hardly like to tell you about their eyes, for fear you should think I am exaggerating, because it really does sound almost incredible. Still, I might as well risk it, so here goes: their eyes are detachable, so that you can take them out when you do not want to see anything and put them back when you do. Needless to say, it is not unusual to find someone who has mislaid his own eyes altogether and is always having to borrow some-one else's; and those who can afford it keep quite a number of spare pairs by them, just in case. As for ears, the Tree-men have wooden ones of their own, and everyone else has to be satisfied with a couple of plane-tree leaves instead.

I must just mention one other thing that I saw in the King's palace. It was a large mirror suspended over a fairly shallow tank. If you got into the tank, you could hear everything that was being said on the Earth, and if you looked in the mirror, you could see what was going on anywhere in the world, as clearly as if you were actually there yourself. I had a look at all the people I knew at home, but whether they saw me or not I really cannot say.

Well, that is what it was like on the Moon. If you do not believe me, go and see for yourself.

Finally we said good-bye to the King and his courtiers, boarded our ship, and set sail. As a parting gift, Endymion presented me with two glass shirts, five copper ones, and a complete suit of lupine armour, but unfortunately they got lost later on. We were also given air-protection by a thousand Vulture-riders, who escorted us for the first fifty miles of our journey.

After sailing past several islands without stopping, we eventu-ally arrived at Lucifer, where we found an advance-party of colonists already in occupation, so we landed there to replenish our water-supply. Then we re-embarked and set course for the Zodiac. This brought us within a few hundred yards of the Sun, and we very much wanted to land there too, but the wind made it impossible. Still, we saw enough to tell us that it was an extremely fertile country, with plenty of rivers and other natural advantages.

While we were coasting along, we were spotted by some Cloud-Centaurs in Phaethon's employment, who dived down and started circling the ship; but when they heard that we were under the protection of an allied power, they went away again. Our escort of Vulture-riders, had, of course, left us already.

We continued on the same course, but losing height all the time, for the next twenty-four hours, and the following evening arrived at a place called Lampborough, which is situated half-way between the Hyades and the Pleiades, and considerably below the Zodiac.

We went ashore, expecting to meet some human beings, but all we saw was a lot of lamps walking about. There were lamps transacting business in the market-place, and lamps working on the ships in the harbour. Most of them were wretched little creatures, who were obviously pretty dim, but there were one or two of immense power and brilliance, who were clearly the leading lights of the community. Each lamp had its own private house with its name on the door, and we could hear them chatting away to their neighbours over the garden fence. They were all perfectly friendly, and we had several offers of hospitality, but none of us quite liked the idea of eating or sleeping with them.

In the middle of the town was a law-court, in which the chief magistrate was holding an all-night session. Various lamps were summoned to appear before him, and those who failed to show up were sentenced to death as deserters: death, of course, meant being blown out. We went in and watched the proceedings for a while, and heard several lamps make excuses for not starting work promptly at lighting-up time. Among those present I suddenly recognized a lamp of my own, so I asked him how things were going at home, and he told me all the latest news.

After spending the night there, we started off again and soon found ourselves among the clouds, where, rather to our surprise, we sighted the famous city of Cloudcuckoobury.[3] The wind was too strong for us to land there, but we gathered that they had just been holding an election for President, and that the successful candidate was a man called Crow.

'So Aristophanes was telling the truth after all,' I said to myself. 'How wrong I was to doubt him!'

Three days later the sea became clearly visible, but there was still no sign of land, except for a few islands in the air, which were much too hot and bright for us to approach. Finally, about noon on the fourth day, the wind gradually subsided and enabled us to make a perfect landing on the surface of the sea.

It was wonderful to be able to dabble our fingers in the water again, and we promptly celebrated the occasion with what was left of our wine. Then we dived overboard and had a glorious swim, for the sea was quite calm and there were no big waves.

But as so often happens, this apparent change for the better was only the prelude to something infinitely worse. The fine weather continued for another two days, but at dawn on the third we suddenly saw a school of whales approaching from the East. The largest was about a hundred and seventy miles long, and he started coming towards us with his mouth open, churning up the water for miles around into a great cloud of foam, and baring his teeth, which were considerably taller than the biggest phallus you ever saw in your life, as sharp as needles, and as white as ivory. We kissed one another good-bye and waited for the inevitable.

The next moment he had gobbled us up, ship and all; but he never got a chance of chewing us, for the ship slipped through one of the gaps between his teeth and sailed straight into his stomach.

At first it was so dark inside that we could not see a thing, but after a while he opened his mouth again and we saw that we were in a sort of cave, which stretched away to an immense distance in every direction and would have been quite capable of accommodating a town with a population of anything up to ten thousand. It was littered with piles of fish and other sea-creatures, all mashed up together with sails and anchors and human bones and the remains of ships' cargoes, and in the middle of it was a tract of land which rose into a range of low hills. I suppose it was the sediment of all the muddy water that the whale had swallowed over the years. By this time it was covered with trees, and lots of other plants and vegetables were growing on it. In fact, the whole area, which was about twenty-seven miles in circumference, appeared to be under intensive cultivation. It was alive with various types of sea-bird, and kingfishers and seagulls were to be seen nesting in the trees.

For a long time we felt far too depressed to do anything, but eventually we pulled ourselves together and put props under the ship, after which we rubbed some sticks together to make a fire, and had as good a meal as we could manage in the circumstances. At least there was no shortage of fish, and we still had some of the water that we had taken on board at Lucifer.

Next morning we spent the first few hours admiring the view through the monster's mouth, whenever he happened to open it. One moment we would catch sight of some land, the next of some mountains. Sometimes there would be nothing to see but sky, sometimes we would have a glimpse of some islands – from all of which we concluded that the whale was dashing about at high speed from one end of the sea to the other. Before long we began to get used to it, and thinking we might as well see all there was to be seen of our new home, I set off with seven others for a stroll through the woods.

We had scarcely gone half a mile before we came across a temple, with an inscription saying that it was dedicated to Poseidon. A little further on we saw some graves, complete with tombstones, and not far off a spring of fresh water. The next moment we heard a dog barking and noticed some smoke rising above the trees. Assuming that it came from a house of some kind, we began to walk faster and suddenly came face to face with an old man and a boy, who were busily engaged in weeding and watering a kitchen-garden.

We came to an abrupt standstill, hardly knowing whether to feel pleased or frightened, and their reaction was evidently much the same, for at first they just stared at us without saying a word. The old man was the first to recover.

'My dear sirs!' he exclaimed. 'Who on earth are you? Are you sea-gods of some kind, or merely unfortunate human beings like us? Oh yes, that's what we are. We were born and bred on dry land like anyone else, but now we seem to have turned into some species of fish, for here we are swimming about inside this great sea-creature! To tell you the truth, I really don't know what's happened to us. I shouldn't be at all surprised to hear that we were dead – but I prefer to think we're still alive.'

'We're human beings too, sir, I assure you,' I replied. 'We haven't been here very long, though – we were only swallowed yesterday – and we were just taking a walk through the woods to see what they were like. However, some good angel seems to have brought us together, so now we've the comfort of knowing we're not the only ones in this situation. But do tell us who you are and how you got here.'

'Let's keep all that', he said, 'until after dinner.'

With these words he took us into his house, which was quite a comfortable one, with built-in bunks and all the usual conveniences, and gave us an excellent meal of fish, vegetables, and fruit. When we had had as much as we wanted, he asked us how we came to be there, so I described the whole series of our adventures, from the beginning of the great storm right up to our arrival in the whale.

'What an amazing story!' he exclaimed when I had finished. 'And now I suppose it's my turn. Well, I'm a Cypriot by birth, and one day, many years ago, I started off on a trading expedition to Italy, taking my son here and quite a lot of my servants with me. I had a varied assortment of goods on board a large vessel – you probably noticed the remains of it in the throat as you came in.

'All went well until we were approaching Sicily, but then we were caught in a gale and three days later found ourselves in the Atlantic. There we met the whale, who swallowed our ship with every man on board, and we two were the only survivors. So we buried all the others, built a temple to Poseidon, and have been here ever since, spending most of our time growing vegetables to eat, and supplementing our diet with fish and fruit.

'On the whole, the conditions aren't too bad. You can see for yourselves, there's no shortage of timber, and there are several vines in the forest, which make quite decent wine. There are plenty of soft leaves to stuff our pillows and mattresses with, and any amount of firewood.

'When we get bored, we amuse ourselves by laying snares for the birds that fly in through the mouth, or climbing out on to the gills and catching some fresh fish – or merely having a shower-bath, for it's an excellent place for that too. Oh yes, and there's a salt-water lake not far from here, about two miles round and full of all sorts of fish. We often go swimming and sailing there – for we've got a small boat, which I built myself.

'It must be twenty-seven years since we were swallowed, so by now we've got quite used to it. The only trouble is, we simply can't stand the neighbours. They're such an uncivilized lot, one really can't have anything to do with them.'

'Do you mean to say', I asked, 'that there are some other people living inside this creature?'

'Of course there are,' he replied. 'Hundreds of them – and an uglier pack of brutes you never saw. The Western, that's to say the tail-end, part of the forest is inhabited by people who look like kippers, except that they have eyes like eels and faces like lobsters. They live on raw meat and are very aggressive. Over towards the right wall of the stomach is a colony of mermen – I don't know what else to call them, for above the waist they're ordinary human beings, and below it they're just plain lizards. Still, they're much less troublesome than some of the others. On the left are some people with claws instead of hands, and some friends of theirs who have heads like tunny-fish. The area in the middle is occupied by crab-like creatures with feet like turbots, who can run very fast and are extremely quarrelsome. Most of the land towards the East, that is, towards the mouth, is uninhabited, as it's liable to be flooded by the sea, but even so those wretched turbot-feet have the impudence to charge me five hundred oysters per annum for the lease of it. Well, that's what the neighbours are like, and the problem is, how can one maintain a reasonable standard of life in such conditions?'

'How many of them are there altogether?' I asked.

'Oh, a thousand at the very least,' he answered.

'What sort of weapons have they got?'

'None whatever, unless you count fishbones.'

'In that case,' said I, 'our wisest plan would be to go to war with them, for we've got all the latest equipment, and if we can once show them who's master, we'll have no more trouble.'

Everyone agreed to this proposal, so we returned to our ship and began to prepare for war. As a quarter-day was approaching, we thought the best way of provoking hostilities would be to refuse to pay the rent. Accordingly, when an official arrived to collect it, we merely sent him away with a flea in his ear. This made the crabmen very angry with Scintharus – for that was our host's name – and they came rushing towards us in full force, howling for vengeance. As soon as we realized that they were on the warpath, we armed ourselves and awaited their attack, having previously arranged an ambush of twenty-five men, who had instructions to fall upon the enemy's rear the moment they had gone past.

Everything went according to plan. Our ambushed troops closed in on the crabmen from behind and started cutting them to pieces, while the other twenty-five of us – for Scintharus and his son were taking the places of our two cross-fertilizers – made a savage onslaught from the opposite direction.

Eventually we managed to rout them, and chased them all the way back to their holes killing a hundred and seventy in the process. Our only casualty was the steersman, who was run through from behind with the rib of a red mullet.

That night we camped out on the battlefield, and stuck up a dolphin's vertebral column by way of a trophy. Next morning the news got round to all the other inhabitants of the whale, who joined forces and renewed the attack. On the right wing were the people who looked like kippers, under the command of Field-Marshal Anchovy, on the left the people with heads like tunny-fish, and in the centre the people with claws instead of hands. The mermen had stayed at home, having decided to remain neutral.

We made contact with the enemy not far from the temple of Poseidon, and immediately came to grips with them, uttering blood-curdling yells that went echoing round and round the whale's cavernous interior. It did not take us long to rout our unarmed opponents and chase them back into the forest, and from then on the whole country was under our control. After a while they sent envoys to arrange for the burial of their dead and discuss terms of peace; but we had no intention of making peace just yet, and next day we systematically destroyed every single one of them except the mermen, who scuttled away through the gills and dived into the sea the moment they saw what was going on.

After that we proceeded to explore the country at our leisure, and now that all hostile elements had been eliminated, we settled down to a life of luxury, in which we spent most of our time playing games, or hunting, or cultivating the vines, or picking fruit off the trees. In fact we were like prisoners in a very comfortable gaol, where the regulations allowed one to do exactly what one liked, except escape.

This went on for a year and eight months, but on the fifth day of the ninth month, at the second opening of the whale's mouth – for he opened his mouth regularly once an hour, which was our only method of telling the time – at two o'mouth precisely, as I said, we suddenly heard a tremendous row going on outside, in which we could distinguish shouts of command and the splashing of oars. We were so intrigued that we clambered right up into the mouth and stood immediately behind the teeth, where we had an excellent view of the most amazing spectacle that I have ever seen: giants three hundred feet high sailing about on islands, just as we do on ships.

I know you will think this part of my story quite incredible, but I am going to tell you about it all the same. The islands in question were extremely long, though not particularly high. Each was approximately eleven miles in circumference, and carried a crew of about a hundred and twenty. Some of these were sitting on either side of the island and rowing in perfect time, not with oars, but with enormous cypress trees, complete with all their original branches and leaves. Behind them, at what you might call the stern, was a steersman standing on the top of a hill and operating a bronze rudder about half a mile long, and at the prow were another forty giants or so, fully armed and exactly like human beings, except that they had flames instead of hair, which enabled them to dispense with helmets.

Each island had a lot of trees growing on it, which bellied out in the wind and enabled the helmsman to move his craft in any direction he chose, but the principal motive power was provided by the rowers, who were kept in time by a man specially detailed for the purpose, and could send their island zooming along at a fantastic rate of knots.

At first there were only two or three of these islands to be seen, but eventually about six hundred made their appearance, and as soon as they had taken up their battle-stations a great naval action began. Some of them collided head-on, others were rammed amidships and started to sink, and several pairs became inextricably entangled, whereupon the troops posted at the prows boarded one another's islands, and desperate hand-to-hand fighting ensued, in which no prisoners were taken.

Instead of grappling irons they used giant octopuses with cables attached to them, which wound their tentacles round the trees of the enemy island and thus prevented it from getting away. They also bombarded one another with oysters the size of farm-carts and sponges a hundred feet in diameter.

Apparently the whole thing had started because Seabooze, the commander of one fleet, had misappropriated a herd of dolphins belonging to Quickswim, the commander of the other, for we could hear them hurling abuse at one another, and each side was using its leader's name as a sort of battle-cry. Eventually Quickswim won, after sinking a hundred and fifty enemy islands and capturing another three, complete with their crews. The rest went full speed astern and lit out for the horizon. Their enemies pursued them for a while, but when it began to get dark they gave it up and came back to deal with the wrecks. After taking control of most of the enemy ones, they proceeded to salvage eighty or so of their own which had been sunk, and finally, to commemorate their victory, they stuck up one of the captured islands on top of the whale's head.

That night they camped out on the creature's back, having moored some of their islands to it with cables and left the rest to ride at anchor nearby. Oh yes, they had anchors too – very strong ones, made entirely of glass. Next morning they held a thanksgiving service, dug graves in the whale's skin and buried their dead in them, and eventually sailed away in excellent spirits singing some sort of triumphal chant.

So much for the battle of the islands.

2

After a while I got rather bored with life inside the whale, and started trying to think of some method of escape. Our first plan was to dig our way out through the creature's right side, but when we had constructed a tunnel nearly half a mile long without getting anywhere, we abandoned that idea and decided instead to set fire to the forest, in the hope that this would kill the whale and thus facilitate our exit. So, working gradually from the tail-end towards the mouth, we began committing systematic arson.

For seven days and nights the monster remained completely unaware of it, but after eight or nine days we gathered that he was feeling rather off colour, because he did not open his mouth quite so much. By the tenth day some of the flesh had gone gangrenous and began to stink, and on the twelfth we suddenly realized to our horror that if we did not jam something between his jaws next time he opened his mouth, we ran a serious risk of being buried alive in a corpse.

So before it was too late we managed to wedge his mouth open with two great wooden beams, after which we proceeded to recommission our ship, stocking up with as much water and other necessaries as possible and inviting Scintharus to take over the job of steersman.

By next morning the whale was thoroughly dead. We hauled the ship up into the mouth, pushed it through one of the gaps between the teeth, and steadying it with ropes belayed round the teeth themselves, lowered it gently into the sea. Then we climbed on to the creature's back, where, beside the trophy commemorating the sea-fight, we made a thank-offering to Poseidon. As there was no wind, we camped out there for the next three days but on the fourth we returned to our ship and sailed away. During the first few hours we came across several corpses left over from the battle of the islands, and actually beached our ship on one of them, in order to take its measurements – which surprised us considerably.

When we had been sailing along for several days with a gentle breeze behind us, a bitter wind sprang up from the north and caused such a sharp drop in temperature that the whole sea froze solid – not merely on the surface, but to a depth of approximately four hundred fathoms, so that one could safely step out of the ship and walk about on the ice.

The wind went on blowing steadily, and we were beginning to find the cold quite unbearable, when Scintharus suddenly had a bright idea. On his advice we dug a huge cave under the water, in which we lit a fire and lived very comfortably for the next four weeks or so on a diet of fish, which we hacked out of the sea around us. When supplies finally ran out, we emerged from our shelter, prised the ship out of the ice, put on full sail, and went skidding along over the slippery surface as smoothly and pleasantly as if we had been sailing in the conventional manner.

Five days later there was a thaw, and the sea turned back into water. We continued our voyage, and about thirty-four miles further on came to a small desert island, where we collected some fresh water – for we had used up the last lot – and shot a couple of wild bulls before putting to sea again. The bulls in question wore their horns immediately below their eyes, in accordance with Momus's recommendation, instead of on top of their heads.

Shortly afterwards we entered a sea of milk, in which we sighted a white island with large numbers of vines growing on it. This island turned out to be an enormous hunk of cheese, of rather tough consistency (as we soon found out when we started eating it) and measuring nearly three miles in circumference. There were plenty of grapes on the vines, but when we tried squeezing them in the hope of making some wine, all that came out was milk.

In the middle of the island someone had built a temple. The inscription informed us that it was dedicated to Galatea, the lady whose complexion has been described as whiter than cream-cheese.[4] We stayed there for five days, living quite literally on the fat of the land and drinking milk from the grapes, and learned that the whole place belonged to the sea-nymph Gorgonzola. Apparently Poseidon gave it to her after their divorce, by way of alimony.

On the morning of the sixth day we started off again, and for the next two days were wafted by a gentle breeze over an almost waveless sea. Then, just as we had noticed that we were no longer sailing through milk, but through salt-water of the normal colour, we saw a lot of people running towards us. They were exactly like ourselves except that their feet were made of cork – and that, I suspect, was the reason why they were called Corkfoots. We were most surprised at first to see them bounding along over the waves instead of sinking through them, but they seemed to take it absolutely for granted. They came up and spoke to us in our own language, explaining that they lived in the Isle of Cork and were in a great hurry to get back there. They trotted along beside us for a while, then, wishing us *bon voyage*, turned off to the left and were soon out of sight.

A few hours later some islands came into view. Quite near us on the left was a town built on top of a huge round cork, which we took to be the place that our fellow-travellers had been making for. Farther away towards the right were five great mountainous islands which looked as if they were on fire, and straight ahead of us, but at least fifty miles away, a long low island appeared on the horizon.

When we got a bit closer to it, we became aware of a wonderful perfume floating about in the atmosphere, of much the same kind, no doubt, as the one that Herodotus describes[5] as emanating from Arabia. To give you some idea how pleasant it was, it was like smelling roses, narcissi, hyacinths, lilies, violets, myrtles, bays, and flowers of the wild vine, all at the same time. It made us feel that our luck had turned at last, and following our delighted noses, we drew gradually nearer and nearer to the island.

Soon we were close enough to make out several large harbours, in which the water was absolutely calm, and several limpid streams flowing gently into the sea. Then we saw meadows and woods, and heard birds singing on the shore and on the branches of the trees. The whole atmosphere of the place was light and airy, owing to a pleasant breeze which kept the trees in perpetual motion and blew through the branches with a delightful humming sound, rather like the effect of hanging up a flute in the open air. And far away in the distance we could hear a confused uproar which was not in the least alarming, for it was only the sort of noise you get at a party, when some of the guests are playing flutes or guitars, and some of them are singing, and the rest are just clapping their hands in time with the music.

We found it all so attractive that we did not hesitate to drop anchor in one of the harbours and go ashore, leaving Scintharus and two others on board to look after the ship. As we were walking across a flowery meadow, we were stopped and arrested by the local police, who handcuffed us with daisy-chains – which are the most powerful form of constraint employed in those parts – and took us off for trial before the chief magistrate. On the way there they informed us that we were on the Island of the Blest, and that the magistrate's name was Rhadamanthus.

When we arrived at the court, we found that there were three other cases to be heard before ours came up. The point at issue in the first was whether Ajax Major should be allowed to mix with the other heroes or not, in view of the fact that he had gone mad and committed suicide. After hearing all the arguments for and against, Rhadamanthus finally decided that the accused should be given a dose of hellebore and remanded for psychological treatment by Hippocrates, until such time as he should recover his sanity, when he should be free to join the other heroes.

The second was a matrimonial case, in which both Theseus and Menelaus claimed conjugal rights over Helen. The verdict was that she should cohabit with Menelaus, on the ground that he had suffered considerable inconvenience and danger on her account, and also that Theseus had three wives already, viz. Hippolyta, Phaedra, and Ariadne.

The third case was a question of precedence between Alexander the Great and Hannibal. Rhadamanthus gave his verdict in favour of Alexander, who was then allotted a throne beside Cyrus the First of Persia.

At last it was our turn, and Rhadamanthus asked us what excuse we could give for daring to set foot in that holy place while we were still alive, so we told him the whole story. He adjourned the case for several hours while he consulted with his colleagues on the bench, who included, among others, Aristides the Just. Having finally made up his mind, he delivered his verdict as follows:

'For your folly in leaving home and for your idle curiosity, you will be called to account when you die. In the meantime you may remain here and share the privileges of the heroes for a period not exceeding seven months.'

As he spoke these words, our handcuffs fell off of their own accord. We were then formally set at liberty, and escorted into the town to join the heroes.

The town in question is built entirely of gold, except for the outer wall, which is of emerald and contains seven gates, each composed of a solid chunk of cinnamon. The whole area inside the wall is paved with ivory, all the temples are constructed of beryl, and the altars, on which they usually sacrifice a hundred oxen at a time, consist of single slabs of amethyst. The town is encircled by a river of best-quality perfume, nearly two hundred feet across and approximately ninety feet deep, so that you can swim about in it without any risk of stubbing your toe on the bottom. By way of Turkish baths, they have large glass houses heated by burning cinnamon, with hot and cold dew laid on.

Their clothes are made of very fine cobwebs, dyed crimson, but they have not any bodies to put them on, for the town is exclusively inhabited by disembodied spirits. However, in-substantial as they are, they give an impression of complete solidity, and move and think and speak like ordinary human beings. Altogether, it is as if their naked souls were walking about clothed in the outward semblance of their bodies, for until you try touching them, it is quite impossible to detect their incorporeal nature. I suppose the best way of putting it would be to say that they are like walking shadows – except, of course, that they are not black.

Nobody grows old there, for they all stay the age they were when they first arrived, and it never gets dark. On the other hand, it never gets really light either, and they live in a sort of perpetual twilight, such as we have just before sunrise. Instead of four seasons they have only one, for with them it is always spring, and the only wind that blows comes from the west. All kinds of flowers grow there, and all kinds of garden-trees, especially shady ones. The vines bear fruit twelve times a year – in other words, once a month – and we were given to understand that the pomegranate-trees, the apple-trees, and all the other fruit-trees bore fruit no fewer than thirteen times a year, for two separate crops were normally produced in the month of Minober. As for the corn, instead of ordinary ears it sprouts mushroom-shaped loaves of bread, all ready to eat.

Scattered about the town are three hundred and sixty-five water-springs, an equal number of honey-springs, five hundred scent-springs (but these, I admit, are rather smaller than the others), seven rivers of milk, and eight rivers of wine. In spite of these urban amenities, however, most of the social life goes on outside the town, in a place called the Elysian Fields, which is a meadow beautifully situated in the middle of a wood. Under the shade of this wood, which is full of all sorts of different trees, a delightful party is permanently in progress.

The guests recline at their ease on beds of flowers, and are waited on by the winds, which do everything but serve the wine. However, there is no difficulty about that, for there are plenty of big glass-trees all round. In case you do not know what glass-trees are, they are trees made of very clear glass, which bear fruit in the form of wine-glasses of every conceivable shape and size. So every guest picks one or two of these glasses the moment he arrives, and puts them down beside him, whereupon they immediately become full of wine. That takes care of the drink problem, and the floral decorations are arranged by the nightingales and other song-birds from the neighbouring meadows, which pick up flowers in their beaks and rain them down over the guests, singing sweetly all the while.

Finally the heroes are even saved the trouble of putting on their own scent by the following ingenious system: specially absorbent clouds suck up perfume from the five hundred springs and from the river, after which they go and hover over the party; then the winds give them a gentle squeeze, and down comes the scent in a fine spray like dew.

After dinner they usually have some kind of musical or literary performance, and their favourite turn is Homer reciting his own poems – for he is generally to be found there, sitting next to Odysseus. They also have choral singing by young boys and girls, conducted and accompanied by someone like Eunomus, or Arion, or Anacreon, or Stesichorus, who has, I am happy to say, been forgiven by Helen for the rude things he wrote about her. When the boys and girls have done their stuff, the floor is taken by a choir of swans and swallows and nightingales, who sing to what you might call a woodwind accompaniment, that is, to the music of the wind blowing through the branches of the trees.

But what really makes the party go with a swing is the fact that there are two springs in that meadow, one of laughter and the other of pleasure. So the first thing a guest does when he gets there is to take a sip from each of these springs, and from then on he never stops laughing and having a wonderful time.

And now I want to tell you about some of the distinguished people that I saw there. Among those present were all the demigods, and all the Greek kings who took part in the Trojan War, except for Ajax Minor, who was said to be on one of the Islands of the Damned, serving a sentence for rape. There were also several foreigners, including both the Cyruses from Persia, Anacharsis from Scythia, Zamolxis from Thrace, and Numa Pompilius from Italy. Then there was Lycurgus from Sparta, and all the Seven Sages except Periander.

I noticed Socrates having a chat with Nestor and Palamedes. He was surrounded by a group of extremely attractive young men, among whom I recognized Hyacinthus, Narcissus, and Hylas. I got the impression that he was in love with Hyacinthus, for he was always firing difficult questions at him; but whatever the motive for them, these discussion-classes of his had apparently made him most unpopular with Rhadamanthus, who had often threatened to banish him from the island if he did not stop talking shop and ruining the atmosphere of the party with his peculiar brand of irony.

There was no sign of Plato, and I was told later that he had gone to live in his *Republic*, where he was cheerfully submitting to his own *Laws*. But hedonists like Aristippus and Epicurus were naturally the life and soul of the party: they were such absolutely charming fellows, and so easy to get along with. Aesop was much in demand for his talents as a *raconteur*, and Diogenes had so far modified his views that he had married Lais, the courtesan, and was always getting drunk and trying to dance on the table.

None of the Stoics were present. Rumour had it that they were still clambering up the steep hill of Virtue, and I heard that Chrysippus would in any case not be allowed on the island until he had taken at least four doses of hellebore.

As for the Sceptics, it appeared that they were extremely anxious to get there, but still could not quite make up their minds whether or not the island really existed. I suspect that they were also rather afraid of what Rhadamanthus might do to them, for having talked so much about 'suspension of judgement', they probably feared that he might turn out to be a hanging judge. In spite of this, several of them had apparently started out in company with people who had in fact arrived, but either they had been too lazy to keep up with the others and so got left behind, or else they had changed their minds and turned back when they were half-way there.

Well, I think that covers all the most interesting people that I met there, and it only remains to say that the most respected member of the community was Achilles, with Theseus a close runner-up.

And now perhaps you would like to hear something about their attitude to sex. They see nothing indecent in sexual intercourse, whether heterosexual or homosexual, and indulge in it quite openly, in full view of everyone. The only exception was Socrates, who was always swearing that his relations with young men were purely Platonic, but nobody believed him for a moment, and Hyacinthus and Narcissus gave first-hand evidence to the contrary. As for the women, they are shared indiscriminately by all the men, and there are no such things as jealous husbands. In that respect at least they are all good Communists. Similarly the boys cooperate freely with anyone who makes advances to them, and never raise the slightest objection.

I had not been there for more than two or three days before I seized an opportunity of going up to Homer and asking him, among other things, what country he really came from, explaining that this was still a great subject of literary research.

'Don't I know it!' he said. 'One school of thought claims that I come from Chios, another from Smyrna, and a third from Colophon. In point of fact I come from Babylon, and my real name is Tigranes, which means "pigeon" in Babylonian. My present nickname dates from an occasion when I was carried off to Greece as a hostage. Within a few days I'd managed to escape and find my way home again, and after that my friends never called me anything but Homer.'

I then asked if the textual experts were right in rejecting certain lines in his poems as spurious.

'Of course not,' he replied. 'I wrote every word of them. The trouble about these wretched editors is that they've got no taste.'

Having satisfied my curiosity on this point, I asked him what was the precise significance of the use of the word *wrath* in the opening sentence of the *Iliad*.

'No significance whatsoever,' he answered. 'It was the first word that came into my head.'

After that I wanted to know if the *Odyssey* was, as many critics think, an earlier work than the *Iliad*.

'Certainly not,' said Homer.

There was no need to ask if he was really blind, for I could see for myself that he was nothing of the sort, but I questioned him closely about several other things, for whenever he seemed to have a free moment I used to go and talk to him, and he was delightfully frank in all his answers – especially after he won that lawsuit of his. You see, Thersites brought an action against him for making fun of him in the *Iliad*, [6] but the plaintiff rather overstated his case by suing him, not for libel, but for assault and battery, and Odysseus, who appeared as Counsel for the Defence, had no difficulty in getting his friend off.

About this time there were two new arrivals. The first was Pythagoras, who after seven transmigrations of soul had finally completed his life-cycle. I noticed that the whole of his right side was made of pure gold. His application for membership was accepted, though there was some doubt whether his name should be entered as Pythagoras or Euphorbus, as it originally was. The second was Empedocles, looking rather the worse for wear after being thoroughly cooked in Mount Etna. In spite of all his efforts to gain admission, this application was turned down flat.

Shortly afterwards the heroes held their annual Funeral Games to celebrate their own deaths. The programme was arranged by Achilles and Theseus, who had both had a lot of experience in that line. It would take too long to go through all the events, but I will just give you a rapid summary. The wrestling competition was won by Heracles' son Carus, who managed to beat Odysseus in the finals. The boxing was a draw between Arius the Egyptian (the one who is buried at Corinth) and Epeius. No prize was offered for all-in wrestling, and who won the mile I simply cannot remember. As for the poetry competition, Homer's entry was by far the best, but for some reason or other the prize was awarded to Hesiod. Incidentally, all the prizes in question were crowns of peacock's feathers.

Just as the games were ending, a report came through that the convicts on the Islands of the Damned had overpowered their warders and broken out, and were heading for the Island of the Blest. The ringleaders were said to be Phalaris, Busiris, Diomedes of Thrace, and a lot of other unpleasant characters like Sciron and Sinis, who used to amuse himself by stringing up passers-by on the tops of pine-trees.

Rhadamanthus immediately instructed the heroes to fall in on the beach, under the command of Theseus, Achilles, and Ajax Major, who had responded satisfactorily to psychological treatment. A battle then took place between the opposing forces, and the heroes won a resounding victory, for which Achilles was largely responsible. Socrates, however, who was stationed on the right wing, also put up a very good show – far better than he did at the battle of Delium, for instead of running away when he saw the enemy approaching, he stood his ground and looked them firmly in the eye, on the strength of which he was afterwards awarded a Garden of Honour in the suburbs, where he collected all his friends and held innumerable discussion-classes. I believe he called it his Academy for the Corruption of the Dead.

The escaped convicts were rearrested and sent back to serve even heavier sentences, and Homer wrote an epic poem on the subject of the battle. When I finally said good-bye to him, he gave me a copy of it for publication over here, but unfortunately it got lost, like everything else. However, I can still remember the first few lines, which went like this:

> Of Hell's first revolution, and the fright
> Of that rebellious crew, when heroes dead
> Repulsed them, and preserved their blissful isle,
> Sing, heavenly Muse!

In accordance with local tradition, we celebrated the victory by eating enormous quantities of baked beans – all except Pythagoras, who registered his disapproval of our bean-feast by sitting apart and refusing to eat a thing.

When we had been there six months and were half-way through the seventh, another sensational incident took place. Scintharus's son, Cinyras, had by this time grown into a very good-looking young man and developed a violent passion for Helen. She was obviously madly in love with him too, for they were always exchanging meaning glances across the dinner-table and drinking each other's healths, or getting up and going for walks in the wood by themselves. Eventually Cinyras felt so desperate about it that he made up his mind to run away with her. She was all for it, and their plan was to go and live on one of the neighbouring islands, either the Isle of Cork or the Isle of Cheese. Three of my most enterprising associates were also in the plot, but Scintharus had not been let into the secret, for his son knew that he would only try to stop him.

So one night, as soon as it got dark – I was in no condition to interfere, for I had fallen asleep over my wine – they slipped away when the others were not looking, took Helen on board our ship, and hurriedly put to sea. About midnight Menelaus woke up and felt for his wife. Finding she had disappeared, he yelled for his brother, and went rushing off with him to tell Rhadamanthus. Just before dawn the coastguards reported that the ship was still in sight, so Rhadamanthus promptly detailed fifty heroes to embark in a fast vessel, constructed of a single stalk of asphodel, and set off in pursuit. The heroes rowed like mad, and about midday overtook the runaway couple just as they were entering the sea of milk – in fact they very nearly got away with it.

Having taken our ship in tow, using a daisy-chain as a tow-rope, the heroes rowed back to the island, where Helen was escorted ashore in floods of tears, feeling terribly embarrassed and covering her face in her hands, while Cinyras and his three accomplices were brought before Rhadamanthus. After satisfying himself that there were no other accessories to the crime he sentenced them to forty strokes of the mallow, and transportation to the Islands of the Damned. The Court also decided to cancel our immigration permit, and give us twenty-four hours notice to leave the island.

I was so depressed at the thought of leaving all those good things behind me and starting off on my travels again, that I burst into tears – until I was informed by the Bench that in a very few years I should come back to them, and that a throne and a couch in the Elysian Fields were being reserved for me in advance. This comforted me a little, and after the trial I went up to Rhadamanthus and begged him to let me know what Fate had in store for me, or at least to give me some help with my navigation. He told me that I had a long way to go yet, and a great many dangers to face, but that I should get home eventually, though he would not like to say exactly when.

'You see those islands?' he said, pointing them out to me. 'Well, those five with the flames coming out of them are the Islands of the Damned, and that sixth one in the distance is the Island of Dreams. Beyond that again is Ogygia, where Calypso lives, but you can't see it from here. If you carry straight on past all seven of them, you'll come to a great continent on the opposite side of the world from where you live. There you'll have some very odd experiences and meet some very peculiar people, most of them quite uncivilized, and in due course you'll find your way back to Europe.'

He then presented me with a mallow which he had pulled up out of the ground, and told me to pray to it in times of danger. He also gave me a lot of good advice on how to behave when I finally got home, such as never to use a sword to poke the fire, never to eat lupines, and never to sleep with boys above the age of eighteen.

'Keep those rules in mind', he concluded, 'and you can be sure of coming back here.'

So I got everything ready for the voyage, and that night the heroes gave us a farewell dinner. Next morning I went up to Homer and asked him to write me a couple of lines suitable for an inscription. He was only too glad to oblige, and I inscribed them on a tablet of beryl, which I put up near the harbour. They read as follows:

> Lucian came here, saw all there was to see,
> Then sailed back home across the wine-dark sea.

In spite of the court-order, we were allowed to spend one more night on the island, but next day we really did have to go, and all the heroes were there to see us off. Just before I went on board, Odysseus came up to me, and when Penelope was looking the other way slipped a letter into my hand, addressed:

> Calypso,
> Island of Ogygia.

Rhadamanthus had thoughtfully sent Nauplius, the famous pilot, with us, in case we landed on one of the Islands of the Damned and the authorities arrested us, under the impression that we were there in a different capacity. The wisdom of this precaution struck us very forcibly when we exchanged the scented atmosphere of the Island of the Blest for a horrible smell of burning. It suggested the simultaneous combustion of pitch, sulphur, and petroleum, combined with the roasting of human flesh, and we found it almost unbearable. The air was black with smoke, and a fine rain of pitch started coming down all over us. Then we began to hear the crack of whips, and the screams of countless souls in torment.

Well, I do not know what the other islands were like, but the one we landed on was surrounded by steep cliffs, all dry and stony, without any sign of trees or water. However, we managed to climb up over the rocks by a path overgrown with thorns and thistles, and picked our way across some incredibly ugly country until we came to the prison itself.

Before going in, we stopped and stared in amazement at its extraordinary topography. The whole area of ground inside it sprouted a thick crop of sharp knives and stakes, and was enclosed by three rivers, the outer one of mud, the middle one of blood, and the inner one of fire. This last was so wide as to be quite impassable, flowed exactly like water, and was furrowed with waves like the sea. There were lots of fish swimming about in it, some like big torches, and others like live coals, which were apparently know as Coaleys.

The only way in was across a narrow bridge spanning all three rivers, which was guarded by Timon of Athens; but Nauplius boldly led the way past him, and started pointing out some of the prisoners who were receiving punishment. Many of them were kings, but just as many were ordinary people like ourselves, and we actually recognized one or two of them. For instance, we saw Cinyras strung up by his offending part over a smoky fire.

We were then taken on a conducted tour of the whole prison, and given a summary of each prisoner's crimes. It appeared that the worst punishments of all were reserved for those who had written Untrue Histories, a category which included Ctesias of Cnidos and Herodotus. As my conscience was absolutely clear in that respect I was able to watch the poor fellows' sufferings without any serious fears for my own future; but it was a horrible sight all the same, so we got away as soon as we could and returned to our ship, after which we said good-bye to Nauplius and set sail for the Island of Dreams.

We soon caught sight of it not far ahead of us, but its outlines remained blurred and shadowy, as though it was still a long way off, and like a dream it kept retreating as we approached and doing its best to disappear in the distance. Finally, however, we managed to overtake it, and late that afternoon we came to anchor in the Harbour of Sleep and landed near the ivory gates, not far from the temple of the Cock. We set off immediately to explore the town, and saw all sorts of dreams walking about the streets; but before I tell you about them, I want to describe the town itself, since nobody but Homer has ever so much as mentioned its existence, and his account is not entirely accurate.

All round the town is a forest of treelike poppies and mandragoras with lots of bats nesting in the branches – for no other form of bird-life is to be found on the island. Close under the city walls, which are very high and all the colours of the rainbow, flows the river of Darkness, and beside one of the city gates is a spring called the Fountain of the Log, and another called the Well of the Eight Hours.

Talking of gates, by the way, Homer was quite wrong when he said that there were only two of them.[7] There are in fact four, two opening on to the Plain of Inertia, one of steel and one of earthenware, and two giving access to the harbour and the sea, one of horn and one of ivory. The landward gates are used as exits for nightmares, and the seaward ones for true and false dreams. Needless to say, we went in by the gate of horn, which is exclusively reserved for dreams of the former type.

On the right as you enter the town is the temple of Night, for she and the Cock are the two great local deities, and on your left is the palace of Sleep, who is the real governor of the island although he delegates some of his authority to a couple of gentlemen called Muddlehead and Wishfulfilment. In the centre of the market-place is a spring called the Fountain of Coma, and just behind it is the temple of Reality and Illusion, where the residents go for analysis by a specially appointed dream-interpreter called Contradiction.

As for the dreams themselves, they varied enormously in character and appearance. Some were tall and handsome, with soft and beautiful complexions, and some were just ugly little toughs. Some seemed to be made of pure gold, and some were obviously cheap and shoddy. One or two of them had wings, and looked genuinely superhuman, while others were merely dressed up to represent kings and gods and so on.

We recognized several of our recurrent dreams, who came up and greeted us like old friends and invited us into their houses. There they put us to sleep and gave us a reception which was royal in every sense of the word, for they promised to make us kings and treated us as if we were kings already. Some of them were even kind enough to take us back to our homes for an hour or two, so that we could see how our families were getting on.

We stayed with them for a month, fast asleep and having a glorious time. Then suddenly there was a great crash of thunder which woke us all up. We jumped out of bed, ran back to our ship, and pausing only to take a fresh stock of food on board, set sail for the island of Ogygia.

We arrived there two days later, but before going ashore I opened the letter that Odysseus had given me and read its contents, which were as follows:

My darling Calypso,

I thought you might like to know what's been happening to me since I said good-bye to you and sailed away on that home-made raft of mine. Well, first of all I was shipwrecked, but a charming young lady called Leucothea saved my life and helped me to get ashore. I landed in Phaeacia, and the people there were good enough to arrange transport back to Ithaca, where I found a lot of young men living at my expense and making passes at my wife. I'd just about finished killing them when I was killed myself by Telegonus, who's apparently a son of mine by Circe, though I didn't know it at the time. So now

I'm on the Island of the Blest, wishing to goodness I'd never left you and kicking myself for turning down your offer of immortality. But as soon as I get a chance I'm going to slip away from here and come and see you.

Yours ever,
ODYSSEUS

There was also a P.S. suggesting that she might like to give us a meal while we were there.

We started walking inland, and it did not take us long to find her cave, for it was exactly as Homer described it, and there she was in the doorway spinning wool. I handed her the letter, and the first thing she did when she had read it was to burst into tears; but after a while she remembered her duties as a hostess and invited us in to dinner. The food was excellent, and while we were eating it she asked us a lot of questions about Odysseus, and also about Penelope – for instance, what did she look like, and was she really as well-behaved as Odysseus used to make out? We gave her the sort of answers that we thought she wanted to hear, and then went and spent the night on the beach beside our ship.

Next morning we set sail in a very high wind, and after battling with it for a couple of days, were unlucky enough to run into some pirates. They were savages from one of the neighbouring islands, who evidently made a practice of attacking all the shipping in their area. Their own ships were made of enormous dried pumpkins, about ninety feet in diameter, hollowed out and fitted with bamboo masts and pumpkin-leaves for sails.

Two of these vessels came bearing down on us and started bombarding us with pumpkin-pips, which wounded many of us severely. However, we managed to give as good as we got, and towards midday we sighted several other vessels coming up behind them, which apparently belonged to some enemies of theirs, for as soon as they saw them they lost all interest in us and prepared to fight them instead. We seized this opportunity to sail away at full speed, leaving them hard at it. It was fairly obvious who was going to win, for the new arrivals outnumbered their opponents by five to two, and their ships were much stronger, consisting as they did of hollowed-out nutshells, which were also about ninety feet in diameter.

As soon as we had got well away from them, we dressed our casualties' wounds, and from then on went fully armed day and night, for we never knew when we might not be attacked. Sure enough, just before sunset twenty more pirates suddenly darted out at us from an apparently uninhabited island. They were mounted on large dolphins, which neighed like horses as they bounded across the waves. The pirates quickly surrounded our ship and started pelting us at close range with dried squids and crabs' eyes, but as soon as we let fly with our arrows and javelins, so many of them were wounded that the whole lot turned tail and fled back to the island.

About midnight, when the sea was very calm, we inadvertently ran aground on a halcyon's nest. It was nearly seven miles in circumference, and the bird that was sitting on it was not much smaller. We interrupted her in the process of incubating her eggs, and she flew up into the air with a melancholy cry, creating such a draught with her wings that she practically sank our ship. As soon as it was light we disembarked and went for a walk round the nest, which consisted of a vast number of trees plaited together to form a sort of raft. On it were five hundred eggs, each about the size of a barrel, from which impatient chirpings could already be heard.

So we broke one open with an axe, and hatched out a chick approximately twenty times as big as a vulture.

A few miles further on we were startled by some most unusual phenomena. The goose-shaped projection at the stern of the ship suddenly started flapping its wings and quacking. Simultaneously Scintharus, who had been bald for years, developed a fine head of hair, and most surprising of all, the mast began putting out branches, and some figs and some black grapes appeared at the top of it – though unfortunately they were not quite ripe. Naturally we were rather taken aback, having no idea what disasters these portents were meant to portend; so we just prayed to the gods to avert them, whatever they were.

We sailed another fifty miles and sighted a huge thick forest of pines and cypresses. They were growing, not on dry land, as we thought at first, but in the middle of the bottomless deep – so of course they had no roots. In spite of this disadvantage, they somehow contrived to keep vertical and stay absolutely still: presumably they were floating. When we got nearer and began to realize what we were up against, we felt completely baffled, for the trees grew too close together for us to sail between them, and by that time it seemed equally impossible to turn back.

I climbed to the top of the tallest tree I could find, to see what happened the other side of the forest, and discovered that after about five miles of it there was open sea again. In the circumstances we decided that our only hope was to get the ship up on top of the trees, where the foliage looked quite thick enough to support it, and somehow carry it across to the other side. So that is what we did. We tied a good strong rope round the prow, then climbed to the top of the trees, and with some difficulty hauled the ship up after us. Once we had got it there, things were easier than we had expected. All we had to do was spread our sails, and the wind pushed us along across the branches – in fact it was just like sailing through the water, only of course rather slower. It reminded me of a striking line in a poem by Antimachus:

> They voyaged onward o'er a sea of leaves.

Having thus solved the problem of the forest, we lowered our ship into the water again, and continued our journey through a clear and sparkling sea until we came to a deep cleft in the ocean, rather like one of those fissures that sometimes develop on land as a result of earthquakes. We hastily took in sail, but our momentum carried us right up to the edge, and we very nearly went over. Peeping down, we saw to our surprise and horror that there was a sheer drop of approximately 600,000 feet, as if the sea had been sliced in half from top to bottom.

However, when we looked around a bit, we saw, not far off on the right, a sort of bridge of water running across from one side to the other. So we rowed towards it, and with our hearts in our mouths just managed to get over – but we never thought we should make it!

Beyond the chasm the sea looked smooth and inviting, and after a while we sighted a small island which offered good landing facilities and appeared to be inhabited. So we went ashore and started walking inland in search of food and water, as our supplies had run out. Well, we soon found some water, but there was no sign of food, except for a lot of mooing in the distance. Assuming that this indicated a herd of cows somewhere, we advanced in the direction of the sound and suddenly came face to face with a crowd of savages. They were human beings with heads and horns like cattle – in fact just like the Minotaur.

The moment they saw us, they put down their heads and charged. Three of us were killed, but the rest of us got safely back to the ship. There we collected some weapons – for we had no intention of letting our friends' deaths go unavenged – and then returned to make a counter-attack. This time we managed to catch them off their guard, for they were just preparing to dine on our late companions, so we let out a sudden yell and fell upon them, killing at least fifty and capturing two prisoners of war, whom we took on board our ship.

As we had still failed to find any food, someone suggested that we should make do with the prisoners, but I would not allow it and insisted on keeping them alive, until eventually the enemy sent ambassadors to discuss terms for their repatriation – at least we gathered that this was what they meant, though they could not do anything but point at the prisoners and moo pathetically. So we handed them over in exchange for a lot of cheese, some dried fish, some onions, and four three-legged deer. The latter had the usual number of back-legs, but only one in front.

We stayed there for the rest of that day, and the following morning put to sea again. Before long there were various indications that we were approaching land – fish swimming closer to the surface, birds flying about, and so on. Shortly afterwards we saw some men practising a most unusual form of navigation, which might be called 'paddling your own canoe', except that you *are* the canoe, and there is no need to paddle. I will tell you how it is done. You float on your back in the water, elevate the appropriate organ – which in their case is suprisingly large – to an angle of ninety degrees, attach a sail to this improvised mast, and go scudding along before the wind, holding the sheet in one hand.

Then we saw some other people sitting on corks and being drawn along by dolphins, harnessed together in pairs. They seemed perfectly friendly and not at all nervous, for they drove straight up to us and inspected our ship from every possible angle, having apparently never seen such a thing before.

That evening we landed on another small island, which appeared to be inhabited exclusively by women. They greeted us in our own language, shook us warmly by the hands, and kissed us. They were all young and pretty, and most attractively dressed in long flowing garments which reached right down to the ground. They told us that the island was called Noholdsbard, and the town itself Waterbitch, and each of them asked one of us to spend the night with her.

I could not help feeling that there was something fishy about this arrangement, so before following my hostess indoors I took a quick look round – and came across a large pile of human bones and skulls!

Well, I did not want to raise the alarm just yet, but I got out my mallow and prayed to it earnestly – for if this was not a 'time of danger' I did not know what was. A few minutes later, as my hostess was bustling about the kitchen getting dinner ready, I spotted that she had donkey's hooves instead of ordinary feet. I immediately drew my sword, grabbed hold of her and tied her up securely, and then subjected her to a thorough cross-examination. At first she refused to say anything, but in the end she confessed that she belonged to a species of mermaid known as Assfeetida, which lives on a diet of human flesh.

'Our usual system', she added, 'is to make our guests drunk, then go to bed with them and kill them while they're asleep.'

On the strength of this information, I climbed on to the roof of the house, leaving her still tied up, and shouted for my companions. As soon as they arrived, I explained the situation, directed their attention to the heap of bones, and took them indoors to see my prisoner – who promptly turned into water and disappeared. Just to see what would happen, I ran the water through with my sword, and it instantly became blood.

That was enough for us. We raced back to the ship and put to sea, and next morning, just as it was getting light, we sighted what we took to be the mainland. So after kneeling down and saying a prayer, we began to discuss our future policy. Some of us wanted to make a token landing, just so that we could say we had been there, and then go straight home. Another suggestion was that we should abandon the ship and start exploring the interior to see what the natives were like.

While we were arguing about it, we were suddenly overtaken by a violent storm, which dashed our ship against the rocky coast and completely broke it up. All we could do was grab our weapons and anything else that came to hand, and strike out for the shore. Thus we finally landed on the continent at the other side of the world; and what happened to us there, I will tell you in another book.

NOTES AND GLOSSARY

NOTES

THE DREAM

1. *Iliad* II, 56–7.
2. *Anabasis* III, i, 11–13.

ZEUXIS

1. *Odyssey* I, 351–2.
2. *Iliad* XVI, 379.
3. *Iliad* XI, 160.

CONVERSATIONS IN LOW SOCIETY

1. See *Iliad* XVIII, 206–14.

CONVERSATIONS IN THE UNDERWORLD

1. *Medea* 230–1, 250–1.

CHARON SEES LIFE

1. Protesilaus (see Glossary).
2. See *Iliad* I, 590–600.
3. *Odyssey* XI, 315–16.
4. *Odyssey* XI, 316.
5. *Iliad* V, 127–8.
6. *Odyssey* V, 291–4.
7. Adapted from *Iliad* III, 226–7.
8. Adapted from *Iliad* III, 226.
9. See *Herodotus* I, 30–3.
10. *Iliad* VI, 146–9.
11. See *Odyssey* XII, 173–7.
12. A Homeric pastiche based on *Iliad* IX, 319–20.
13. e.g. *Odyssey* I, 2; *Iliad* II, 141; *Iliad* II, 570.

MENIPPUS GOES TO HELL

1. Euripides, *Heracles Mainomenos* 523–4.
2. Euripides, *Hecuba* 1–2.

3. From a lost play.
4. From the *Andromeda*, a lost play of Euripides.
5. Adapted from *Odyssey* XI, 164–5.
6. i.e. of the Mysteries (see Glossary).
7. *Works and Days* 289–92.
8. Adapted from *Odyssey* X, 570.
9. Adapted from *Iliad* IX, 457.
10. *Iliad* XX, 61.
11. e.g. *Odyssey* X, 521.
12. Adapted from *Odyssey* XI, 539.

ICAROMENIPPUS

1. Heraclitus (see Glossary).
2. e.g. Pythagoras (see Glossary).
3. e.g. Socrates (see Glossary).
4. *Odyssey* IX, 302.
5. e.g. Halm text 7, 184 (Penguin Fable 130).
6. *Iliad* XIII, 3–6.
7. Adapted from *Odyssey* XI, 309.
8. *Odyssey* XVI, 187.
9. *Iliad* XVIII, 483–608.
10. *Iliad* I, 222.
11. The moon-goddess, Artemis, was the sister of the sun-god, Apollo.
12. *Odyssey* X, 98.
13. *Odyssey* I, 170.
14. It was begun in the fifth century B.C., completed in the second century A.D.
15. Aratus *Phaenomena* 2–3.
16. Adapted from *Iliad* XVI, 250.
17. *Iliad* V, 341.
18. Adapted from *Iliad* II, 1–2.
19. *Iliad* XVIII, 104, etc.
20. *Iliad* II, 202.
21. *Iliad* I, 528.

AN INTERVIEW WITH HESIOD

1. *Theogony* 30–3.
2. Hesiod, *Theogony* 46; *Odyssey* VIII, 325.

3. *Works and Days* 482.
4. As Calchas did (*Iliad* I, 93–6; II, 329).

SOME AWKWARD QUESTIONS FOR ZEUS

1. *Iliad* XXIV, 209–10; *Theogony* 217–19, 904–6.
2. *Iliad* XX, 336.
3. *Iliad* VIII, 19–27.
4. i.e. the Epicureans (see Glossary).
5. For the whole story, see *Herodotus* I, 34–43.
6. Euripides, *Phoenissae* 18–19.

PHILOSOPHIES GOING CHEAP

1. $1 + 2 + 3 + 4$.
2.   1
          2 2
        3 3 3
      4 4 4 4
3. Because 'God is a number' (see p. 102, and Glossary under Pythagoras).
4. Euripides, *Hippolytus* 612.
5. e.g. in the *Electra* of Euripides.

FISHING FOR PHONIES

1. A parody of *Iliad* II, 363.
2. Adapted from *Iliad* VI, 112.
3. From a lost play.
4. *Iliad* XXII, 262.
5. A parody of *Iliad* VI, 46–50.
6. A parody of *Iliad* X, 447–8.
7. From an unknown play.
8. Euripides, *Bacchae* 386–8.
9. *Iliad* III, 57.
10. Plato, *Phaedrus* 246 E.
11. e.g. in *The Clouds* of Aristophanes.
12. Euripides, *Phoenissae* 1764–6.
13. A parody of *Iliad* XVIII, 507–8.
14. Adapted from *Iliad* II, 468.
15. As human beings are said to have been in *Symposium* 191 D (see Penguin translation pp. 59–62).

THE PATHOLOGICAL LIAR

1. *Odyssey* I, 5.
2. *Iliad* IV, 218–19.
3. The Greek Rip van Winkle.

ALEXANDER

1. *Odyssey* IV, 230.
2. Thucydides, *Peloponnesian War* II, i, 1.
3. *Odyssey* XIX, 211.
4. i.e. one drachma and two obols (about 11d.).
5. A.D. 165–168.
6. *Iliad* II, 855.

THE TRUE HISTORY

1. The Straits of Gibraltar.
2. *Iliad* XVI, 459–60.
3. An aerial town built by birds in *The Birds* of Aristophanes.
4. Theocritus, *Idylls* XI, 20.
5. *Histories* III, 113.
6. *Iliad* II, 212–77.
7. *Odyssey* XIX, 562.

GLOSSARY

ACADEMICS: members of the Academy, the school of Plato (see PLATO). Its doctrine included elements of Scepticism (see SCEPTICS).

ACHILLES: the hero of the *Iliad*. He is the best fighter on the Greek side. In XXIII he organizes funeral games for Patroclus.

ACROPOLIS: a rocky plateau, 200 feet high, in the middle of Athens.

ADMETUS: a king of Pherae in Thessaly. Apollo had to work for him for nine years, as a punishment for killing the Cyclops.

AEACUS: one of the three judges in the Underworld.

AESCHINES (about 390–314 B.C.): an Athenian orator. At first he denounced the aggression of Philip of Macedon, but was bribed or otherwise persuaded to support his cause at Athens.

AESOP (sixth century B.C.?): a writer of moral fables about animals.

AGAMEMNON: a king of Mycenae, Commander-in-chief of the Greeks in the *Iliad*.

AJAX MAJOR: a Greek hero who competed with Odysseus for the right to inherit the arms of Achilles. Odysseus won, and Ajax went mad with disappointment, massacred a flock of sheep, and committed suicide.

AJAX MINOR: a Greek hero who raped Cassandra during the sack of Troy.

ALCINOUS: a king of Phaeacia in the *Odyssey*. Odysseus repays his hospitality by telling him the story of his adventures (IX–XII).

AMPHIARAUS: an Argive hero and prophet. He was swallowed up by the earth while retreating from an unsuccessful attack on Thebes.

ANACREON (sixth century B.C.): a lyric poet, famous for his love-poems and drinking-songs.

ANCHISES: a member of the Trojan royal family. Aphrodite fell in love with him, and slept with him on Mount Ida. Hence Aeneas, the hero of the *Aeneid*.

ANTIOCHUS SOTER: a king of Syria (281–261 B.C.). He fell in love with his stepmother, Stratonice, and got his father's permission to marry her.

ANTISTHENES (born about 440 B.C.): the founder of the Cynic school (see CYNICS).

ANUBIS: a dog-headed Egyptian god.

APHRODITE: the goddess of love. She was the daughter of Zeus, the wife of Hephaestus, and the mistress of Ares. The myrtle was sacred to her. One of her stock epithets in Homer is 'golden'.

APIS: an Egyptian god, incarnated in a series of sacred bulls.

APOLLO: the god of music, poetry, prophecy, archery, and the sun. He had oracles at Delphi, Claros, Delos, and Branchidae. He was beardless and had long hair as a sign of his eternal youth, for Greek boys did not cut their hair until they grew up.

APOLLONIUS OF TYANA (born about 4 B.C.): a Pythagorean philosopher and mystic who claimed to work miracles.

AREOPAGUS: a hill to the west of the Acropolis at Athens; also a criminal court which sat there.

ARION: a semi-mythical poet and musician, famous for being saved from drowning by a music-loving dolphin.

ARISTIPPUS OF CYRENE (early fourth century B.C.); founder of the Cyrenaic school of philosophy. He regarded pleasure as the chief good, a doctrine which was taken over by Epicurus. He lived for a time at the court of Dionysius, dictator of Syracuse, in Sicily.

ARISTOPHANES (about 448–380 B.C.): the first great writer of Athenian comedy.

ARISTOTLE (384–322 B.C.): the founder of the Peripatetic school, so called from his habit of walking about while teaching. He explained difficult subjects to his students in the mornings, and gave simpler talks to the general public in the afternoons. These two types of lecture were known as Esoteric and Exoteric respectively. His ethics regarded virtue as a mean between two extremes, and distinguished three types of good: (1) of the soul, (2) of the body, (3) of the external world. Type (3) explicitly included wealth, hence the suggestion that Peripatetics were rich and interested in making money. He also did research into physics, biology, and zoology.

ARRIAN (about A.D. 95–175): a Greek author who wrote a summary of the doctrines of Epictetus.

ARTEMIS: the Greek equivalent of Diana, worshipped at Ephesus as a fertility-goddess (see Acts 19: 27–35).

ASCLEPIUS: the son of Apollo and Coronis, and god of medicine. His cult was extremely popular during the second century A.D. His symbol was a snake.

ATHENE: the goddess of wisdom, and the protectress of Athens. Her father, Zeus, swallowed her mother, for fear she might give birth to a son stronger than himself, so Athene was born from his head. She was a warlike virgin, who normally wore full armour and a helmet. Her stock epithet in Homer is 'grey-eyed'.

ATLAS: a Titan punished for rebelling against the gods by being used to prop up the sky. Heracles took the weight off his shoulders for a bit, so that he could go and fetch the Apples of the Hesperides. Perseus later turned him into a stone with the Gorgon's head, and he became the Atlas Mountains.

ATTIS: a Phrygian god, the son of the fertility-goddess, Cybele, who grew jealous when he wanted to get married, and sent him mad, so that he castrated himself.

AUGEAN STABLES: see HERACLES.

BACCHANTS: companions of Dionysus, who danced round him in a wild state of intoxication.

BRANCHIDAE (or DIDYMA): a place on the coast of Ionia, where there was an oracle of Apollo.

BUSIRIS: a king of Egypt who used to sacrifice all foreigners to Zeus.

CALCHAS: a prophet attached to the Greek forces in the Trojan War.

CALLISTO: a nymph loved by Zeus. She was turned into a bear, either by Hera, out of jealousy, or by Zeus, to cover his tracks and keep Hera from finding out.

CALYPSO: a nymph with whom Odysseus has an affair in the *Odyssey*.

CASTALIAN SPRING: a spring on Mount Parnassus, sacred to Apollo. Those who drank from it were inspired to write poetry.

CERBERUS: a three-headed dog that guarded the entrance to the Underworld.

CERCOPES: mischievous gnomes who tried to rob Heracles when he was asleep. He caught them, but found them so amusing that he let them go.

CHARON: a squalid old man who rowed the dead across the Styx in a leaky boat. Corpses were buried with an obol in their mouths to pay their fare.

CHIMAERA: a lion-headed, goat-bodied, dragon-tailed monster.

CHRYSIPPUS (about 280–204 B.C.): a philosopher who systematized the doctrines of Stoicism (see STOICS).

CIRCE: a beautiful witch with whom Odysseus has an affair in the *Odyssey*.

CLAROS: a town on the coast of Ionia, where there was an oracle of Apollo.

CLOTHO: one of the three Fates (see FATES).

COCYTUS: the River of Wailing in the Underworld.

CODRUS: the last of the legendary kings of Athens.

COLOSSUS OF RHODES: a huge statue of the sun-god at the entrance to the harbour of Rhodes.

CORONIS: the mother of Asclepius by Apollo. The name is connected with the Greek word for crow (*corone*).

CORYBANTS: companions of the Asiatic goddess Cybele.

CRATES (late fourth century B.C.): a Cynic philosopher (see CYNICS).

CROESUS: the last king of Lydia (560–546 B.C.), famous for his wealth. He tested various oracles by asking them what he was doing on a certain day. He was in fact doing the most unpredictable thing he could think of: boiling a lamb and a tortoise together in a bronze caldron. Only the Delphic oracle replied correctly. Later he asked it if he should cross the River Halys and invade Persia. It replied that by doing so he would destroy a great empire. He therefore went ahead with the invasion, and was utterly defeated. The Lydian Empire was destroyed by Persia, and Croesus was taken prisoner by Cyrus.

CTESIAS OF CNIDOS (fourth century B.C.): a physician who wrote a history of Persia, and a book about India. Neither has survived.

CYNICS: philosophers of the school of Antisthenes and Diogenes. The name means *dog-like*, in the sense of *shameless*, because they deliberately flouted convention in both speech and behaviour. Believing that nothing mattered except virtue, they practised extreme asceticism. They lived like tramps, and developed a special style of popular preaching, in which they savagely criticized all non-Cynics, and jeered at their 'illusions'. Their uniform was a single blanket, a stick, and a knapsack. They prided themselves on their cosmopolitanism and sincerity. Their patron-saint was Heracles, as the type of self-reliance and endurance.

CYRUS THE GREAT (died 529 B.C.): the founder of the Persian Empire. He defeated and captured Croesus.

CYRUS THE YOUNGER (died 401 B.C.): brother of Artaxerxes, king of Persia, against whom he led the expedition described by Xenophon in the *Anabasis*.

DAEDALUS: an Athenian technical expert who made self-moving statues. He also constructed wings from feathers stuck together with wax for himself and his son Icarus (see ICARUS), and flew from Crete to Sicily.

DANAE: the daughter of Acrisius. He was told that her son would kill him, so he kept her locked up in a brazen tower.

DAPHNE: a nymph loved and chased by Apollo, who got herself turned into a bay-tree just in time.

DARIUS: the king of Persia (521–485 B.C.) who started the First Persian War against Greece.

DELOS: an island in the Aegean, where there was an oracle of Apollo.

DELPHI: an oracle of Apollo on the south-west slope of Mount Parnassus. Responses were given by a priestess seated on a tripod over a fissure in the rock, from which intoxicating gases were said to rise.

DEMETER: the goddess of corn and agriculture.

DEMOCRITUS OF ABDERA (born about 460 B.C.): a materialist philosopher. He invented the atomic theory which was taken over by Epicurus, and was known as 'the laughing philosopher' because he ridiculed human folly.

DEMOSTHENES (383–322 B.C.): a great Athenian orator.

DIDYMA: see BRANCHIDAE.

DIOGENES (fourth century B.C.): the most famous Cynic philosopher (see CYNICS). He was said to have lived in a tub.

DION (assassinated 353 B.C.): the brother-in-law of Dionysius (see DIONYSIUS OF SYRACUSE). He was a man of great integrity, and an admirer of Plato.

DIONYSIA: an Athenian festival of Dionysus, at which tragedies and comedies were performed.

DIONYSIUS OF SYRACUSE (430–367 B.C.): a tyrannical dictator of Syracuse in Sicily, who was also a patron of literature and philosophy. He was visited by Plato in about 389 B.C.

DIONYSUS: the son of Zeus and Semele, and the god of wine.

DRACHMA: a silver coin, worth about 8d.

ECHO: a nymph loved by Pan, who became a disembodied voice in order to escape his attentions; but Lucian makes Pan tell the story rather differently.

EMPEDOCLES (fifth century B.C.): a philosopher and scientist who committed suicide by jumping into the crater of Mount Etna.

ENDYMION: a handsome youth who was sent permanently to sleep by the Moon, so that she could come down and kiss him whenever she liked.

EPEIUS: the man who wins the boxing-match in *Iliad* XXIII.

EPHIALTES: a young giant who, with his brother Otus, tried to pile Mount Ossa on Olympus, and Mount Pelion on Ossa, so as to climb up to heaven and attack the gods.

EPICTETUS (about A.D. 60-140): a Stoic philosopher (see STOICS).

EPICURUS (341-270 B.C.): the founder of the Epicurean school of philosophy. His physics were based on the atomic theory of Democritus. His ethics, derived from Aristippus, regarded pleasure as the chief good. For him, however, pleasure did not mean physical indulgence, as was often supposed, but peace of mind, freedom from anxiety caused by excessive desires, fears of death, and fears of the supernatural. So while admitting that gods existed, he denied that they interfered in human life. Epicureans were therefore regarded as atheists, for they opposed all forms of religious observance.

ERICHTHONIUS: a legendary Athenian hero, the son of Hephaestus and of the Earth.

EUPATOR: a king of the Bosporus (about A.D. 154-171).

EUPHORBUS: the Trojan who first wounds Patroclus in the *Iliad*. See PYTHAGORAS.

EURIPIDES (about 480-406 B.C.): the third great Athenian writer of tragedy.

EURYBATUS: an Ephesian employed by Croesus, who embezzled some money and betrayed his employer's plans to the enemy.

EURYTUS: a king of Oechalia who was killed by Apollo, for challenging him to an archery-match.

FATES: three aged goddesses called Clotho, Lachesis, and Atropos, who spun the threads of human life.

FURIES: snake-haired goddesses who pursued the guilty and avenged crime.

GANYMEDE: a beautiful boy, related to the Trojan royal family, who was carried up to heaven by Zeus, in the form of an eagle, to be, among other things, his cup-bearer.

GIANTS: monstrous sons of the Earth who rebelled against the gods, but were defeated and imprisoned underground.

GORGONS: snake-haired women so hideous that the sight of them turned one to stone.

GORGONZOLA: a name unknown to Lucian, but substituted on page 274 for Tyro, which has cheesy connotations in Greek.

HANNIBAL (247–182 B.C.): the Carthaginian general in the Second Punic War against Rome.

HECATE: a goddess of the Underworld.

HELEN: a beautiful woman, the daughter of Zeus, in the form of a swan, and Leda. She was kidnapped by Theseus before she was ten, and carried off to Athens; but her brothers, Castor and Pollux, got her back by force. She then married Menelaus, king of Sparta, but later eloped with Paris to Troy, thus causing the Trojan War.

HEPHAESTUS: the god of fire and metal-work. He was lame because his father, Zeus, once threw him down from heaven to earth, for siding with his mother, Hera, in an argument.

HERA: the wife and sister of Zeus. Her stock epithets in Homer are 'white-armed' and 'ox-eyed'.

HERACLES: a hero famous for his strength. He was the son of Alcmene and Zeus, who made the night he spent with her three times the normal length. In his youth two allegorical females called Pleasure and Virtue asked him whether he would prefer a life of enjoyment, or one of hard work and fame. He chose the latter. Later, as an expiation for killing his wife and children in a fit of insanity, he had to do various impossible jobs, known as the Labours of Heracles. One was to fetch the Apples of the Hesperides, which involved holding up the sky while he sent Atlas to get the apples (see ATLAS). Another was to go down to the Underworld and bring up Cerberus (see CERBERUS). Another was to kill the Nemean Lion, an invulnerable monster that he had to strangle with his bare hands. From then on he always wore its skin; he also carried a club. Another Labour was to clean out of the Augean Stables the excrement of 3,000 cattle that had accumulated over thirty years. He did it by diverting the River Alpheus through the buildings. He also stole the Oxen of Geryon, which doubtless explains why he was able to supply Lucian with meat in the *Icaromenippus*.

HERACLITUS (early fifth century B.C.): a philosopher who, because of his melancholy view of life, was known as 'the weeping philosopher'. His ideas were expressed in very obscure metaphorical epigrams. He held that everything is in a state of flux; that conflict and tension between opposites are essential parts of reality; and that the universe is guided by an Ever-Living Fire, from which all things proceed, and into which they are perpetually returning.

HERMES: the son of Zeus, the messenger of the gods, and the conductor of the dead to the Underworld.

HERODOTUS (about 480–425 B.C.): the first great Greek historian, though many of his stories sound rather unhistorical.

HESIOD (eighth century B.C.?): a poet who wrote the *Works and Days*, a didactic poem on agriculture, the *Theogony*, a history and genealogy of the gods, and the *Catalogue of Women*, a collection of stories about mythical heroines.

HIPPOCRATES (born about 460 B.C.): the most famous ancient authority on medicine.

HOMER (eighth to ninth century B.C.?): the traditional author of the *Iliad* and the *Odyssey*, said to have been blind. His birthplace was unknown, but a famous hexameter lists some of the places suggested:

Smyrna, Chios, Colophon, Salamis, Rhodos, Argos, Athenae.

His name was the Greek word for *hostage*, on which Lucian puns in *The True History* (p. 280), where I have invented an equally silly English equivalent. Critics like Zenodotus (about 285 B.C.) and Aristarchus (about 156 B.C.) tried to establish a reliable text of Homer by collating manuscripts, and rejecting certain lines as spurious. They also speculated on the order in which the two poems were written, and subjected them to what the New Criticism would call 'close reading', in order to discover occult significance in his choice of words.

HYACINTHUS: a beautiful boy accidentally killed with a quoit by his lover, Apollo. From his blood grew the hyacinth.

HYLAS: a beautiful boy-friend of Heracles. While fetching water, he was dragged down into a river and drowned by over-affectionate water-nymphs.

HYPERBOREANS: a mythical people who lived in the far north.

ICARUS: the son of Daedalus (see DAEDALUS). While flying away from Crete with his father, he went too near the sun, so that the wax melted, the feathers dropped out, and he fell into the sea, which was then named after him.

IDEAS: a technical term in the philosophy of Plato (see PLATO). For each individual object or concept in the world, there was an ideal pattern, called the Idea, laid up in heaven. All actual beds, for instance, were merely poor imitations of the Idea of Bed. The Ideas, which could only be perceived intellectually, were eternal, and the sole realities, whereas everything in the Phenomenal world, i.e. the world of sense-perception, was transient and unreal.

IRUS: a greedy beggar who fights Odysseus in *Odyssey* XVIII.

ISIS: an Egyptian goddess.

ISTER: the ancient name for the Lower Danube.

IXION: a Thessalian who roasted his father-in-law in a pit of burning coals, and later tried to seduce the goddess Hera. He was punished in the Underworld by being tied to a perpetually revolving wheel.

LAIS: the name of two famous courtesans, one from Corinth and the other from Sicily.

LAIUS: the father of Oedipus and husband of Jocasta. Being told by an oracle that his son would kill him, he had Oedipus exposed at birth on a mountain, but he was rescued by a shepherd, and brought up by the king of Corinth. Later, while driving his chariot along a narrow road, Oedipus was stopped by a chariot coming from the opposite direction. After some argument about right of way, he lost his temper and killed the other driver, who was in fact his father Laius. He then drove on to Thebes, and shortly afterwards married his mother Jocasta.

LAOMEDON: a king of Troy, who employed Apollo and Poseidon to build the walls of his town and then refused to pay them.

LEDA: the wife of Tyndareus, the king of Sparta. Zeus fell in love with her, and visited her in the form of a swan. The result was two eggs, one containing Castor and Pollux, and the other Helen and Clytaemnestra. (The latter egg, like the curate's, was only good in parts, for Clytaemnestra became a murderess.)

LEPIDUS (second century A.D.): an Epicurean who lived at Amastris. It appears from an inscription that in spite of his philosophical creed he was a priest of the Roman state religion.

LETHE: the River of Oblivion in the Underworld. Souls about to be reincarnated drank from it, and forgot their former lives.

LEUCOTHOE: a sea-nymph who saves Odysseus from drowning in *Odyssey* V.

LYCEUM: a gymnasium at Athens, where Aristotle taught; hence the philosophical school of Aristotle (see ARISTOTLE).

LYCURGUS: the legendary originator of the Spartan constitution.

LYNCEUS: a man with such good eyesight that he could see through the earth.

MALLUS: a town in Cilicia where there was an oracle of Amphilochus.

MARATHON: a plain twenty-two miles north-east of Athens, where the Persian invaders were defeated in 490 B.C.

MARCUS AURELIUS (A.D. 121–180): a Stoic Roman Emperor. For several years he was at war with the Quadi, the Marcomanni, and other German tribes. In A.D. 174 he decisively defeated the Quadi, but was still directing operations against the Marcomanni when he died.

MELETUS: one of the three men whose charges resulted in the execution of Socrates.

MENANDER (about 343–262 B.C.): the second great writer of Athenian comedy.

MENELAUS: a king of Sparta. He was the son of Atreus, the grandson of Pelops, the brother of Agamemnon, and the husband of Helen.

MENIPPUS (third century B.C.): a Cynic philosopher who invented a new form of prose satire. He is thought to have influenced Lucian, but none of his works survive. One of them was called *The Sale of Diogenes*, so it may have been the source of *Philosophies Going Cheap*.

METRODORUS (died about 277 B.C.): an Epicurean philosopher (see EPICURUS).

MIGHTY MOTHER: another name for the Asiatic nature-goddess, Cybele. Her rites included wild orgiastic dances.

MILO (sixth century B.C.): an athlete who won the wrestling match at the Olympian Games six times in succession.

MINA: the sum of 100 drachmas, i.e. about £3 6s. 8d.

MINOS: a legendary king of Crete, who became one of the three judges in the Underworld. He was the son of Zeus by Europa. His own son, Glaucus, was smothered in a jar of honey, a fact of which Minos was first informed by a soothsayer called Polyidus.

MINOTAUR: a monster, half-man and half-bull, resulting from the intercourse of Pasiphae, the wife of Minos, with a bull.

MOMUS: the god of criticism and satire, much given to finding fault with existing arrangements.

MUSES: nine goddesses who inspired literature and the arts.

MYRMIDONS: the people commanded by Achilles in the *Iliad*. His grandfather, Aeacus, had lost all his subjects through an epidemic, and Zeus had replaced them with human beings produced out of ants (*myrmekes*).

MYRON (fifth century B.C.): a Greek sculptor, famous for his *Discobolus* (man throwing a discus).

MYSTERIES: secret rites of Demeter at Eleusis, ten miles north-west of Athens. Initiates were sworn to silence about them.

NARCISSUS: a boy so beautiful that he fell in love with his own reflection in a pool, and became rooted to the spot in the form of a narcissus.

NEMEAN LION: see HERACLES.

NESTOR: a garrulous old Greek in the *Iliad* and the *Odyssey*.

NIOBE: a mother of fourteen children who jeered at the goddess Leto for having only two, Artemis and Apollo. So the two killed the fourteen, and Niobe wept for them until she turned into a column of stone, down which tears contined to flow.

NIBEUS: the best-looking Greek in the *Iliad*, except Achilles.

NUMA POMPILIUS: the legendary successor of Romulus as king of Rome. Owing to his great wisdom, which he owed to frequent consultations with the goddess Egeria, his reign was a Golden Age.

OBOL: a copper coin worth one-sixth of a drachma, i.e. just under 1½d.

ODYSSEUS: the hero of the *Odyssey*, proverbial for his intelligence. In *Odyssey* XI he goes down to the Underworld to consult Tiresias. In *Iliad* X he goes on a night commando-raid with Diomede, for which he wears a leather helmet with a felt skull-cap inside it.

OLYMPIAS (fourth century B.C.): the wife of Philip of Macedon, and the mother of Alexander the Great, whose father was said to have been, not Philip, but a huge serpent that crept into her bed one night.

ORITHYIA: the daughter of Erechtheus, a king of Athens. The North Wind fell in love with her, and whisked her off to Thrace, where she had four children by him.

ORPHEUS: a legendary musician who went down with his lyre to the Underworld to bring back his dead wife Eurydice. He was later torn to pieces by Thracian women.

OTHRYADES: the only survivor of 300 Spartans who fought 300 Argives for the possession of the Plain of Thyrea. He was ashamed to go home alone, so he put up a trophy, wrote an inscription in his own blood, and committed suicide on the battlefield.

OTUS: see EPHIALTES.

PALAMEDES: one of the Greek heroes in the Trojan War. He was something of an intellectual, for he was said to have added some new letters to the alphabet, and invented lighthouses, measures, scales, dice, and the game of draughts.

PAN: the god of flocks and shepherds. He was a goat from the waist down, and also had horns and a goatee beard, which was possibly why the nymphs that he admired ran away and got changed into something else (see ECHO, PITYS). One of them, Syrinx, turned into a reed, with which he then invented the Pan-pipe. He lived in Arcadia, but turned up at Marathon to help the Athenians (see MARATHON), and from then on was worshipped at Athens.

PARIS: a son of Priam, king of Troy. He was exposed at birth on Mount Ida, because of a prophecy that he would cause the destruction of Troy, but was brought up by shepherds and became one himself. He had an affair with the nymph Oenone, but was later helped by Aphrodite to elope with Helen, and thus cause the Trojan War.

PEGASUS: a winged horse.

PELEUS: the father of Achilles.

PELOPS: a grandson of Zeus, and grandfather of Menelaus and Agamemnon.

PENELOPE: the wife of Odysseus. In the *Odyssey* she is a model of chastity, who resisted the advances of 108 suitors over a period of twenty years' grass-widowhood. But some stories gave her a different character, and made her the mother of Pan, either by Hermes, or by all the suitors. She was also said to have married her stepson Telegonus after he killed his father.

PENTHEUS: a king of Thebes who was torn to pieces by Bacchants in the *Bacchae* of Euripides, as a punishment for trying to put down the worship of Dionysus.

PERIPATETICS: the followers of Aristotle (see ARISTOTLE).

PERSEPHONE: the wife of Pluto, god of the Underworld.

PERSEUS: the son of Danae. With a sickle he cut off a Gorgon's head, and then used it to turn his enemies to stone (see GORGONS).

PHAEACIA: the country of Alcinous, where Odysseus landed after being shipwrecked in *Odyssey* V.

PHAETHON: the son of the Sun.

PHALARIS (sixth century B.C.?): a cruel Sicilian tyrant, who roasted people alive in a brazen bull.

PHAROS: a small island off Alexandria, where the first lighthouse was erected by Ptolemy II (285–246 B.C.).

PHIDIAS (born about 500 B.C.): an Athenian sculptor, famous for a colossal ivory-and-gold statue of Zeus at Olympia.

PHILIP OF MACEDON (about 382–336 B.C.): the husband of Olympias, and the father of Alexander the Great. By a mixture of force and diplomacy he gradually extended his power over most of Greece, chiefly at the expense of Athens.

PHILOMELA: the daughter of a king of Athens. She was raped by her brother-in-law, Tereus, so she and her sister Procne punished him by serving him his son Itys for dinner. When he realized what he had eaten, Tereus rushed at the sisters with a sword; but before he could do any damage, he was changed into a hoopoo, Philomela into a swallow, and Procne into a nightingale (in Latin mythology, the sisters exchanged birds).

PHINEUS: a blind prophet of Thrace.

PINDAR (about 518–443 B.C.): a Greek lyric poet. His *Olympian Odes* are so called because they celebrate victories at the Olympian Games, but Lucian seems to think their title makes them suitable for recitation before an audience of Olympian gods.

PIRAEUS: the port of Athens, five miles south-west of the town.

PITYS: a nymph loved by Pan, who turned into a pine-tree to get away from him; but Lucian makes Pan end the story differently.

PLATO (427–348 B.C.): the founder of the Academic (or Platonic) school of philosophy. Most of his works are dialogues in which Socrates is the principal speaker, so Lucian attributes the same ideas to Socrates and Plato indiscriminately. In the *Republic*, Plato's most important work, Socrates sketches an ideal community, in which everything, including women and children, is public property. In the *Laws* Plato outlines a constitution and legal system for an imaginary new colony. The two features of Plato's philosophy to which Lucian alludes are his theory of Ideas (see IDEAS), and his doctrine of the immortality of the soul, for which he gives several arguments, particularly in the *Phaedo*. His best works have great literary charm, abound in quotations from poets, especially Homer, and employ a form of irony for which Socrates is also famous. In certain dialogues (e.g. *Gorgias, Protagoras*) he depreciated sophists like Gorgias, Protagoras, Hippias, and Prodicus. On three occasions he visited the court of Dionysius of Syracuse, where he had a disciple in Dion.

PLUTO: the god of the Underworld.

PODALIRIUS: a son of Asclepius, mentioned in the *Iliad* as a Greek army doctor who came from Tricce. The first syllable of his name means 'foot' in Greek, a sense on which Lucian puns in the *Alexander* (p. 247). To make an equivalent pun in English, I have had to give Alexander an extra (but not unsuitable) disease.

POLYCLITUS (fifth century B.C.): a sculptor famous for a bronze figure of a boy tying a ribbon round his head, the *Diadumenos*, and a huge ivory-and-gold statue of Hera.

POLYCRATES (sixth century B.C.): a tyrant of Samos. During the Persian Wars he was betrayed into the power of the Persian Satrap, Oroetes, and crucified (522 B.C.).

POLYXENA: a daughter of Priam, loved by Achilles, and sacrificed on his tomb, in accordance with instructions from his ghost. The episode occurs in *Hecuba*, a play by Euripides.

POSEIDON: the brother of Zeus, and god of the sea. He built the walls of Troy for Laomedon, who then refused to pay him.

PRAXITELES (born about 390 B.C.): an Athenian sculptor, famous for his *Hermes*.

PRIAM: the king of Troy during the Trojan War.

PROMETHEUS: a Titan who stole fire from heaven and gave it to human beings. He was punished by being chained to a rock in the Caucasus mountains. All day an eagle pecked away at his liver, which grew again during the night.

PROTESILAUS: the first Greek killed in the Trojan War. He was allowed to return from the dead for three hours to comfort his widow, Laodamia.

PTOLEMY: the name of several kings of Egypt. Ptolemy Philadelphus (285–246 B.C.) and Ptolemy Euergetes II (146–117 B.C.) both married their sisters.

PYRIPHLEGETHON: the River of Fire in the Underworld.

PYRRHO (about 365–275 B.C.): the founder of the school of Scepticism. He held that, in view of the contradictory evidence presented by the senses and by intellectual processes, certain knowledge was impossible, so the only thing to do was to preserve an open mind and suspend judgement.

PYTHAGORAS (born about 580 B.C.): the founder of the Pythagorean school of philosophy. He was born in Samos, but migrated to Croton in Magna Graecia, Italy, where he founded a school. His doctrine was of a mystical religious character, but included the study of mathematics (especially geometry), astronomy, and music. He discovered the numerical relation between the length of strings and the musical note that they sound when vibrating, and hence decided that the whole universe was best explained as a harmony, expressed in mathematical terms. He believed in the transmigration of souls, and claimed that he had been Euphorbus (see EUPHORBUS) in a previous incarnation, since he recognized that hero's shield when he saw it in a temple. He did not, as Lucian implies, teach the doctrine of the four elements, which was the contribution of Empedocles. Pythagoras made his disciples wear their hair long, practise vegetarianism (except that beans were taboo), and preserve a five-year period of silence. He was said to have had a golden thigh, but there were also equally apocryphal stories representing him as an unscrupulous charlatan. In *Philosophies Going Cheap* he speaks in the Ionian dialect: nowadays I feel he would have a Viennese or Zurichian accent.

RHADAMANTHUS: one of the three judges in the Underworld.

RUTILIANUS (about A.D. 106–175): a Roman diplomat. He was consul between 150 and 155, Governor of Moesia Superior between 155 and 158, and finally Proconsul of Asia Minor.

SABAZIUS: a Phrygian and Thracian deity, whose cult became popular in Italy during the early Empire.

SARDANAPALUS: an Assyrian king who reigned at Nineveh from 668 B.C. He was famous for his wealth, and according to a probably unhistorical tradition was an effeminate and voluptuous tyrant, whose shocking behaviour caused his subjects to rebel against him.

SCEPTICS: philosophers of the school of Pyrrho (see PYRRHO).

SCIRON: a brigand who used to make passers-by wash his feet, and while they were doing so, kicked them into the sea.

SCYLLA: a monster with twelve feet, and six heads each containing three rows of teeth, encountered by Odysseus in *Odyssey* XII.

SEVEN SAGES: famous legislators and philosophers of the period 620–550 B.C. The list always included Thales of Miletus (born about 624) and Solon (about 640–558). Periander was sometimes on it, sometimes not, having been a partly benevolent, partly malevolent tyrant.

SEVERIANUS (about A.D. 105–161): a Belgian, who was Governor of Cappadocia during the Parthian War. He was ordered to invade Armenia (Lucian is unfair in suggesting that he had any option), was defeated at Elegeia, and committed suicide.

SIBYL: a prophetess inspired by a god, usually Apollo.

SILENUS: an elderly, drunken, semi-goatlike deity.

SINIS: a brigand killed by Theseus. He used to bend down a couple of pine-trees, tie a victim to the tops of them, and then let them go.

SIRENS: musical but predatory females in *Odyssey* XII, who sit on an island and lure passing sailors to destruction with their singing. Odysseus successfully by-passes them by putting wax into the ears of his crew, and having himself tied to the mast.

SIRIUS: the dog-star.

SISYPHUS: a cunning king of Corinth, punished in the Underworld by having to roll a huge stone up a hill. It always rolls down again just as he is getting to the top (*Odyssey* XI).

SOCRATES (469–399 B.C.): an Athenian philosopher, the teacher of Plato (see PLATO) and chief speaker in most of his dialogues. He was the son of a sculptor; fought at the battle of Delium (424) where the Athenians were routed by the Boeotians; and was executed, by being made to drink hemlock, on charges brought against him by Meletus, Anytus, and Lycon. Though he often speaks approvingly of homosexuality, he was not in fact a practising homosexual: in the *Symposium* Alcibiades describes how he once slept under the same cloak with Socrates, who took no advantage of the situation. In person, Socrates was bald, snub-nosed, thick-lipped, and pot-bellied. One of his eccentricities was to swear 'By Dog!' or 'By Plane-tree!' Like Plato he was famous for his irony. He was satirized by Aristophanes in the *Clouds*.

SOLON (about 640–558 B.C.): an Athenian statesman who reorganized the Athenian constitution. Herodotus makes him visit Croesus when the latter was at the height of his power (which is chronologically impossible).

STESICHORUS (about 640–555 B.C.): a lyric poet. He was said to have been struck blind for writing a poem against Helen, and to have regained his sight when he published a palinode in which he invented the theory that not Helen, but a phantom-double of hers had eloped with Paris.

STOA: a painted colonnade in the market-place at Athens, frequented by Zeno, the founder of Stoicism: hence the name.

STOICS: the followers of Zeno (early third century B.C.) and of Chrysippus (280–204 B.C.) In their ethical theory, virtue was all that really mattered; but external circumstances, though of secondary importance, were divided into three categories: (1) 'Preferable', i.e. the sort of things, like health, that a sensible person would choose, all other things being equal; (2) 'Non-Preferable', e.g. sickness; (3) 'Indifferent', i.e. things that did not matter either way, like life and death. This concentration on virtue was expressed in a series of paradoxes about the Wise Man, i.e. the Stoic. One was: 'The Wise Man is the only true king, etc'. Another was: 'All but the Wise

Man are insane', which is why Chrysippus recommends three doses of hellebore (p. 161), the traditional cure for madness. The Stoics laid great stress on logical theory and minor technical problems connected with it. In their theory of sense-perception, an object was accurately perceived only if the mind achieved an Imaginative Grasp of the object – whatever that might mean. The Stoic uniform included a long beard and an air of great solemnity, both of which, according to Juvenal as well as Lucian, often served to screen secret immorality, especially of a homosexual kind, though the Stoics prided themselves on their 'manliness'. Their patron-god was Heracles (see HERACLES); their favourite image was that of climbing to the top of the Hill of Virtue (from Hesiod's *Works and Days* 289–92). Stoicism was immensely popular during the second century, partly because the Emperor Marcus Aurelius was a Stoic.

STYX: the Hateful River in the Underworld, over which the dead have to be ferried by Charon.

SULLA (138–78 B.C.): a Roman dictator with a taste for art and literature. He visited Greece in 87 B.C., while on active service in the war against Mithridates, and took home from Athens several famous pictures and a library of books by Aristotle.

TALENT: the sum of sixty minas, i.e. about £200.

TALUS: a brazen man who guarded the shores of Crete.

TANTALUS: a man punished in the Underworld by being made to stand in a pool of water, which dried up whenever he tried to drink it, under boughs laden with fruit, which was blown out of reach whenever he tried to pick it (*Odyssey* XI).

TELEGONUS: a son of Odysseus by Circe. He was shipwrecked on the coast of Ithaca, and started helping himself to the local produce. Odysseus and Telemachus went out to protect their property, and Telegonus ran his father through with a spear, not knowing who he was.

TELEMUS: a soothsayer.

THAMYRIS: a Thracian poet and musician who was blinded for his effrontery in challenging the Muses to a singing competition.

THEBANS: a people who claimed descent from five *Spartoi*, or Plantmen, who grew from dragon's teeth sown in the ground by Cadmus.

THERSITES: a Greek soldier described in *Iliad* II as the ugliest man that went to Troy. Odysseus hits him with a staff, for making insubordinate remarks about his superior officers.

THESEUS: a legendary king of Athens. He abducted Helen, while still a nymphet; had an affair with Ariadne, whom he deserted on Naxos; and later married the Amazon Queen Hippolyta, and the Cretan Princess Phaedra.

THETIS: a sea-goddess, the mother of Achilles.

TIMON (fifth century B.C.): an Athenian misanthrope.

TIRESIAS: a Theban who was temporarily turned into a woman, as a result of hitting a snake. When Zeus and Hera were arguing about which sex got more pleasure out of love, they referred the matter to Tiresias, in view of his special experience. He sided with Zeus, which annoyed Hera so much that she struck him blind, but Zeus gave him the power of prophecy and long life to make up for it. Odysseus consults him in the Underworld in *Odyssey* XI.

TITYOS: a giant killed by Apollo and Artemis for trying to rape their mother Leto, and punished in the Underworld by having his liver pecked perpetually by vultures (*Odyssey* XI).

TRIPTOLEMUS: a favourite of Demeter, who gave him a chariot drawn by winged dragons, in which he flew over the earth scattering wheat-seeds, and diffusing the knowledge of agriculture.

TROPHONIUS: a man who was swallowed up by the earth at Lebadeia in Boeotia, where he was afterwards consulted as an oracle in an underground cave.

URANUS: the Sky, the grandfather of Zeus. He was castrated by his son Cronus, and each drop of blood shed in the process developed into a Giant.

XENOPHON (about 430–355 B.C.): an Athenian soldier and historian, author of the *Anabasis*, in which he describes how he brought safely home the survivors of the 10,000 Greeks trapped in enemy territory after the failure of Cyrus's Persian expedition (see CYRUS THE YOUNGER). On the night after the leaders of the expedition had been treacherously captured, Xenophon dreamed that his father's house was set on fire by a thunderbolt. Interpreted as 'a great light from Zeus' it seemed a good sign; but it might also

symbolize being at the mercy of a King – in this case, Artaxerxes. Either way, it stimulated Xenophon to take command of the situation himself, with splendid results.

XERXES: a king of Persia (485–465 B.C.) who was responsible for the Second Persian War against Greece.

ZAMOLXIS (or ZALMOXIS): a Thracian slave of Pythagoras (see PYTHAGORAS). When given his freedom he became a Pythagorean missionary in Thrace.

ZEUS: the king of the gods, husband and brother of Hera, and father of Athene, Aphrodite, and Hermes. On page 50 there may be an allusion to *Iliad* II, where Zeus suffers from insomnia, and *Iliad* XIV where Hera deliberately uses sex as a form of soporific. Lucian's other references to Zeus are usually concerned with his curious love-life, which nearly always involved a transformation into a bird or animal (see GANYMEDE, LEDA, CALLISTO).

ZEUXIS (fifth century): a painter (said to have died of laughing at a funny picture of an old woman that he had painted).

ZOROASTER (or ZARATHUSTRA): the founder of the Magian religion (from which we get the word *magic*). He was probably a Persian of the sixth century B.C.